The Sociology of U.S. Agriculture

IOWA STATE UNIVERSITY PRESS / AMES

The Sociology of U.S. Agriculture

AN ECOLOGICAL PERSPECTIVE

Don E. Albrecht • Steve H. Murdock

Don E. Albrecht is associate professor and Steve H. Murdock is professor and head, Department of Rural Sociology, Texas Agricultural Experiment Station, Texas A&M University System, College Station, Texas. The authors' names are listed in alphabetical order to indicate equal coauthorship of the work.

© 1990 Iowa State University Press, Ames, Iowa 50010
All rights reserved
⊗ This book is printed on acid-free paper.
Manufactured in the United States of America

First edition, 1990

Library of Congress Cataloging-in-Publication Data

Albrecht, Don E.
    The sociology of U.S. agriculture : an ecological perspective / Don E. Albrecht, Steve H. Murdock. — 1st ed.
        p. cm.
    Includes bibliographical references (p.).
    ISBN 0–8138–0192–3
    1. Agriculture — United States — Sociological aspects. 2. Agricultural ecology — United States. 3. Human ecology — United States. 4. United States — Rural conditions. I. Murdock, Steve H. II. Title. III. Title: Sociology of US agriculture. IV. Title: Sociology of United States agriculture.
HD1765.A43 1990
306.3′49′0973 — dc20   89–77423

Contents

Acknowledgments

Numerous persons and agencies have been invaluable in the completion of this work. First, the Department of Rural Sociology and the Texas Agricultural Experiment Station have provided the financial backing for this effort and receive our sincere appreciation.

In the preparation of this book numerous persons have provided assistance in data collection and manuscript preparation. The extensive programming efforts of Darrell Fannin are gratefully acknowledged. In addition, special appreciation is extended to Donna Nunez, Tonia Roberts, Phyllis Owens, and James DeGuzeman for their dedication and patience in typing the numerous drafts of this volume. Patricia Bramwell displayed her usual high level of dedication in supervising the staff and seeing to details, and as always her assistance is gratefully appreciated. Numerous others assisted in the preparation of base data. We wish to especially thank Ken Backman, Edli Colberg, Nancy Lugo, Lloyd Potter, and Beverly Pecotte.

Several people have read all or part of various drafts of this manuscript and their comments and suggestions have made this manuscript much better than it would be otherwise. Our thanks are extended to Jim Copp, Kathy Schifflet, Gary Green, Peter Korsching, and Eldon Schriner in this regard.

Finally, our greatest appreciation is extended to Rita R. Hamm. Rita spent many long hours editing various drafts of this volume. Rita also made numerous helpful suggestions for substantive changes. We owe her a special debt of gratitude.

The Sociology of U.S. Agriculture

The Changing Structure
of U.S. Agriculture

To even the most casual observer it is apparent that farming in America has experienced an enormous transformation during recent decades. During the 1930s, for example, farms in the United States numbered more than 6 million and averaged about 150 acres each. At that time the farm population exceeded 30 million people, which meant that about one in every four Americans was living on a farm. Typically, the farmer and his or her family provided the majority of the labor on their farm, and the farm was generally the sole or primary source of the family's livelihood.

By 1982 the number of farms declined to about 2.2 million, and the farm population was 5.6 million—only 2.4 percent of the total U.S. population (Banks and Mills 1983). The average farm in 1982 was 440 acres—about three times as large as during the 1930s. Further, nearly one-half of the farm operators reported their primary occupation was something other than farming. In addition, agricultural production had become increasingly concentrated on a few very large, commercial farms. By 1982 only about 1.2 percent of the farms in the United States had gross farm sales of $500,000 or more, but these farms accounted for nearly one-third of the nation's gross farm sales.

The causes of these transformations in U.S. agriculture are numerous and varied and the consequences are dramatic (Babb 1979). Many families have been forced to leave their farms and move to urban locations without the skills or training necessary to pursue nonfarm occupa-

3

4   tions. Many rural communities that are dependent on farmers for their survival face declines in their populations and service bases. Cities struggle to keep up with the growth resulting from the immigration of persons from rural areas, and concern exists about the potential health problems and environmental disruptions resulting from advanced farming practices (Buttel et al. 1981; Pimentel et al. 1976; Paarlberg 1980). At the same time, changes in American agriculture have allowed the American farmer to become the most efficient food and fiber producer the world has ever known. This contributes to a relatively safe and cheap diet for Americans and allows the overall standard of living in American society to be enhanced (Penn 1979; Samualson 1964).

In sum, agricultural change in the United States over the years has profoundly affected both the producer and society as a whole. The history of that change is characterized by several long-term patterns (such as the continual decline in the number of farms and a corresponding increase in the size of farms) that have pervasive and continuous effects on agricultural producers and American society. On the other hand, several recent developments in agriculture in the United States show marked departures from the patterns of the past, and it is uncertain how these changes will affect the future structure of agriculture and the nature of its relationships with American society. For example, during the 1980s farmers in the United States were faced with their most severe financial crisis since the Great Depression. As a result of low commodity prices, high interest rates, decreasing export markets, falling land values and other factors, the number of farmers forced from agriculture was high (U.S. Department of Agriculture 1984a; Leholm et al. 1985; Murdock and Leistritz 1988; Murdock et al. 1985; Murdock et al. 1986). In addition, major breakthroughs in areas such as biotechnology promise to drastically change agriculture in the United States (Buttel 1985; Buttel et al. 1983; Kloppenburg 1984). Thus the future of agriculture in the United States, like its past, is likely to be one in which both farming patterns and their interrelationships to American society are constantly changing.

Increased understanding of the causes and consequences of past changes in the structure of agriculture provides the bases of knowledge necessary to anticipate the future structure of agriculture in the United States and the relationship between agriculture and the rest of society.[1] However, many of the dimensions essential for obtaining this knowledge base have not been adequately examined. Thus, many of the most critical issues affecting both the past and future of agriculture in the United States are related not to technical aspects of agricultural production but to social, economic, and policy issues (Paarlberg 1980). In particular, sociological analysis of the interrelationships between changes in the structure of agriculture in the United States and American society appear to be critical (Schwarzweller 1984), if such issues as the effects of alternative agricultural policies on farm producers, the distribution of the benefits of new technologies, and the effects of a decreasing number of farms on the viability of rural communities are to be adequately addressed.

Despite the long history of agriculture research and the rapid patterns of change in agriculture in the United States, the sociological dimensions of agriculture have received only limited attention even in the discipline of rural sociology. Thus, although the formation of the discipline and its major journal, *Rural Sociology,* resulted from concerns about the plight of American farmers during the Great Depression (Christenson and Garkovich 1985; Schwarzweller 1984; Falk and Gilbert 1985; Gillette 1913; Slocum 1962), rural sociologists' interest in agricultural topics has waxed and waned over the years. During the period from 1936 to 1945 *Rural Sociology* published fifty-two articles (14.5 percent of all articles published) dealing specifically with agriculture.[2] However, during the period from 1956 to 1965, the number declined to twenty-three (7 percent of all articles). Although articles on related topics such as the adoption and diffusion of agricultural innovations received extensive attention during this period, interest in adoption also began to decline after 1960 (Fliegel and van Es 1983).[3] Only recently (since the late 1970s) has interest in the structure of agriculture been revived with over eighty articles (22.7 percent of the articles) appearing from 1976 to 1985. Attention to the issues surrounding agricultural production has thus not been a consistent concern of even that group of sociologists whom one would expect to be most concerned with agriculture.

Even during the recent period of revived interest in the topic, the examination of issues central to understanding agriculture has been uneven. Although a large number of journal articles, agricultural experiment station and extension service publications, and numerous books address issues related to the past, present, and future structure of agriculture in the United States (Wimberley and Bebee 1980), a surprisingly small number of recent works look specifically at the sociological dimensions of the structure of agriculture in a conceptually grounded, system-

6   atic, and integrated manner. In fact, nearly all existing works suffer from one or more of the following three weaknesses: (1) they are edited books with articles that have not been systematically integrated; (2) they examine only a single dimension of the sociology of agriculture; or (3) they are atheoretical and fail to provide a conceptual basis for tracing the interdependence among the various components of agriculture. Thus, despite the existence of many excellent recent works (e.g., Rodefeld et al. 1978; Schertz 1979; U.S. Department of Agriculture 1979; Berardi and Geisler 1984; Friedland et al. 1981; Summers 1983; Buttel and Newby 1980; Busch and Lacy 1983), there is no recent general work examining the multiple dimensions of the sociology of agriculture through the use of a systematically applied theoretical framework.

There are several reasons why such a work is needed. First, as in any field of study, the use of a theoretically informed approach ensures that the concepts used in an analysis are systematically defined and that the major premises and suppositions surrounding a given explanation of a phenomenon are clearly delineated (Stinchcombe 1968). In addition, a theoretically informed work provides the basis for integrating diverse phenomena and provides a basis from which alternative futures can be evaluated. Several scholars in the sociology of agriculture have clearly noted both the atheoretical nature of past evaluations of agricultural phenomena and the benefits of the use of theoretically informed analyses (Berardi and Geisler 1984; Buttel and Newby 1980; Dunlap and Martin 1983).

Equally important is the need for a work that examines multiple dimensions of the structure of agriculture using a single perspective. Agriculture in the United States exists in a complex context in which the organizational structure of American society, its diverse technological bases, its nonfarm and urban industrial base and numerous other dimensions affect both the structure of agriculture and its future course of development. Such factors need to be examined using a single perspective that provides a means of integrating such dimensions. A theoretically informed description of the sociological structure of agriculture in the United States is thus clearly essential if an increased understanding of those events that have shaped agriculture in the past, and that are likely to affect it in the future, is to be obtained.

This book provides a theoretically informed general reference that describes key dimensions of the structure of agriculture in the United States, integrating these dimensions to provide a coherent perspective on

the past, present, and possible future structure of agriculture in the 7
United States. The perspective used to organize the work is that of human ecology. Using this perspective as an organizing and synthesizing mechanism, the factors that form key dimensions of the structure of agriculture or that affect the formation of that structure are described. The intent is twofold: first, to provide a useful single-source description of the multiple dimensions affecting the structure of agriculture in the United States and the societal consequences of agricultural change; second, to provide an exposition of the use of the ecological framework for explaining the sociological dimensions of agricultural phenomena.

Although numerous perspectives may be used to organize and synthesize a work on the sociological dimensions of agriculture in the United States, we believe the use of an ecological perspective is merited by several factors. First, this perspective is recognized within the sociology of agriculture as having utility for examining agricultural issues (Dunlap and Martin 1983; Albrecht and Murdock 1984, 1985a; Murdock and Albrecht 1985) and has a long tradition in sociology (Theodorson 1961; Micklin and Choldin 1984). As such, human ecology has both a sufficient empirical base as well as a level of substantive content necessary to support such an effort.

Second, we believe that the framework allows a number of dimensions central to the understanding of past and possible future events in U.S. agriculture to be addressed in a systematic fashion and in a way that provides new insights concerning the causes and consequences of changes in the structure of agriculture. Thus, the role of future technologies in agriculture, the effects of organizational changes in agricultural practices on the environment, and the evolving interdependence between agriculture and rural communities are issues that have ecological components and can be usefully interpreted using ecological concepts.

Third, human ecology is obviously a framework with which we are intimately familiar and which we believe can be useful in understanding agricultural phenomena. Thus, we concur with the premise of Schnore (1961, 128) that "the study of social organization is the central focus of the entire sociological enterprise" and maintain that social organization should be the central focus of the sociology of agriculture. Furthermore, we maintain with Duncan (1961, 140) that organizational questions "can best be illuminated . . . by stating them and attacking them as ecological problems." Finally, because of the interdisciplinary nature of the human ecological perspective (Hawley 1986; Micklin and Choldin 1984), we

8   believe that a more complete exposition of an ecological perspective on the sociology of agriculture in the United States may provide a useful basis for the integration of sociological dimensions with other physical and biological approaches to the examination of agricultural phenomena.

In sum, we believe there are advantages in using an ecological perspective. However, in describing the human ecological perspective on agriculture we attempt only to establish the utility of the ecological framework for explaining agricultural phenomena and not its superiority relative to other perspectives.

LIMITATIONS OF THE EFFORT

The present effort is limited in several ways. First, the analysis is clearly focused on dimensions of agriculture as practiced in the United States since 1900. Issues such as those related to the class structure of peasant agriculture, migrant farm labor, and the role of women in development are given little attention, not because they are not important to understanding the past and present structure of agriculture but simply because of the need to focus the effort given space limitations.

Second, the focus is on the sociological dimensions of U.S. agriculture and particularly on those concerns most closely related to the changing structure of U.S. agriculture. Analyses of the key economic and physical science dimensions affecting agriculture, though clearly essential to obtaining a complete understanding of agriculture in the United States, are largely beyond the scope of the work. In like manner, some attention is given to the social psychological determinants and consequences of agricultural practices, but the major emphases are macrostructural and organizational.

Third, as with any single effort, we examine only some of the many dimensions affecting agriculture in the United States, and the work likely reflects our biases and experiences gained primarily from firsthand knowledge of agriculture in the western United States. We thus believe that this endeavor makes a contribution to understanding the sociology of the structure of agriculture in the United States.

ORGANIZATION OF THE TEXT   9

The book is organized into this introduction and eight additional chapters. Chapter 2 develops the theoretical framework used to examine the causes and consequences of agricultural change. The chapter begins with an overview of the human ecological approach, then compares and contrasts human ecology with other theoretical approaches that have been used previously in the sociology of agriculture. The discussion presents several examples of the use of human ecology to explain the structure, and changes in the structure, of agriculture in the United States. Overall, the discussion in this chapter provides a description of the major concepts in human ecology and how these concepts can be applied to agriculture.

The third chapter describes the present state of agriculture and the historical developments through which it reached its present stage of development. Much of this discussion is based on historical data available from the census of agriculture. Some of the structural issues discussed in this chapter include the size and number of farms, the degree of agricultural dualism, the extent of farm concentration, the extent of part-time farming, and the form of tenure, organization, and labor relationships in agriculture in the United States.

Chapter 4 is the first of several chapters that examine ecological factors that influence and are influenced by the structure of agriculture and changes therein. Specifically, Chapter 4 examines the agricultural environment. Only recently have sociological researchers recognized the importance of environmental resources for agricultural structure and change (Ashby 1982; Dunlap and Martin 1983), and several recent articles have established that the availability of critical natural resources has important consequences for agriculture and rural society (Albrecht and Murdock 1984, 1985b, 1986a, 1986b; Albrecht and Ladewig 1985). This chapter explores the effects of the availability of natural resources on the structure of farm organizations and the commodities produced. In addition, the chapter discusses the consequences of changes occurring in the availability of critical natural resources for agriculture and rural society. Finally, some potential environmental consequences of modern agriculture in the United States are examined.

The fifth chapter describes the relationship between technology and agriculture. This chapter reviews some of the important technological developments that have occurred in the past and the consequences of

10   these developments for agriculture and rural society. Unlike most previous treatments of the topic, this chapter does not merely describe the consequences of past technological developments; rather, it establishes a framework for explaining the consequences of previous technological developments and for projecting the consequences of future technological breakthroughs. This is done by showing that the impacts of new forms of technologies vary by the types of interdependence that exist between a technology and the environmental and organizational bases in an area (Murdock and Albrecht 1985). Examples clarify the ecological premises underlying this chapter and describe some of the likely consequences of future technological developments in agriculture.

In addition to environmental resources and technology, the structure of agriculture is also dramatically influenced by numerous forms of nonfarm organizations. The effects of these organizational forms are the topic of Chapter 6. Specifically, this chapter discusses four types of nonfarm organizations — government, financial and economic institutions, agribusiness, and organizations that represent farmers.

One of the most obvious and discussed consequences of agricultural change is the effects of these changes on rural population trends. This relationship is the topic of Chapter 7. During the past several decades the industrialization of agriculture greatly reduced the labor needs of farming and resulted in a vast out-migration of farm people. This out-movement from farming did not occur evenly across the agricultural spectrum. For example, the likelihood of leaving farming has been greater among tenant farmers, small farmers, and black farmers than among other segments of the farm population. Consequently, the demographic structure of rural America is vastly different today than it has been in the past. This chapter contains a discussion of the historical population trends and also an examination of the size, distribution, and composition of the rural population today. In addition, the likely implications of future agricultural changes for the rural population are discussed.

During the 1940s Walter Goldschmidt (1946, 1978b) maintained that the structure of farming in an area had a major influence on numerous economic, fiscal, community service, and social aspects of nearby rural communities. Since that time many other studies have examined the relationship between agricultural change and the rural community (e.g., Leistritz and Ekstrom 1986; Leistritz et al. 1986; Heffernan 1982a). Chapter 8 reviews this literature and uses human ecological theory to examine the implications of agricultural change for socioeconomic conditions in rural communities.

Chapter 9 is the concluding chapter. It examines future research topics that must be examined if the issues affecting the future structure of agriculture in the United States are to be addressed. It also uses the theoretical framework developed in Chapter 2 and the findings from the other chapters to describe alternative possible future structures of agriculture in the United States. It includes a discussion of both the nature of these future trends and their likely consequences. Finally, we make suggestions about improving the theoretical development of the sociology of agriculture, arguing that the field's conceptual base must receive further development if we are to improve our understanding of the issues and to project future changes in agriculture in the United States.

This work, then, is both an attempt to provide a useful single-source overview of some of the key issues affecting agriculture in the United States and an attempt to show the relevance of human ecology for integrating explanations bearing on such issues. We believe the work is both descriptively useful and conceptually insightful. We hope that its legacy will be one of inspiring additional works aimed at both refuting and confirming the suppositions we propose.

NOTES

1. Farm or agricultural structure refers to factors such as the size and ownership of the farm operation, the organization and use of resources in farming, the commodities produced, the form of business organization and the manner in which business decisions are made, the manner in which the farming unit procures its inputs and markets its products, the ease of entry into farming as an occupation, and the extent to which operators depend on farm income (as opposed to nonfarm income) (Penn 1979).

2. The data provided here is a result of examining each article in the first fifty volumes of *Rural Sociology* (1936–85). Each article was examined to determine whether or not the focus was on an agricultural issue. If other individuals evaluated these articles undoubtedly the results would be slightly different. However, our purpose was to examine broad trends. Also, articles dealing with the sociology of agriculture have outlets in addition to *Rural Sociology,* and no effort was made to enumerate these articles. For fifty years *Rural Sociology* has been the major outlet for research in the sociology of agriculture, and the publications covered therein provide a general reflection of the interest of rural sociologists and others interested in rural issues (Christenson and Garkovich 1985; Sewell 1965).

   3. Articles dealing with the adoption and diffusion of farm practices were counted separately. The totals are as follows: 1936–45, one article; 1946–55, eighteen articles; 1956–65, forty-two articles; 1966–75, thirty-three articles; 1976–85, nineteen articles. While adoption-diffusion research could be considered a branch of the sociology of agriculture, the focus of these articles is substantially different. For example, although adoption-diffusion research is concerned with the adoption of a specific farm practice, the focus emphasized in this book is broader, examining the consequences of the spread of that particular farm practice. Earlier researchers studying adoption and diffusion issues were generally not concerned with the structural or social aspects of the spread of these practices and technologies (Fliegel and van Es 1983; Goss 1979).

2

Human Ecology and U.S. Agriculture

A s noted in Chapter 1, we believe the human ecological framework provides a useful theoretical perspective for understanding and explaining many of the characteristics of, and changes which have affected, the historical development of agriculture in the United States. We also maintain that its basic premises and concepts may prove useful in anticipating future changes in U.S. agriculture. The purpose of this chapter is twofold — to present the basic premises, concepts, and structure of human ecological theory and to demonstrate its utility for understanding historical and future patterns of change in U.S. agriculture.

In describing the elements of ecological theory we also present a brief history of the ecological perspective and compare its basic premises to those of other widely used perspectives. In attempting to demonstrate the utility of the ecological framework for understanding agricultural phenomena, our analysis is admittedly selective and inclusive of only some of the major processes and events that have shaped the structure of agriculture in the United States. We hope, however, that by presenting an overview of the basic concepts of the ecological framework, other scholars may be led to further expand the tenets and to provide additional interpretations of the events shaping U.S. agriculture using a human ecological framework. Our intent then is to lay the foundation for the further expansion of the use of human ecological theory in the sociology of agriculture while providing a limited number of examples of

13

14   its applicability. We thus seek to establish the utility of the key concepts that are used to organize the remainder of the text.

THE HUMAN ECOLOGICAL FRAMEWORK

Historical Development of Human Ecology

The framework of human ecology is a product of the nineteenth century's emphasis upon biological evolution and naturalism. As Hawley (1950, 5) comments:

> The basis of modern ecology, as of all other branches of the biological sciences and to a large extent of the social sciences as well, lies in the work by the great biologists, Darwin and Wallace. In particular, Darwin's *Origin of Species,* published in 1859, and his *Descent of Man,* 1871, set the stage for a new era in biological research. Attention shifted from a preoccupation with cosmological problems, such as the ultimate meaning of each form of life for every other which followed from the assumption of immutability of species to a search for specific causes responsible for the existence of species, based upon accumulated evidence of change in the organic world. Final causes were forsaken in favor of necessary and sufficient causes. In the ferment of biological empiricism of the 19th century a scientific natural history began to take form.

In this regard, human ecological theory is not very different from more traditional forms of sociological theory stemming from the works of Durkheim and others. Thus, Appelbaum (1970, 15) indicates:

> Strongly influenced by Darwin's work in biological evolution, theorists often sought a sociological analogue to the living organism. Although the earlier theories were highly evaluative in defining progress in terms of Western industrial society, Spencer and Durkheim developed a model of organismic evolution that has strongly influenced sociological thinking to the present day.

What distinguishes ecological theory from other sociological perspectives is its continued emphasis on the applicability of basic ecological concepts to human society. Hawley (1950, 66) notes:

Much of this section is derived from Steve H. Murdock, Ecological expansion in southern Appalachia: A theoretical and empirical assessment (1975).

Ecology begins, as we have seen, with the problem of how growing,   **15**
multiplying beings maintain themselves in a constantly changing but
ever restricted environment. It proceeds, in other words, with the
conception of life as a continuous struggle for adjustment of organisms to environment, a struggle initiated and continued essentially
by the differential modes of change of these two components of the
life process.

This aspect of the perspective has often led social scientists to perceive the perspective as a form of biological determinism (Theodorson
1961; Micklin and Choldin 1984). However, it is a distinctly human
ecology although it employs concepts from basic ecology. As Hawley
(1950, 68–69) observes:

> Man is an organism, to be sure, and as such he has much in common
> with other forms of organic life.
> But at the same time he is capable of an extraordinary degree of
> flexibility and refinement in behavior. This is to be observed in
> man's extensive control over his surroundings, as manifested in the
> degree to which he modifies and reconstructs his environment
> through invention and the use of tools and again in the complex
> cooperative arrangements entered into with his fellow man. Further-
> more, man's great facility for devising and accumulating methods of
> coping with life situations is evidence of a dynamics in human be-
> havior that is without counterpart elsewhere in the animate world. It
> is this that constitutes man as an object of special inquiry and makes
> possible a human as distinct from a general ecology.

And Duncan (1964, 77) states:

> You cannot throw away what is distinctively human—communica-
> tion with symbols, custom and the artificial or cultural transforma-
> tions man makes in his environment—and treat the residue as the
> ecology of the species. . . . A partitioning of the world of human
> affairs into the ecological and the nonecological is not used. When
> examined from an ecological standpoint, social evolution and social
> organization are subject matter for human ecology.

Nearly from its beginning, however, the history of human ecology
has been characterized by reactions and overreactions to its biological
roots. The impact of human ecology on general sociology was perhaps at
its strongest during the 1920s and 1930s when it formed a major part of
the theoretical basis for the development of the Chicago School of So-

16   ciology. Ecological theory was used to explain the location of areas of crime and vice within cities (Reckless 1926; Levin and Lindesmith 1937), to explain the growth and structure of urban areas (Burgess and McKenzie 1925), to examine the nature of neighborhoods (Zorbaugh 1926), and even to explain the incidence of mental illness in urban areas (Dunham 1937). Within this school, however, one of its founders, Robert Park, was to assert that human ecology was only applicable to a part of human existence.

> The facts seem to be, then, that human society, as distinguished from plant and animal society, is organized on two levels, the biotic and the cultural. There is a symbiotic society based on competition and a cultural society based on communication and consensus. . . . Human ecology is, fundamentally, an attempt to investigate the processes by which, when the biotic balance and the social equilibrium are disturbed, the transition is made from one relatively stable order to another (Park 1936, 13–14).

In like manner Quinn (1939, 168) characterized human ecology as:

> A specialized field of sociological analysis which investigates (1) those impersonal subsocial aspects of communal structure — both spatial and functional — which arise and change as the result of interaction between men through the medium of limited supplies of the environment, and (2) the nature and forms of the processes by which this subsocial structure arises and changes.

This division of the social world into the subsocial and the social, with the ecological framework being limited to explanation at the level of the subsocial, was the dominant perspective on ecology in the Chicago School. Because of this emphasis during this early evolution of the ecological framework, its concepts and perspective were seen as primarily applicable to social phenomena that had a spatial or temporal referent or that could be seen as resulting from the basic concept of competition (e.g., invasion and succession of ethnic groups in urban neighborhoods). It is this form of human ecology that remains prominent in the minds of many sociologists (e.g., Swanson and Busch 1985) when they think of human ecological theory. This form of human ecology has been referred to by Theodorson and others (Murdock and Sutton 1974; Murdock 1979; Albrecht and Murdock 1985a) as the "old" school of human ecology and was the subject of widespread criticism (Alihan 1938; Davie

1938; Firey 1945) even during the height of its development.

The work of Amos Hawley ushered in another period of rapid development of human ecology. This era has been referred to as the "new ecology" by Theodorson (1961) and others (Murdock and Sutton 1974; Murdock 1979) and has been characterized by a rejection of the limitation of ecology to the subsocial, to competitive processes, and to the analysis of temporal and spatial patterns. In a classic article (1944) and in his subsequent book (1950) based on his work and that of McKenzie, Hawley reasoned that such limitations were not endemic to the human ecological framework.

> But to be more specific, responsibility for the existing chaos in human ecology, it seems to me, rests upon certain aberrant intellectual tendencies which have dominated most of the work that has been done. The most significant of these may be described as: (1) the failure to maintain a close working relationship between human ecology and general or bioecology; (2) an undue preoccupation with the concept of competition; and (3) the persistence in definitions of the subject of a misplaced emphasis on "spatial relations" (Hawley 1944, 399).

Hawley argued that human ecology should utilize the more advanced concepts of general ecology, should not be limited to processes to which only competition applied, but is equally applicable to processes reflecting cooperation (thus reflecting not only symbiotic but commensalistic relationships as well) and other social processes. Spatial and temporal patterns, he maintained, are merely convenient abstractions by which to measure activities and relationships.

> The subject of ecological inquiry then is the community, the form and development of which are studied with particular reference to the limiting and supporting factors of the environment. Ecology, in other words, is a study of the morphology of collective life in both its static and its dynamic aspects. It attempts to determine the nature of community structure in general, the types of communities that appear in different habitats, and the specific sequence of change in community development (1944, 403).

In addition, Hawley (1944, 405) noted:

> The distinctive feature of the study lies in the conception of the adjustment of man to habitat as a process of community develop-

18   ment. Whereas this may be an implicit assumption in most social
science disciplines, it is for human ecology the principal working
hypothesis. Thus human ecology might well be regarded as the basic
science.

Hawley's conception was holistic, which placed human ecology clearly
within the domain of the social sciences.

The basic premises and concepts of the new ecology were further
developed by Hawley (1950) and by Duncan (1961, 1964), Duncan and
Schnore (1959), and Schnore (1961). Duncan and Schnore (1959) in an
attempt to expand the applicability of the ecological framework consolidated the major concepts of ecology under the heuristic device referred
to as the POET variables (population, organization, environment, and
technology), or the ecological complex. Although more frequently used
by nonecologists than ecologists, and in fact, often criticized for its
generality by ecologists (Gibbs and Martin 1959; Micklin and Choldin
1984), the POET variables are the most frequently used conceptualiza-
tion in human ecology. Although the development of this and other
concepts of the new ecology served to further expand the applicability of
human ecological factors to a diverse range of societal phenomena, only
a few theoretical developments since Hawley's classic work have attempted to add to the conceptual basis of human ecology (Duncan 1964;
Hawley 1986; Micklin 1973).

Since the early 1960s a majority of the developments in human
ecological theory have involved applications of the expanded ecological
framework of the new ecology to the analysis of a diverse set of factors.
Thus, such factors as urban systems (Hawley 1971; Berry and Kasarda
1977), the evaluation of demographic processes such as migration (Sly
1972; Sly and Tayman 1977), the analysis of characteristics of organizations (Hannan and Freeman 1977; Kasarda and Bidwell 1984; Carroll
and Huo 1986), the examination of patterns of criminal activity (Cohen
and Felson 1979), the synthesis of community theory (Murdock and
Sutton 1974), the systematization of community impact analysis (Murdock 1979), and the analysis of agricultural phenomena (Dunlap and
Martin 1983; Albrecht and Murdock 1984, 1985a) have all been approached through the use of a human ecological framework.

Human ecology has developed over nearly a century into an increasingly holistic framework but remains an infrequently used social science
perspective. Few theoretical works surveying sociological theory give it

more than passing attention, and it remains tainted by its close association with biological ecology, by its founders' tendencies to limit it to the subsocial dimensions of human existence, and by the tendency of some to confuse it with perspectives such as that of sociobiology (Wilson 1975) that view social behavior as biologically determined. As we attempt to demonstrate, its concepts are applicable to basic social processes and forge needed linkages between environmental and social factors.

Basic Assumptions of Human Ecology

From Hawley's (1950, 66–67) assertion that

> ecology begins, as we have seen, with the problem of how growing, multiplying beings maintain themselves in a constantly changing but ever restricted environment. It proceeds, in other words, with the conception of life as a continuous struggle for adjustment of organisms to environment, a struggle initiated and continued essentially by the differential modes of change of these two components of the life process. In the ecological view, however, life is not an individual but an aggregate phenomenon. Hence the underlying assumption of ecology is that adjustment to environment is a mutual, in fact a communal, function. The adjustment of a population to its physical world occurs not through the independent actions of many individuals but through the coordination and organization of individual actions to form a single functional unit.
>
> The inevitable crowding of organisms upon limited resources produces a complex interaction of organism with organism and of organism with environment in the course of which individuals adjust to one another in ways conducive to a more effective utilization of the habitat.

and from the view that

> man is an organism, to be sure, and as such he has much in common with other forms of organic life.
>
> But at the same time he is capable of an extraordinary degree of flexibility and refinement of behavior. This is to be observed in man's extensive control over his surroundings, as manifested in the degree to which he modifies and reconstructs his environment through invention and the use of tools and again in the complex cooperative arrangements entered into with his fellow man. Furthermore, man's great facility for devising and accumulating methods of

coping with life situations is evidence of a dynamics in human behavior that is without counterpart elsewhere in the animate world. It is this that constitutes man an object of special inquiry and makes possible a human as distinct from a general ecology (Hawley 1950, 68–69).

the three basic premises of human ecology can be derived. These premises are (Murdock 1975): (1) that the central and most important problem of organic existence involves adaptation to a set of environmental factors, (2) that it is only through the development of an interdependent collective organization that adaptation is possible, and (3) that man's adaptive capacity is indeterminate and he tends to preserve and expand life to the full extent permitted by environmental limitations.

These assumptions have numerous ramifications for the use of the ecological framework and its application to diverse types of sociological phenomena and have been referred to by Hawley (1986, 7) as the adaptive, growth, and evolution propositions of human ecology. The first assumption, that the adaptation of organisms to the environment is the central problem of life, led to a theoretical and empirical emphasis upon sustenance activities (Gibbs and Martin 1959) and upon the organizational configurations that typically follow from different sustenance functions (Duncan et al. 1960; Eberstein and Frisbie 1982; Micklin and Choldin 1984).

The second major assumption of human ecology, that of the collective nature of adaptation, also affected the nature of the ecological enterprise and its theoretical and empirical development. Perhaps the primary result of this emphasis is that ecologists have come to center their attention upon the structural aspects of social existence and to neglect the social psychological realm of human behavior. Limiting emphasis to structural factors is not shared by anthropologists (Hardesty 1980) who apply ecological principles to the study of the characteristics of human cultures and is also being questioned by some sociologists (Hwang and Murdock 1983; Hwang 1983). However, the tendency of ecological analysis to remain at the structural level endures. At the same time, this assumption points to interdependence as the key to organizational adaptation. "Interdependence is the inescapable and fundamental aspect of human existence. Such, at any rate, is the elementary assumption of social science generally and of human ecology in particular" (Hawley 1950, 177). The task of discerning the manner in which people interrelate

in order to achieve a satisfactory state of adaptation to a set of environ- **21**
mental conditions is central to human ecology.

The third assumption of human ecology addresses the qualitative difference between humans and other animate life. It denotes that humans are more flexible, more adaptive, and more expansive than any other creatures. The impact of this assumption has been to move human ecology into the mainstream of social science and to dispel the perceptions of the framework as applicable to only the subsocial dimensions of human existence. It is this assumption that specifies the differences between general and human ecology and that brings culture and the systems with which it interrelates into the realm of human ecology (Duncan 1964; Hawley 1986).

Taken together, then, these assumptions establish that human ecology is a social science framework that concentrates primarily on the explanation of the organization and structure of social life. They establish the importance within human ecology of the physical and social environment and of the adaptive process by which human societies cope with environmental characteristics and change. These premises thus establish that the human ecological framework is one that links the classic concerns of the social sciences with the importance of the environment as recognized in general ecology.

Basic Concepts of Human Ecology

Having described the origins of ecology, its assumptions, and their implications, we present the basic concepts of human ecology in this section. Many of these follow quite directly from the major assumptions outlined above.

Environment. From the first of the basic assumptions it is clear that the environment is the starting point for the human ecologist.

> Environment is a generic concept under which are subsumed all external forces and factors to which an organism or aggregate of organisms is actually or potentially responsive. The very breadth of the concept restricts its use for purposes of precise description. In general, however, environment refers to the medium in which an organism exists. Environment comprises the raw materials of life

and the conditions both favorable and unfavorable, that affect the use of those materials. The supply of necessary materials and the circumstances which attend their use are such as to constitute an ever-present problem for living creatures (Hawley 1950, 12–13).

Environment is thus a very broad and inclusive concept and one which requires internal differentiation. Such differentiation must be limited, however.

Any attempt to enumerate the components of environment involves one in an endless task; for each species and type of life responds to a variety of stimuli in a way more or less peculiar to itself. It is possible for general purposes, however, to avoid the extreme multiplicity of factors included in the meaning of environment by reverting to the simple classification . . . namely: (1) inorganic; and (2) organic. In the former are included all the mechanical and nonliving conditions that surround the organism such as light, air, pressure, humidity, temperature, minerals, topography, etc. The latter, the organic environment, comprises all manifestations of life whose activities impinge upon the individual or group of individuals. This includes other members of the same species present in the area. Thus man's organic environment is composed of the vegetation which impedes his movements, animals which prey upon him and upon which he preys, domesticated plants and animals and what is often most important, his fellow men (Hawley 1950, 17).

Environment then may be simplistically divided into inorganic and organic components. The concept of environment so defined and delineated is still extremely broad and inclusive and, as shall be shown presently, is constantly redefined and expanded by the organisms adapting to it (Hawley 1986, 11). Its differentiating feature lies in its relative fixity and unalterability relative to other factors operating at a given period of time. It is a relative fixity because the environment is ultimately alterable by nonhuman and human agents and because the degree of alterability varies with the elements of the environment in question. Thus, the inorganic environment is less alterable than the organic sphere. In sum then, to define environment is to ask what are the fixed, not immediately alterable factors present at a given period of time that serve as limiting, conditioning, and predisposing influences upon the behavior of organisms.

Population. The concept of population is derived from both the first **23** and second major assumptions of human ecology. It refers to both the living elements that adapt to environment and to the group nature of adaptation. It must, however, be seen in relation to environment for "the relation between the two is a fundamental dependence of one on the other" (Hawley 1950, 14). It is that living element that, through various modes of aggregation of its units, adapts to a set of environmental factors. It refers, in the demographic sense, to a spatially delimited aggregate.

The distinctive characteristic of population is its relative alterability by comparison to the environment. It, rather than the environment, is the dynamic, active, adaptive element of the environment-organism dualism. This distinction is essential and prevents the confusion of the ecological concept of population with the whole realm of demographic phenomena. In a strict conceptual sense the classic demographic phenomena of population size, distribution, and composition are the result of past changes in population elements, and because of their relative fixity to change at a given point in time, might best be seen as a set of environmental factors limiting the modes of possible adaptation. Population change and the demographic processes of fertility, mortality, and migration, on the other hand, because of their relative alterability, are dynamic factors symbolic of the constant process of adaptation and should be viewed as population variables. This distinction is clearly a subtle one because of the constant interaction of environment and population and is one that we shall largely ignore, but it demonstrates the care that must be taken to carefully delineate the concepts of human ecology.

Adaptation. Adaptation is the process referred to in the first assumption of human ecology. Adaptation is the process that links other phenomena to environmental factors. It involves a process of adjustment by which a population maintains itself in a given set of environmental conditions. "Adaptation is the securing and conserving of control over the environment" (Hawley 1950, 16). "As a process, adaptation means nothing more than a striving to establish a working relationship; as a state of being, adaptation is simply that which exists at the moment" (Hawley 1950, 18).

It is essential that adaptation be considered as a striving toward a working relationship and as that which exists at the moment, and that

24   evaluative connotations concerning the correctness of the adaptation be avoided. By so doing, one avoids the tautological situation of insisting that because a state of affairs exists, it is the correct adaptive state, and the reason one knows it is correct is because it exists. Adaptation is a continuous, never-ending process because the factors to which it is a reaction are constantly changing. The state of adaptation present at any given time may represent the ideal state for some elements of a population, but at the same time it may represent a less than adequate state of adaptation for other elements.

Interdependence. Interdependence is the key process referred to in the second major assumption of human ecology. Interdependence refers to the fact that populations and organisms within populations, in order to exist and survive within an environmental nexus, must relate their members to one another in various dependent modes. Two different types of interdependence are emphasized in ecological theory. One is the symbiotic form. It refers, in its strict biological configuration, to relationships in which unlike life forms cooperate for their mutual benefit. Within the human sphere, it refers to relationships in which persons performing unlike activities cooperate to perform specific functions. The complex division of labor so characteristic of modern industrial societies is one of the most prevalent forms of a symbiotic relationship.

The second form of interdependence is the commensalistic form. In nature this consists of those relationships between like life forms that function for their mutual benefit. In human societies its most common forms are the associations between people with similar characteristics such as social classes and informal organizations.

Interdependence in either form represents a set of indispensable relationships. These relationships make each organism dependent upon the other, increase the survival chances of each organism, and promote a greater quantity and quality of life goods.

Technology. Technology is a concept derived from the major assumptions and from the concepts delineated above. It refers to all those techniques, practices, and tools utilized by humans to facilitate their environmental adaptability and to expand the dimensions of their environment. In general, two modes of technology may be distinguished **25** (Murdock 1975) — mechanical-scientific and cultural innovation.

The mechanical-scientific mode refers to the application of mechanical techniques and scientific findings to environmental problems to promote environmental expansion. It is this mode that has markedly changed the limits and realm of the environment. It has decreased the effects of the inorganic and organic environment by developing mechanisms that moderate the influence of the environment (e.g., cooling and heating systems that moderate the effects of temperature extremes or transportation technologies that decrease the cost and time delays entailed in transversing physical distances) or that bring new environmental resources to bear on the limitations of the environment (e.g., new energy sources such as gas, oil, and coal that allowed fossil fuel power to be substituted for animal power).

Closely related to the mechanical form of technology and mutually interactive with it is the mode of technology we refer to as cultural innovation. The concept denotes the shifts in patterns of behavior that facilitate various types of adaptation. The routinization of time schedules is an example of this form of technological development. Its development marked an essential change in ordering the functions of modern industrial society. The development of many aspects of the mechanical-scientific forms of technology were dependent in part upon such cultural innovations as rational-scientific thought. These two forms of technology — the mechanical-scientific and cultural innovation — have worked interactively to produce dramatic changes in the environment and to increase humans' adaptability to the environment.

Organization. "Organization is assumed to be a property of the population that has evolved and is sustained in the process of adaptation of the population to its environment, which may include other populations" (Duncan and Schnore 1959, 136). It is that "system of relations among interdependent parts through which a population adapts to an environment" (Boland 1966, 1) and an "organization of activities, arranged in overlapping and interpenetrating series of activity constellations or groups" (Duncan and Schnore 1959, 137). It is thus the total set of interdependences resulting from a population's adaptation to a set of environmental and technological factors. Thus, organization reflects en-

26   vironmental limitations, population changes, technological factors, adaptation, and interdependence.

Organization involves the complex interaction of many factors and is often seen as the fourth element of the ecological complex, the other three elements of this complex being population, environment, and technology (Duncan 1959). As noted previously, these POET variables are often used as a convenient rubric for explaining ecological phenomena. Using these terms, organization must be seen "as reciprocally related to each of the other elements of the ecological complex." In fact, to define any of the elements of this complex adequately one has to take into account their relationship with organization (Duncan and Schnore 1959, 136). Organization is thus the key ecological variable. It is that variable that most clearly portrays the meaning of the ecological complex. To show its general relationship to other factors is to show, at least in part, that the ecological complex is operating upon such factors.

Organization does not subsume the other elements of the complex, however, for although these four elements are interactive, there are important distinctions among them. Population refers to the unit of analysis and the human element that must adapt; technology refers to the techniques for adaptation; and organization refers to a set of interrelated social activities utilized in, and resulting from, a population's adaptation to an environment. In relation to environment, it may be asserted that "environment is relevant to organization as it is defined and regulated by organization. Hence the environmental substance is the organizationally relevant environmental substance" (Boland 1966, 3). Environment provides the context in which organization develops. Thus, despite the interactive nature of the ecological complex, the four elements of it do have distinctive characteristics by which they can be delineated both empirically and theoretically.

The characteristics of organization that are seen as central to ecological analyses include functionality, differentiation, key function, dominance, and isomorphism. Functionality is an important aspect of ecological organization.

> Units are not usually regarded as organization unless they are active in the performance of one or more functions. . . . That by organization we mean an arrangement of differentiated parts suited to the performance of a given function or set of functions. . . . That ecological organization is the broad and general term used to refer to the complex of functional interrelationships by which men live (Hawley 1950, 178).

One of the chief functions of organization is that of adaptation, and it is in the examination of the general forms of this functional adaptation that ecological research has found one of its central problems. Functionality is an essential aspect of organization, and to be an organizational element is to fulfill or assist a population in pursuing an adaptive function.

Differentiation is yet another critical aspect of organization. "Organization necessarily presupposes differentiation. Only when divergent though mutually complementary units are articulated in some sort of system of working relationships may we properly use the term organization" (Hawley 1950, 195). Differentiation is a widely recognized social science concept and is usually discussed in terms of the division of labor, which is one of its symbiotic interdependent forms. "The occupational division of labor is the economically determined skeleton on which the flesh of modern social organization develops" (Kahl 1959, 39). Its presence, as indicated in the diversification of roles, duties, and responsibilities, is symbolic of its importance as an essential element of ecological organization.

Organizations are also characterized by key functions. These refer to the central activities of an organization that most closely link it to its environment. In terms of sustenance organization, they convey the connotation of major economic activity. Systems are characterized as agrarian, industrial, and so on. Such key functions determine much about the nature of social organization and its effects upon other phenomena and thus form essential elements of the concept of organization.

The characteristic of dominance refers to the tendency for organizations to develop hierarchies of influence. It refers to the tendency for elements to become differentiated in terms of their ability to manipulate one another. It is closely linked with the concept of power as used in general sociology (Hawley 1968). Generally, dominance centers on the key function, with those elements associated with the key function also becoming the dominant ones. Thus, in an area rich in minerals, mining often becomes the key function, while in an area with fertile soils and a favorable climate, agriculture often becomes the key function.

The characteristic of isomorphism refers to common patterns of organization that arise in response to various environmental, population, and technological conditions. Even in the face of environmental diversity certain common organizational responses may appear in each organizational complex. Thus, though the degree to which the division of labor has proceeded may differ from one area to another, there is little

28 doubt that some division of labor will be present in all areas. Isomorphism allows generalization and cross-sectional comparisons and is the central concept legitimizing the formation of various forms of typologies such as those involved in the functional classifications of cities (Tarver 1972; Berry and Horton 1970).

These five characteristics define essential aspects of organization. They point to the breadth and inclusiveness of the concept as used in human ecology and give a clear indication of why the concept of organization has become the central concern of ecological theory and research.

Ecosystem. The ecosystem refers to a territorially delineated system in which population, environmental, and technological factors interact to produce an organizational complex. It consists of the elements of the ecological complex given a spatial and temporal referent. Thus, to define an ecosystem requires asking the questions of where and when. Central to this concept is that of the ecosystem as providing a context for an interrelated set of factors that serve to control the simultaneous flow of three factors—materials, energy, and information (Duncan 1964). An ecosystem can be seen as "any unit that includes all the organisms in a given area interacting with the physical environment so that a flow of energy leads to clearly defined trophic structure, biotic diversity, and material cycles (i.e., exchange of materials between living and nonliving parts) (Odum 1971, 8). As Hawley notes (1986, 26) "an ecosystem is an arrangement of mutual dependencies in a population by which the whole operates as a unit and thereby maintains a viable environmental relationship." The ecosystem is thus the total system of study for the human ecologist.

Ecological Expansion. Ecological expansion is the ecological concept of change. Whereas the concept of ecosystem refers to the ecological organizational complex at a given point in time, ecological expansion refers to the process of change in the ecological complex. Expansion involves "change of a developmental character in which a community is enlarged and extended, becoming not only more inclusive but also increasingly complex in its internal structure" (Hawley 1950, 322). It involves the variables of the ecological complex and is characterized by "technological accumulation at an accelerated rate; intensified exploita-

tion of environment; demographic transition and organizational revolu-   **29**
tion" (Duncan 1964, 75). Although Hawley also delineated the change
concepts of ecological conversion and contraction (1950, 322), it is the
concept of expansion that has been central to ecological analysis.

These concepts, as described, form the basis of any application of
ecological theory to a substantive area and are thus the basis used in this
work to examine the changing nature of U.S. agriculture. However,
before delineating some of the areas in agriculture in which ecological
dimensions may be of significance, it is useful to delineate how ecological perspectives utilizing such concepts compare to other widely used
sociological frameworks.

Human Ecology and Other Sociological Frameworks

Before applying the framework of human ecology to agricultural
phenomena it may prove useful to discuss its characteristics relative to
several other widely used frameworks in sociology and to provide at least
some evaluation of the utility of the ecological framework in comparison
to these frameworks. The intent of this section is not to suggest that
ecological theory is somehow better than alternative frameworks but
rather to suggest that its use allows one to address standard sociological
concerns while including dimensions not usually addressed by traditional
sociological perspectives.

Space limitations allow only a few comparisons to be made. Thus,
we compare human ecology and three other frameworks—functional
theory, conflict (and by association, critical) theory, and symbolic interactionism. In making these comparisons we follow the comparative
dimensions delineated by Kinloch (1977). He notes that sociological
theories can be compared on the basis of their

1. ontological assumptions about the nature of society
2. ontological assumptions about the nature of the individual relative to society
3. focus of analysis (individual versus society or structural components of societies)
4. epistemological assumptions about the processes by which societies emerge
5. assumptions about the mechanisms through which a society
maintains itself

6. assumptions about the dominant social processes (e.g., consensus, conflict, and interaction) in societies

7. assumptions about the mechanisms by which societies change

Although somewhat arbitrary, these dimensions should prove useful for delineating the characteristics of human ecology relative to other sociological perspectives. In making these comparisons the characteristics of each framework are drawn from the works of their chief proponents. Thus, functionalism is delineated in a manner consistent with the work of Parsons (1937) and Merton (1968), conflict theory from the work of Marx (Bottomore 1964), Dahrendorf (1958), and Coser (1956), and symbolic interactionism from the works of Mead (1934), Cooley (1964), and Blumer (1969), while the ecological dimensions are those noted previously.

When a comparison is made using the dimensions outlined by Kinloch (1977), it can be maintained that each of the ecological, functional, and conflict perspectives hold to the reality of societal factors. Symbolic interactionists, on the other hand, maintain that the reality that exists is largely created by individuals in interaction. Ecologists stress that some environmental factors are largely beyond the control of individual organisms or interrelated sets of organisms, and thus, human ecology grants greater primacy to the environment than any of the other perspectives.

In regard to the relative role of individuals versus society, both functionalism and conflict theory stress the codetermination of social phenomena by groups and individuals. Symbolic interactionism tends to stress the individual and to see societal processes as arising due to the interaction of individuals. Human ecology stresses the primacy of the collective of the group or population. It is the collective adaptation of organisms that creates the characteristics of the ecosystem.

The level of analysis emphasized by the functional and conflict perspectives is the structural with secondary emphasis on the individual. Symbolic interactionism focuses on the individual and the processes of interaction between individuals. Human ecology places clear emphasis on group-level or aggregate analysis of populations. Although individuals are emphasized in some anthropological analyses of ecological phenomena (Bennett 1976), the ecological framework clearly emphasizes aggregate-level analysis.

The suggested answers to the question of how society emerges also differentiate the various perspectives. Functionalists tend to perceive so- **31** ciety arising as a result of individuals and groups responding to environmental, societal, and cultural factors. Environmental factors have primacy only in very primitive societies while in more developed societies a codetermination of societal characteristics through environmental, social, and cultural factors occurs. For conflict theorists the genesis of society lies in conflicts among groups over the control of key resources, both environmental and symbolic. For symbolic interactionists, society is the sum total of interactions among individuals. For human ecologists, society arises as a collective attempt of a population to adapt to the physical and social environment. Thus, the ecological and functional show clear similarities, but the environment is defined more restrictively in functionalism and is given a more limited role in the determination of social forms; whereas in human ecology, the broad and inclusive concept of environment is granted a greater degree of primacy.

For both the functionalist and the human ecologist the maintenance of society is obtained through the development of a relative equilibrium between forces in the system or ecosystem. Unlike the functionalist, however, the ecologist stresses the continuous alteration in that system through the processes of expansion, conversion, and contraction. Systems increase in complexity through expansion rather than by simply evolving to a new form (as has sometimes been maintained in functional descriptions of social evolution [Appelbaum 1970]). From the conflict perspective the maintenance of society results from coalitions and alliances of groups during conflicts with other groups for resources and access to the means of production. Finally, from the viewpoint of symbolic interactionism society is maintained through a routinization of symbolic patterns of interaction that come to control individuals' actions.

Although each of the perspectives emphasizes multiple social processes, they may be differentiated on the basis of their relative emphasis on various processes. Functionalism has been characterized as placing an overemphasis on consensus, while conflict theories have tended to emphasize conflictual processes. Interaction is the process most emphasized by symbolic interactionists. The perspective of human ecology stresses that interdependence arises from two alternative interactive processes, one based primarily on consensual processes between like organisms (commensalism) and the other involving organisms creating alliances on the basis of complimentary needs (symbiotic interdependence) that allow them to compete more effectively with other collectivities. For the ecologists, then, social phenomena are the result of a constant process of interaction between organism and environment in which commensalistic and symbiotic forms of adaptation are used.

For the functionalist, social change is a result of changes in functional needs. However, the explanation of what causes changes in functional needs has not been adequately explained by functionalists. From the conflict perspective change is continuous as groups struggle for control of resources. For the symbolic interactionist, social change occurs through the alteration of interaction patterns between individuals. From the human ecological perspective societies change either because of changes in the environment or because of technological and other factors that alter the relationships between organizations and environments that in turn may alter the very nature of the environment. Change for the ecologist is continuous and reflects the constant need for organisms to adapt to an ever-changing physical and social environment.

Although admittedly simplistic, the above comparisons clearly show the ecological perspective to be very different from the symbolic interactionistic perspective with ecology stressing group-level analysis and the realism of the physical and social environment in conditioning interaction. Ecology shares with conflict theory a realization that conflict and competition over resources may significantly affect societal patterns, but unlike conflict theory, ecology emphasizes the equally strong role of consensus. The ecological perspective is perhaps most similar to the functional perspective sharing with it an emphasis on systems and of functions within social organizations. It places greater emphasis on the role of the environment in the genesis of social organization, however, and grants greater influence to social conflict than the functional perspective. Unlike the functional perspective, social change is not difficult for the ecologist to explain but is part of the ongoing adaptive process that characterizes all natural systems. Finally, the ecological perspective differs from all of the other perspectives in its inclusion of concepts that allow it to interface more easily with biological and other sciences, in its greater emphasis on the collective nature of social life and in its conception of society as being the complex result of interactions between the characteristics of populations and environments, both physical and social. In sum, the ecological perspective can be seen as largely inclusive of the other sociological perspectives and as having the potential to more

effectively link social dimensions with phenomena reflecting the physical **33**
and biological environment (Duncan 1961; Hawley 1986; Siegel 1984).

HUMAN ECOLOGICAL DIMENSIONS OF AGRICULTURE

Having examined the concepts and dimensions of human ecology in some detail in previous sections of this chapter, we now turn our attention to the description of the relevance of ecological theory for use in examining the structure and patterns of change in U.S. agriculture. We do this first by briefly describing general areas of congruence between ecological theory and agricultural phenomena. We then attempt to demonstrate the utility of the ecological framework for understanding present and potential future patterns in agriculture by applying it to several key dimensions of the structure of American agriculture.

General Relevance of Ecological Concepts to American Agriculture

The general concepts of human ecology clearly have relevance for explaining agricultural patterns. Foremost among these is the concept of environment. Dunlap and Martin (1983) clearly note that environmental factors are of key importance in understanding differentials in the structure of agriculture. Such physical environmental factors as differentials in rainfall, soil type, temperature, and length of growing season are clearly consequential in determining the type and relative productivity of agriculture that predominates in different regions of the nation (Coughenour 1984).

The ecological concept of population is equally relevant. This concept of population emphasizes that phenomena occurring at the macrostructural rather than the individual level are largely responsible for the changes that occur in an ecosystem. In this regard, the size, composition, and distribution of the farm population are greatly influenced by such processes as the mechanization of agricultural production, the adoption of government policies that have controlled agricultural production, and the changing patterns of crop exports. In like manner, the fact that the adaptations to these processes have been similar in different regions of the nation suggests that aggregate patterns of adaptation tend to pre-

34   dominate and points to the isomorphic nature of this adaptation.

The role of technology in altering the characteristics of agriculture is obvious. The mechanization of agriculture with its subsequent reduction in labor needs has been perhaps the most dominant factor in changing agriculture in this century. The concept of technology in both its mechanical-scientific form (e.g., new harvesting machines, the tractor, pesticides) and as cultural innovation and education (the agricultural extension service) has dramatically affected the course of agriculture in the United States.

The concept of adaptation is, as noted previously, also of clear relevance to agriculture. Few economic groups have had to make such dramatic adaptations as farmers and ranchers in the United States. Increasing farm size, increased levels of capital investment, and increased specialization are only some of the forms of adaptation that have occurred. In like manner, the continual decline in farm population as farmers have been forced from farm to nonfarm employment is evidence of the consequences of farmers adapting to changing circumstances.

All of these ecological processes have clearly interacted to form the present organizational structure of U.S. agriculture, and as with other organizational forms, the characteristics of organizational structures and processes are evident. Thus, the functions of agriculture have shifted largely from the production of foods for the producer's own use to the provision of food for worldwide markets. Differentiation and concentration have simultaneously affected agriculture as producers have increasingly specialized in the production of single commodities and have consolidated their resource bases to increase farm size. Larger farms have become increasingly dominant in terms of the overall level of production, and the role of agriculture as the key function in many rural areas in the nation has been lost as rural economies have diversified into manufacturing and service-related industries (Bender et al. 1985). The ecosystem in which agriculture now operates has become specialized and differentiated and has been coupled with a decreasing niche for agricultural production in the way of life of rural areas.

Finally, it is clear that a process of ecological expansion is occurring in agriculture as the range of competitors with American farmers has expanded to include producers from across the world. Farm commodities have become key components in international systems of exchange and their control a mechanism for responding to international conflicts. The material, information, and energy bases of agriculture are also expanding rapidly so that the biological matter (e.g., through bioengineering), the range of information available for guiding farm management decisions (through computerized farm management systems), and the potential for alternative energy systems for agriculture (e.g., biomass) require the producer to constantly seek continuing education. For farmers in the United States, then, the ecosystem has expanded to include the competition and information systems resulting from a worldwide system.

As the above discussion indicates, the concepts of human ecology appear to be clearly relevant to the understanding of the events that have in the past and that are presently affecting American agriculture. Thus, an ecological analysis of American agriculture is both useful and desirable. The discussion that follows provides further and more systematic support for this premise.

Examples of the Use of Ecology in Agriculture

The potential utility of ecological theory for understanding agriculture phenomena in the United States is also apparent when one examines specific examples of some of the patterns that have affected the development of agriculture in the United States. We briefly examine

1. the impact of irrigation technology on agriculture in the Great Plains
2. the increase in part-time farming in the United States
3. the potential impact of biotechnology on the structure of U.S. agriculture
4. the decline in tenant farming in the United States

For each of these four examples we present an ecological explanation for the patterns that have evolved (or that may evolve) and suggest insights provided by the use of a human ecological framework that are unlikely to be revealed by the use of more traditional perspectives on these phenomena.

Impact of Irrigation Technology

The effects of irrigation technology on agriculture-dependent areas provide a dimension in which an ecological framework suggests effects on rural populations not apparent from a simple examination of existing demographic data. Using an adaptation of the ecological complex applied by Sly (1972) to the study of migration, Albrecht and Murdock (1986b) suggest that ecological factors may explain transformations in U.S. agriculture and the consequences thereof. Sly maintained that population change is a direct response to organizational change, with exogenous environment and technology changes influencing population indirectly through organizational changes (see also, Poindexter and Clifford 1983; Sly and Tayman 1977; Frisbie and Poston 1975, 1976; Heaton et al. 1981). Applying such a framework to agriculture presupposes that technological developments and/or changes in the availability of environmental resources will result in changes in the organization (structure) of agriculture. The changing structure of agriculture will, in turn, cause change in the population of the ecosystem through migration and natural increase as the population seeks equilibrium with existing sustenance bases. This fundamental tenet of sociological human ecology (Hawley 1968, 1986; Frisbie and Poston 1975) suggests that irrigation technology will affect the populations of rural areas through an effect both on the environment and organization.

Viewed ecologically, irrigation can be seen as an adaptive form of technology that is used to increase the level of exploitation of the environmental resource base of an ecosystem. Using the ecological model depicted by Sly (1972), Albrecht and Murdock (1986b) suggest that a change in the amount of irrigation in an ecosystem can be viewed as a change in the technological/environmental component of that ecosystem. Such change should result in changes in the organizational structure of agriculture and in subsequent changes in the population of that ecosystem. Albrecht and Murdock (1986b) hypothesize that by removing an ecological constraint to increased production, irrigation should increase the carrying capacity of an area (Steward et al. 1955; Hardesty 1977; Wittfogel 1957). Thus, irrigation should result in higher standards of living and population growth (or retention). Using data on the impacts of irrigation in the Great Plains on population growth, Albrecht and Murdock (1986b) found considerable support for their ecological explanation for the impacts of irrigation on rural population change. Since the role of irrigation in retaining rural population had previously been largely ignored, the use of an ecological framework served to suggest an innovative approach for explaining alternative levels of population change in rural areas.

Part-time Farming

One of the most striking changes in American agriculture in recent decades has been the rapid increase in the importance of part-time farming (Buttel and Larson 1982; Cavazzani 1979; Larson 1981; Singh 1983; Wimberley 1983). Albrecht and Murdock (1984, 392–93) suggest that this increase can be explained by ecological factors.

> From a human ecological perspective, part-time farming may be viewed as a component of the organizational structure of agriculture (O). The prevalence of this particular type of organizational adaptation can be expected to be a result of the environmental base in an area (E), the amount and type of technology used to adapt to that environmental base (T), and the subsequent differentiation of sustenance activities (Gibbs and Martin 1962). . . . The prevalence of part-time farming is viewed as a result of a farm population's adaptation to the farm and nonfarm environment, farm and nonfarm technological bases, and the diversity of farm and nonfarm sustenance bases. Both direct and indirect effects of environmental factors, technology factors, and sustenance diversity from both the farm and the nonfarm sectors are seen as affecting the prevalence of part-time farming. The ecological organizational niche of part-time farming is seen as being the result of a complex of environmental, technological, sustenance, and other factors from both the farm and nonfarm components of an ecosystem.

Using data for all counties in the United States, Albrecht and Murdock (1984) find considerable support for their proposed ecological explanation of part-time farming. In addition, they suggest that rather than being seen as a marginal form of production, part-time farming must be seen as reflecting an adaptive mode of behavior allowing many producers to remain in agricultural production (see also Swanson and Busch 1985; Albrecht and Murdock 1985a).

Biotechnology and Agriculture

The potential impact of biotechnological developments on the future structure of American agriculture is receiving increasing attention among rural sociologists (Kloppenburg 1984, 1988; Buttel et al. 1983; Molnar and Kinnucan 1989). In general, it is maintained that the growth of biotechnology will increase the competitive advantages of larger producers relative to moderate-sized producers and thus further accentuate

38 the growing dualism in the structure of U.S. agriculture. Recently, however, Murdock and Albrecht (1985) have provided an alternative perspective on the future impact of biotechnology based on the use of the ecological perspective (additional discussion of this argument is provided in Chapter 5). Using the ecological concepts of symbiosis and commensalism, Murdock and Albrecht (1985) maintain that the nature of the relationship between a form of technology and the environment will determine its impact. Technologies that form commensalistic relationships with the environment allow existing resources to be used more efficiently. Thus, technologies such as mechanization serve largely to make agriculture more efficient, resulting in a need for fewer persons to produce the same levels of commodities. Technologies that form a symbiotic relationship with the environment tend to alter the environmental resource base and related forms of organization by bringing to bear techniques and practices that make previously unavailable resources, or resources whose use was previously economically unfeasible, available and feasible for use by society. This expansion in resources, in turn, allows for an expansion in population and in the complexity of social organization. These authors view biotechnology as being likely to form a symbiotic relationship with the environment and as thus having the potential to retard the loss of farms and of related population, provided the dissemination of biotechnology can be made sufficiently inexpensive (or its use is adequately subsidized) for use by smaller producers. Here again, the use of an ecological perspective suggests an interpretation that is substantially different from that provided by prevailing perspectives (Buttel et al. 1983) and one with clearly important pragmatic and policy implications.

Tenant Farming

Tenant farming has shown a dramatic evolution in the history of American agriculture (Albrecht and Thomas 1986; Brunner and Kolb 1933; Gee 1942; Kloppenburg and Geisler 1985). After increasing from roughly 25 percent of all farmers in 1880 to 42 percent of all producers in 1930, the number of tenant farmers has declined dramatically since 1930 with only 12 percent of all producers being tenant farmers by 1982 (see Chapter 3). As a result, such numerous tenant farmer categories as the southern sharecropper have largely disappeared. During the period from 1930 to 1980 land remained relatively inexpensive and its increasing value ensured that its owners had a positive equity position that made increasing expansion possible for owner-operators. Most analyses have suggested that this expansion of ever-larger, more capital-intensive farms provides little indication that tenant farming will ever again be a significant part of U.S. agriculture (Kloppenburg and Geisler 1985).

Human ecological theory can be used both to suggest the underlying mechanisms for the recent decline in tenant farming and to indicate that tenant farming could again become a significant part of the structure of U.S. agriculture. The decline in tenant farming can be seen ecologically as having resulted from the increase in dominance of other organizational forms that were able to adapt more successfully to a changing set of technological and organizational conditions in agriculture. The increase in capital-intensive agricultural technologies as well as the rise of policies and forms of organizational assistance that were not scale neutral (Busch and Lacy 1983) but rather favored larger owner-operators, produced an ecosystem that was favorable to the growth and increased dominance of owner-operated farming units and that placed tenant producers at a competitive disadvantage. As the larger producers prospered, their ability to dominate the ecosystem and subsume tenant producers' operations increased accordingly. Thus, the decline in the number of tenant producers since 1930 can be seen to reflect ecosystem conditions that favored other types of producers and placed tenant producers at a disadvantage.

The recent economic crisis in U.S. agriculture (Johnson et al. 1985a; Leholm et al. 1985; Murdock et al. 1985) suggests that circumstances favor a significant increase in the number of farmers with major proportions of their operations involving tenantlike organizational arrangements. Thus, present circumstances suggest that the locus of dominance in the present ecosystem of U.S. agriculture may be shifting. The types of farmers that have been most successful in the past have been those who were risk-taking and who used their assets to expand their land resources, but these producers may also be among the most likely to fail because of high levels of debt (Murdock et al. 1986). The assets of those producers who fail are being absorbed by large governmental and private financial organizations. These organizations may fill a new organizational niche (that of landlord) in the ecosystem of agriculture. If so, rather than being characterized by large owner-operator controlled production units, agriculture could again develop a structure in which dominance is exerted by large-scale interests based outside of agricul-

40   ture. If these interests choose to retain their agricultural holdings and to seek to obtain rental income from them, the incidence of tenant farming could increase substantially.

These four examples are only some of those that could be used to suggest the relevance and utility of the human ecological perspective for examining the structure of U.S. agriculture. While some are speculative, empirical analyses that are beyond the scope of the present volume can establish the extent to which past and future events support or fail to support the ecological premises that underlie them. The fact that each example raises significant questions about traditional explanations of these phenomena while providing a plausible ecological explanation for both past and potential future patterns, however, suggests that ecological explanations merit closer attention.

CONCLUSIONS

In this chapter we have described the ecological framework that is used as the organizational base for this volume. The history, the basic assumptions, the concepts, and the relevance of human ecology to other theoretical perspectives have been described, and an attempt has been made to demonstrate the potential utility of the ecological framework for explaining past, present, and potential future patterns in U.S. agriculture. The remainder of this volume can provide only a very limited evaluation of the potential of the ecological framework to address issues of relevance to U.S. agriculture. In order to be of maximum utility this volume must contain a substantial amount of description that is largely atheoretical. However, the intent is that from this and the chapters that follow, the reader will obtain insight into the potential of the ecological framework for analyzing agricultural phenomena.

Historical Patterns of Change
in the Structure of U.S. Agriculture

The ecological processes and patterns described in the preceding chapter have interacted to determine the current structure of agriculture in the United States. The expanding land and environmental resource base of the nation from its founding through the end of the nineteenth century and the increasing range of technologies that substantially improved farm productivity, especially in the twentieth century, resulted in both a rapidly decreasing farm population base and a rapidly changing organizational structure for U.S. agriculture. In order to understand the present and the likely future structure of agriculture in the United States, it is essential to examine historical patterns.

This chapter traces historical patterns of change. The intent is to demonstrate that key ecological factors have operated to alter the organizational structure of agriculture and to provide a context for understanding trends and effects delineated in the remainder of the text. Only patterns for selected factors are presented. Those selected have been widely identified as among the most significant in shaping the structure of agriculture in the United States (Cochrane 1979; Schlebecker 1975) and the most crucial for clarifying the ecological processes that will be the major focus of subsequent chapters. Specifically, the five factors to be examined include (1) changes in the number and size of farms, (2) levels of farm concentration and part-time farming, (3) types of farm organizations, (4) farm tenure patterns, and (5) level and prevalence of

41

different types of farm labor. These factors are representative of the population and organizational components of U.S. agriculture, and the changes in them are described as they have been affected by the changing environmental and technological base in agriculture. What follows is largely a description of the organizational and demographic implications of expansion in the environmental and technological complex of agriculture in the United States.

MAJOR CHANGES IN THE STRUCTURE OF U.S. AGRICULTURE

Number of Farms and Farm Size

The effects of changes in environment and technology are especially prominent when discussing trends in the number of farms and farm size. The first European immigrants to America in the early 1600s brought with them a form of agriculture that was very primitive by twentieth-century standards. Virtually everyone lived by subsistence farming. Nearly everything the family was able to produce was consumed by the family with very little surplus remaining to be sold in the marketplace. Nearly everyone in the population was engaged in agriculture by necessity. In addition, farms were relatively small since the number of acres a family could effectively manage was limited (Schlebecker 1975).

During the next century and a half developments in American agriculture occurred slowly. Through immigration and natural increase the population grew, and as the population grew the number of farms increased. The boundaries of civilization were expanded and more land was brought under cultivation. Farmers were able to better adapt to existing environmental conditions in different parts of the country, and the standard of living gradually improved. However, it remained necessary for nearly everyone in the population to be involved in agricultural production. In fact, when the first United States census was taken in 1790, 96 percent of the U.S. population (a total of about 4 million people) was rural. Although farmers were not enumerated separately, it is generally thought that most of the rural residents at that time were living on farms (Fite 1981).

The nineteenth century was a period of vast expansion for American agriculture. This expansion included both increases in the land area available for farming (environment) and improvements in the farming techniques (technology) utilized (Peterson 1980). At the beginning of the **43** nineteenth century a large majority of the U.S. population was located between the eastern seaboard and the Appalachian Mountains. A vast and largely untouched domain lay between the Appalachians and the Mississippi River. Then in 1803 the Louisiana Purchase nearly doubled the nation's size. Within another half century, either through war or by treaty, Florida, Texas, Oregon, and the American Southwest were brought within U.S. boundaries (Fite 1981). These abundant land resources allowed the nation to expand westward, and extensive fertile lands were brought into agricultural production. As a result, throughout the nineteenth century the number of farms in the United States increased steadily. This provides an excellent example of a population's adjustment to environmental expansion.

The first Census of Agriculture was taken in 1840.[1] This census was very limited, and it was not until 1850 that a count was made of the number of farms in the United States.[2] The 1850 census revealed a total of nearly 1.5 million farms in the United States with less than 300 million acres in farms (Table 3.1). Largely because of westward expansion and the development of previously undeveloped land, there was a rapid increase between 1850 and 1900 in the number of farms and the amount of land in farms. By 1900 there were over 5.7 million farms (an increase of

Table 3.1. Changes in selected farming characteristics in the United States, 1850–1982

Year	Number of farms (1,000)	Acres in farms (1,000)	Percentage of land in farms	Average farm size (acres)
1850	1,449	293,561	15.6	203
1860	2,044	407,213	21.4	199
1870	2,660	407,735	21.4	153
1880	4,009	536,082	28.2	134
1890	4,565	623,219	32.7	137
1900	5,740	841,202	37.0	147
1910	6,366	881,431	38.8	139
1920	6,454	958,677	42.2	149
1930	6,295	990,112	43.6	157
1940	6,102	1,065,114	46.8	175
1950	5,388	1,161,420	51.1	216
1959[a]	3,711	1,123,508	49.5	303
1969	2,730	1,063,346	47.0	390
1982	2,241	986,797	43.6	440

Source: Data from 1850 to 1969 are obtained from *Historical Statistics of the United States: Colonial Times to 1970* (U.S. Department of Commerce, Bureau of the Census 1975). The 1982 data are from the *1982 Census of Agriculture* (U.S. Department of Commerce, bureau of the Census 1984a).

[a]Data for Alaska and Hawaii are included for the first time.

44   nearly 300 percent from 1850) and 841 million acres of land in farms (an increase of nearly 200 percent from 1850). The percentage of land in farms increased from 15.6 percent in 1850 to 37.0 percent in 1900 (Table 3.1).

Not only was there a rapid increase in the number of farms and the land in farm production in the nineteenth century, there were also major strides made in agricultural technology (Berardi 1981; Hamilton 1939). During the nineteenth century several major technological break-throughs were made that substantially increased the capacity of the individual farmer. Some of these breakthroughs included the iron mold-board plow, the grain drill, the mechanical grain reaper, and the grain-threshing machine (Cochrane 1979). These and other developments made it possible for some farmers to produce a substantial surplus, which released many from the necessity of farming.

As a result of such technical developments and the expansion of the nation's land base, by 1880 when the farm population was enumerated separately for the first time 21,973,000 people lived on farms. This was a little less than one-half (43.8 percent) of the total U.S. population (Table 3.2). As the number of farms continued to increase in the last two decades of the nineteenth century, there was a corresponding increase in the farm population. By 1900 there were nearly 30 million farm residents, but they comprised a slightly reduced share of the total U.S. population (41.9 percent).

By 1900 most of the potential farmland in the United States was

Table 3.2.   Farm population in the United States, 1880–1985

Year	Farm population (1,000)	Percentage of total U.S. population
1880	21,973	43.8
1890	24,771	42.3
1900	29,875	41.9
1910	32,077	34.9
1920	31,974	30.1
1930	30,529	24.9
1940	30,547	23.2
1950	23,048	15.3
1960	15,635	8.7
1970	9,712	4.8
1980	6,051	2.7
1985	5,355	2.2

Sources: Data from 1880 to 1910 are from *Historical Statisitics of the United States: Colonial Times to 1970* (U.S. Department of Commerce, Bureau of the Census 1975). Data for 1920–1985 are from Kalbacher and DeAre (1986).

being used for farm production. However, between 1900 and 1910 both the number of farms and the farm population experienced substantial increases as more remote and marginal land was brought into production. By 1910 there were more than 6 million farms, and the farm population surpassed 30 million people. These figures remained virtually constant through the 1940 census. During this thirty-year period, the size of the average farm increased as more land was brought into farm production (Table 3.1). Also, while the farm population remained stable through these years, the total population in the United States was increasing. This meant that the proportion of the U.S. population living on farms steadily decreased. By 1940 slightly less than one-fourth (23.2 percent) of the U.S. population was living on farms (Table 3.2).

The period since 1940 has been one of rapid change in American agriculture. Technological developments in agriculture have continually replaced human labor in the production process and have made it possible for an individual farm operator to cultivate many times the number of acres cultivated by earlier producers (Paarlberg 1980). The major breakthrough in this technological revolution was the development of the all-purpose tractor in the late 1920s (Bertrand 1978). The continual improvement of the tractor, associated with the development of other machines, has changed the very nature of farmwork. It is estimated that in 1930 there were 23 billion hours of farm labor. However, the total hours used for farm work per year has steadily declined (Durost and Bailey 1970; Bertrand 1978), and by 1984 only 3.7 billion hours of farmwork were required.

In addition to these laborsaving technological breakthroughs, technological developments (such as chemical fertilizers and pesticides and hybrid seeds) greatly increased per acre productivity. Thus, not only did the number of acres that an individual farmer could operate increase, but per acre productivity also increased. In 1900 the average farmworker produced enough to supply food and fiber to 7 other persons. By 1940 production had only increased slightly and the average farmer was able to produce enough for 10.7 persons. Since that time the increases have been dramatic. In 1970 the average farmer produced enough food and fiber to supply 47.9 persons, and by 1984 one farmworker could supply food and fiber for 77 people. Today, one hour of farmwork produces fourteen times what it did in 1920 (Poincelot 1986).

An examination of Table 3.1 makes the consequences of these changes apparent. In 1982 the average farm in the United States was

46   about 440 acres, which was more than three times larger than the average farm in 1910. The consolidation of farms into larger and larger units led to a rapid decline in the number of farms. By 1982 there were only about 2.2 million farms, a 65 percent decline from 1940.

    The declining number of farms in the United States resulted in a rapid farm population loss. The farm population declined from 30.5 million in 1940, to 23.0 million in 1950, to 15.6 million in 1960, to 9.7 million in 1970, to 6.0 million in 1980, and finally to 5.3 million in 1985 (Kalbacher and DeAre 1986). This represents an 82 percent decline in the farm population in a period of forty-five years. Once a majority of the U.S. population, farmers comprised only 2.2 percent of the American population in 1985. The decline of the farm population is a function of declining family sizes as well as a declining number of farms. For example, in 1910 there was an average of 5.04 persons per farm. By 1982 this number had declined to 2.41.

Farm Concentration

    The variables of the ecological complex have played a major role in the increased concentration of U.S. agriculture. Technological developments have made it possible for some farms to become extremely large and labor efficient. For the most part these technologies are extremely dependent upon environmental resources (in particular, fossil fuels). Also, the physical environment has an important influence on the spatial variations in agricultural activities such as productivity and the type of crop grown. This is important because concentration is much more apparent in the production of some types of farm commodities than others. Finally, an expanding nonfarm sector has provided an increased number of part-time jobs to farm operators that have allowed them to make a living while maintaining a small farm.

    In 1982 only 1.2 percent of the farms in the United States had gross farm sales of $500,000 or greater, yet these farms contributed nearly one-third of our nation's total farm sales (Table 3.3). Further, only about 13.5 percent of the farms had gross sales of $100,000 or more, but these farms had nearly three-fourths of the farm sales. At the opposite extreme almost half (49 percent) of the farms in the United States in 1982 had gross farm sales of less than $10,000. These farms, however, had less than 3 percent of the total farm sales (Table 3.3). Obviously, production in American agriculture is extremely concentrated, and these levels of concentration have increased rapidly in recent years.[3]

Table 3.3. Number of farms and total farm sales by farm sales categories, 1982

Total farm sales categories	Number of farms	Total sales ($1,000)	Percentage of farms	Percentage of total sales
Less than $5,000	814,535	1,557,326	36.4	1.2
$5,000–$9,999	281,802	2,008,511	12.6	1.5
$10,000–$19,999	259,007	3,694,306	11.6	2.8
$20,000–$39,999	248,825	7,142,112	11.1	5.4
$40,000–$99,999	332,751	21,641,796	14.8	16.5
$100,000–$499,999	274,580	52,781,375	12.3	40.1
$500,000 or more	27,800	42,764,189	1.2	32.5
Total	2,239,300	131,589,615	100.0	100.0

Source: 1982 Census of Agriculture (U.S. Department of Commerce, Bureau of the Census 1984a).

An examination of Table 3.4 shows that in 1900 the medium-sized farm was the backbone of American agriculture. At that time 64 percent of the farms were between 50 and 499 acres, and these farms accounted for 62 percent of the land in farms. Over one-half of the farmland acreage was in farms between 100 and 499 acres in size. Even in 1900, however, there was evidence of some farm concentration as less than 1 percent of the farms were 1,000 acres or larger, but these farms controlled nearly one-fourth (23.8 percent) of the land in farms.

Table 3.4. A comparison of the percentage of farms and percentage of land in farms for size categories, 1900–1982

Farm size	1900	1940	1969	1982
	%	%	%	%
10 acres or less				
Number of farms	4.7	8.3	5.9	8.3
Land in farms	0.2	0.3	0.1	0.1
10–49 acres				
Number of farms	29.0	29.2	17.4	20.1
Land in farms	5.6	4.5	1.2	1.3
50–99 acres				
Number of farms	23.8	21.1	16.9	15.4
Land in farms	11.7	8.8	3.2	1.8
100–499 acres				
Number of farms	39.9	37.0	46.4	39.9
Land in farms	50.6	41.6	27.2	21.4
500–999 acres				
Number of farms	1.8	2.7	7.9	9.1
Land in farms	8.1	10.5	13.9	14.4
1,000 or more acres				
Number of farms	0.8	1.7	5.5	7.2
Land in farms	23.8	34.3	54.4	61.0

Sources: Data for 1900–1969 are from Historical Statistics of the United States: Colonial Times to 1970 (U.S. Department of Commerce, Bureau of the Census 1975). Data from 1982 are from the 1982 Census of Agriculture (U.S. Department of Commerce, Bureau of the Census 1984a).

48   By 1940 the trend toward larger farms and greater concentration was evident. The percentage of farmland held by farms of 50 to 499 acres decreased from 62 percent to 50 percent, while the proportion of the farmland held by farms of 1,000 or more acres increased to 34 percent (Table 3.4). The trend toward larger farms accelerated between 1940 and 1969. By 1969 over half of the land in farms was in those of 1,000 or more acres, while the proportion of the land controlled by farms with 50 to 499 acres declined to 30 percent. Between 1969 and 1982 there was an increase in the number of very small and very large farms, while the trend toward a decreasing number of medium-sized farms continued. By 1982 the structure of American agriculture could be described as dualistic. At one extreme a large and growing number of small farms consisted primarily of part-time, hobby, or recreational farms. At the other end of the continuum was a smaller but growing number of large-scale, commercialized farms (Green and Heffernan 1984; Paarlberg 1980; Stockdale 1982). In 1982 farms with 1,000 or more acres controlled 61 percent of the land in farms. Continuing to decline was the medium-sized farm. In 1900 these farms had controlled 62 percent of the land, but this proportion had declined to 23 percent in 1982.

Part-time Farming

At one time in this country the farm was the sole source of income for most farmers and their families. The 1940 Census of Agriculture, for example, estimated that about 15 percent of all farm operators had one hundred or more days of off-farm employment. Typically, off-farm work was considered to be a temporary condition for those involved. It was reserved for those trying to accumulate capital and skills for entrance into farming on a full-time basis or as a mechanism for easing the exit of retiring or marginal producers from agriculture (Albrecht and Murdock 1984; Heffernan et al. 1981).

Today part-time farming appears to be a stable component of the farm structure and a relatively permanent life-style (Paarlberg 1980). In recent decades the prevalence of part-time farming has increased steadily. As shown in Figure 3.1, the proportion of farm operators with one hundred or more days of off-farm employment increased from 15 percent in 1940 to 43 percent in 1982. Not only does a larger proportion of the farm population have off-farm jobs, but those who work off the

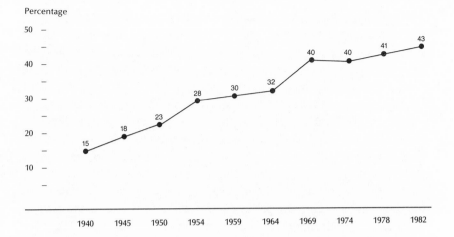

Percentage

Fig. 3.1. Percentage of farm operators with 100 or more days of off-farm employment, 1940 to 1982 (Data for 1940–1969 are from *Historical Statistics of the United States: Colonial Times to 1970* [U.S. Department of Commerce, Bureau of the Census 1975]. Data for 1974–1982 are from the *1982 Census of Agriculture* [U.S. Department of Commerce, Bureau of the Census 1984a]).

farm do so for longer periods of time. In addition, female members of farm families are becoming increasingly important in the nonfarm labor force (Coughenour and Swanson 1983; Maret and Copp 1982). It is estimated that 92 percent of farm families in the United States had some type of nonfarm income in 1977 (Carlin and Ghelfi 1979). Off-farm employment has increased in importance until, in 1977, only 39 percent of the income of farm persons came from the marketing of crops and livestock (Paarlberg 1980).

While the importance of part-time farming has increased throughout the country, it is more prevalent in some parts of the country than in others and is especially important among particular segments of the farm population (Leistritz et al. 1985). In particular, part-time farming is most common in the South and least common in the Great Plains (Carlin and Ghelfi 1979; Leistritz et al. 1985). Not surprisingly, the prevalence of part-time farming is much more pronounced among farmers operating small farms than among farmers operating larger farms. Generally, small farmers have more time available for off-farm work and also have a greater need for additional income to supplement their farm earnings.

Ecological factors can be seen as playing an important role in both the increased prevalence of part-time farming nationwide and in the wide variations in the proportion of part-time farmers in different parts of the country. In an ecological analysis of part-time farming using county-level data, Albrecht and Murdock (1984) found that part-time farming is least common in areas where available resources are conducive to agricultural production and where the employment structure lacks diversity (see also Swanson and Busch 1985; Albrecht and Murdock 1985a). In other words, farmers become part-time farmers where it is difficult to make a living in agriculture and where off-farm employment opportunities are available. Recent analyses have also shown that off-farm employment may provide farm families with the economic stability to survive during periods of financial stress (Breimyer 1977; Leistritz et al. 1986), and thus the ability of an area to retain a relatively stable farm population may be dependent on the ability of the area to provide farm residents with off-farm work.

Business Organization of Farming

From our nation's inception the family farm has always been proclaimed the cornerstone of American agriculture. Historically, nearly all farms have been operations for which the family provided most of the management, labor, and capital (Paarlberg 1980). The technological revolution in American agriculture in recent decades, however, has enabled some farms to become very large and highly specialized and some commodities to be produced in an assembly line fashion (Albrecht and Ladewig 1982). This potential has encouraged many corporations, including some corporations that specialize in nonfarm enterprises, to enter agriculture. Some observers have concluded that this will result in "factories in the field" and in the decline and eventual replacement of the family farm (Barnes and Casalino 1972; Hightower 1971). Concern with corporate farming is rather recent, and a question about the organization of farming was not included in the Census of Agriculture until 1969.

The rise of corporate farming and the differential concentration of corporate farming in particular segments of the farm sector can be seen as a result of ecological factors. For example, sectors of the farm economy that can be categorized as technological or capital intensive have been more likely to adapt to changes by adopting a corporate structure than the more land-intensive enterprises.

Table 3.5 presents data from the 1982 Census of Agriculture on the

Table 3.5. Type of farm organization by selected farm characteristics for the United States, 1982

Selected farm characteristics	Sales ($1,000,000)	Family	Partnership	Family-held corporation	Non-family-held corporation
Farms:					
Number		1,945,639	223,274	52,652	7,140
Percentage[a]		86.9%	9.7%	2.4%	0.3%
Average size of farm (acres)		330	680	2,143	2,024
Land in farms (1,000 acres)		642,380	151,860	112,858	14,451
Percentage		68.9%	16.3%	21.1%	1.6%
Value of agricultural products sold					
Total ($1,000,000)		77,907	21,520	22,902	8,578
Percentage		59.2%	16.4%	17.4%	6.5%
Average per farm ($1,000)		40.0	96.4	435.0	1,201.5
Commodities:					
Total cattle and calves	31,516	48.6%	13.9%	24.0%	13.0%
Calves only	3,739	76.6%	14.0%	7.3%	1.0%
Fattened cattle only[b]	17,047	29.8%	12.1%	35.1%	22.7%
Poultry and poultry products	9,788	59.2%	10.2%	20.4%	10.0%
Grain	36,378	72.4%	16.4%	10.0%	0.1%
Nursery and greenhouse products	3,820	22.4%	8.4%	51.2%	17.9%
Fruit, nuts, and berries	5,842	36.1%	20.3%	29.0%	13.2%
Vegetables, sweet corn, and melons	4,135	33.4%	20.7%	34.1%	11.6%
Dairy products	16,265	68.7%	21.8%	8.3%	0.8%
Hogs and pigs	9,841	69.3%	17.1%	10.3%	2.9%
Cotton	3,220	50.8%	23.7%	19.4%	5.3%

Source: 1982 Census of Agriculture (U.S. Department of Commerce, Bureau of the Census 1984a).

[a]Percentages do not total 100 because some types of farms (such as estates or trusts) are not included.

[b]Fattened cattle are defined as cattle fattened on grain on concentrates for 30 days or more and sold for slaughter.

characteristics of farms by the type of organization. This table shows that of the more than 2.2 million farms, the large majority of these farms were family farms. Of the remainder 9.7 percent were partnerships and 2.7 percent were corporate farms. However, nearly all of the corporate farms (88.1 percent) were family held. These family-held corporate farms are very similar to large family farms except in their legal arrangements (Reimund 1979). In most cases family-held corporate farms rely on the capital, labor, and managerial decisions of the family in a manner similar to the typical large family farm. In most cases the decision to incorporate was made because of tax or inheritance reasons.

Although family farms remain dominant, the number of corporate farms has increased. The 1969 Census of Agriculture estimated that there were 21,513 corporate farms in the United States. By 1978 this number had increased to 50,231, and in 1982 there were 59,792 corporate farms, an increase of 178 percent since 1969. This happened during a period when the total number of farms decreased by 18 percent. Family and nonfamily corporations were not differentiated until 1978. In 1978 there were 5,818 nonfamily corporate farms in the United States. This number increased to 7,140 by 1982.

Although small in number, corporations do make a substantial contribution to American agriculture when viewed in terms of the amount of land in farms and value of agricultural products sold. Corporate farms (average size of 2,129 acres) were much larger on the average than were family farms (average size of 330 acres) in 1982. Thus, corporations comprised 2.7 percent of the total number of farms but controlled about 23 percent of the total land farmed. Nearly 89 percent of the land in corporate farms was held by family corporations, however.

The impact of corporate farms on agriculture becomes even more evident when the market value of agricultural products sold is examined. In 1982 sales from corporate farms constituted 24 percent of the total value of agricultural products sold in this country. In comparison, family farms contributed over 59 percent of the total farm sales. About 6.5 percent of the total farm sales came from nonfamily corporate farms. Nearly three-fourths of corporate farm sales were from family-held corporations. Sales from the average corporate farm totaled more than $526,000 in 1982 compared to about $40,000 from the average family farm. The average nonfamily corporate farm had agricultural sales totaling more than 1 million dollars in 1982.

Thus, while corporate farms have become an important part of

American agriculture, the role of nonfamily corporate farms remains   **53**
limited. The importance of corporate farms is not uniformly distributed
across all agricultural commodities. In 1982, 92 percent of the corporate-
farm cash receipts were from the sale of nine commodities. The most
important commodity produced by corporate farms was cattle and
calves. This involvement, however, was primarily limited to the fattening
of cattle in feedlots rather than calf production (Table 3.5). In fact,
nearly one-half of the cash receipts received by nonfamily corporate
farms in 1982 came from the marketing of fattened cattle.

Of the other commodities listed in Table 3.5, corporate-farm sales
surpass family-farm sales for only three—nursery and greenhouse products; fruits, nuts, and berries; and vegetables, sweet corn, and melons.
Conversely, the production of cotton, poultry products, grain, dairy
products, and hogs and pigs was largely dependent on family farms.

Farm Tenure

The perceived opportunity for landownership lured many landless
and land-hungry European settlers to the United States and later pulled
them westward across the continent (Cochrane 1979). The privilege to
own land became enshrined in the Declaration of Independence and the
Bill of Rights, and has been historically the basis of American farm
policy (Kloppenburg and Geisler 1985). The Homestead Act perhaps
best symbolizes the American ideal of providing land to the farmer and
has, along with other legislation, attempted to establish a system of
medium-sized, owner-operated family farms.

Despite such legislative efforts, the tenant farmer has always played
an important role in American agriculture.[4] Table 3.6 presents information showing the number of farms, percentage of farms, and percentage
of land in farms by tenure status from 1880 to 1982. This table shows
that in 1880 when tenure status information was first obtained in the
Census of Agriculture, about one in every four American farms was
operated by a tenant farmer. For several decades the prevalence of tenant farms steadily increased to 28 percent in 1890, 35 percent in 1900, 37
percent in 1910, 38 percent in 1920, and finally to 42 percent in 1930.
With these high and increasing rates tenancy issues became one of the
major concerns of U.S. agricultural researchers a half-century ago
(Brunner and Kolb 1933; Gee 1942; Harris 1941). Researchers and policy
makers of the day expressed concern that the American farmer, like the

Table 3.6. Number of farms, percentage of farms, and percentage of land in farms by tenure of farm operator, 1880–1982

Year	Full-owners			Part-owners			Tenants		
	Number of farms	Percentage of farms	Percentage of land in farms	Number of farms	Percentage of farms	Percentage of land in farms	Number of farms	Percentage of farms	Percentage of land in farms
1880	2,984,306	74.4	—	—	—	—	1,024,601	25.6	—
1890	3,269,782	71.6	—	—	—	—	1,294,913	28.4	—
1900	3,202,643	55.8[a]	51.4	451,515	7.9	14.9	2,026,286	35.3	23.3
1910	3,355,731	52.7	52.9	593,954	9.3	15.2	2,357,784	37.0	25.8
1920	3,368,146	52.2	48.3	558,708	8.7	18.4	2,458,554	38.1	27.7
1930	2,913,052	46.3	37.6	657,109	10.4	24.9	2,668,811	42.4	31.0
1940	3,085,491	50.6	35.9	615,502	10.1	28.2	2,364,923	38.8	29.4
1950	3,091,666	57.4	36.1	825,670	15.3	36.4	1,447,455	26.9	18.3
1959	2,116,594	57.8	30.8	834,470	22.5	44.8	735,849	19.8	14.5
1969	1,705,720	62.5	35.3	671,607	24.6	51.8	352,923	12.9	12.9
1982	1,325,773	59.2	34.7	656,249	29.2	53.8	258,954	11.6	11.5

Sources: Data for 1880–1969 are from *Historical Statistics of the United States: Colonial Times to 1970* (U.S. Department of Commerce, Bureau of the Census 1975). Data for 1982 are from the *1982 Census of Agriculture* (U.S. Department of Agriculture, Bureau of the Census 1984a).
[a]Percentages do not total to 100 between 1900 and 1959 because managers are excluded.

European farmer, would become a landless peasant (Kolb and Brunner 1935; Schmieder 1941).

These concerns increased when researchers during the 1930s and 1940s compared the tenant farm with the full-owner farm and generally found the tenant farm to have numerous disadvantages (Dickins 1937; Schuler 1938). Specifically, tenant farms were typically found to be smaller and less productive than full-owner farms, and the farming practices followed on tenant farms were poorer and more likely to result in soil erosion and other problems. Further, they found that extensive tenancy was likely to be problematic for communities as tenants were less involved in community affairs, had less education, and had lower incomes than farm owners (Bertrand 1958; Gee 1942; Gillette 1936; Hoffsommer 1937; Kolb and Brunner 1935; National Resources Committee 1937).

Since 1935, however, the number and proportion of tenant farms steadily declined (Kloppenburg and Geisler 1985; Neal and Jones 1950). As described in Chapter 2, the decline in the proportion of tenant farms can be explained ecologically. Resulting from technological developments and steadily escalating land prices, the prevalence of tenant farms decreased to 39 percent of all farms in 1940, to 27 percent in 1950, to 20 percent in 1959, to 13 percent in 1969, and finally to 12 percent in 1982. Overall, a 91 percent decline in the number of tenant farms has occurred since 1935 (Hottel and Harrington 1979). This has included the almost total elimination of the southern sharecropper, who was generally considered to be the most disadvantaged tenant farmer (Johnson et al. 1935; Mandle 1983). In 1930 sharecroppers comprised 29 percent of all tenant farmers and 43 percent of the tenant farmers in the South. With mechanization the labor provided by sharecroppers was increasingly less important and many were forced from the land. In 1959 the census reported the number of sharecropper farms for the last time. Their numbers had become so few that their contributions to agricultural production in the United States had become insignificant.

To a large extent the decline in the proportion of tenant farms has been accompanied by a corresponding increase in the proportion of part-owner farms. In 1900 only about 8 percent of the farms were part-owner farms, but by 1982 this proportion had increased to 29 percent (Table 3.6). In 1982 part-owner farms were substantially larger on the average than either full-owner or tenant farms. At that time the average part-owner farm was 809 acres, compared to 258 acres for the average full-owner farm and 439 acres for the average tenant farm.

56   With the decline in the number and proportion of tenant farms research on tenancy issues declined as well. Thus, other than the aggregate census statistics, little is known today about the characteristics of farmers with different tenure characteristics. A recent study by Albrecht and Thomas (1986) retested historic findings, comparing farmers of different tenure characteristics on a variety of factors. Their findings were in direct contrast to the research of the 1930s and 1940s, as it was found that farmers who rent most or all of their farmland, compared to other farmers, had the largest and most productive farms, used better farming practices, and were more involved in community affairs. In sum, major transitions in the tenure characteristics of U.S. farmers can be viewed as a means of adaptation by farmers to a changing economic, legal, and social environment with the effects of the adaptations on other ecological factors (such as environmental quality) varying with the characteristics of the total ecological complex in which the adaptations occur.

Farm Labor

The history of agricultural labor in the United States is largely a history of adjustments to technological developments, the availability of a population to do the work, and environmental and organizational variations. Historically, American agriculture developed under conditions of plentiful land and scarce labor (Dorner 1983). Thus, securing and maintaining an adequate work force has long been a major problem faced by farm producers (Pfeffer 1983). These labor problems in agriculture are exacerbated by the unique nature of farm production. In contrast to other parts of the American economy farm production takes place sequentially as opposed to simultaneously (Brewster 1950). In a typical factory operation, for example, production flows through a series of stages, all of which can proceed simultaneously at spatially separated points. In contrast, farm production consists of stages that are typically separated by waiting periods because the biological processes involved take time to complete (Madden 1967). Further, unlike production in other industries where commodities are produced continuously throughout the year, crop production is seasonal.

These aspects of farming create several serious labor management problems. First, farmers need extensive amounts of labor at some points and relatively little at others. Employers are unlikely to be willing to pay workers during periods of inactivity, but if workers are not paid, they will likely seek alternative employment. Thus, farmers have a problem of securing a sufficient work force during the production cycle and from year to year (Pfeffer 1983). Also, because of the sporadic nature of farm work, those attracted to farm work are often those who have few options elsewhere.

Historically, solutions to this problem have been numerous and diverse. Pfeffer (1983), for example, discusses three different solutions in different parts of the United States. He notes that in California the farm labor force has consisted of successive groups of immigrant and minority workers that were disadvantaged to the point that they had few other options to farm labor. These groups have included the Chinese, Japanese, Filipino, and Mexican workers as well as white Americans migrating from the Dust Bowl in the late 1930s. In the American South the initial solution was black slaves. After their emancipation most black and some poor white persons became sharecroppers (Zeichner 1939). The sharecropping system guaranteed the planter a steady and reliable labor force, and also allowed the planter to share some of the risks with the cropper since the cropper generally received about half of the proceeds. The cropper thus bore many of the costs of crop loss and/or falling prices (Pfeffer 1983). In the Great Plains large landholders such as the railroads parceled out much of their land to family farmers who provided the labor and bore much of the risk of production. The solution to the farm labor problem sought in these different circumstances can be seen as partially influenced by the combination of resources that largely determined the type of crops produced, combined with the labor requirements and technology available for these various crops.

While a variety of solutions have been tried in respect to obtaining adequate farm labor, the adoption of laborsaving technology as it develops has been the emphasis in American agriculture (Berardi and Geisler 1984). Mechanization thus represents an alternative to farm labor and has displaced millions of farm workers. Mechanization has also resulted in larger and fewer farms in this century as producers themselves have been forced from farming. Table 3.7 presents information showing change in agricultural employment from 1910 to 1982 in the United States. This table shows a steady decline in total farm employment throughout this century. These declines are especially prominent for family workers. Although the number of hired farm workers declined by 54 percent from 1910 to 1982, the number of family workers declined by 81 percent.

Table 3.7. Agricultural employment (in thousands), 1910–1982

Year	Total farm employment[a]	Family workers[a]	Hired workers
1910	13,555	10,174	3,381
1920	13,432	10,041	3,391
1930	12,497	9,307	3,190
1940	10,979	8,300	2,679
1950	9,926	7,597	2,329
1960	7,057	5,172	1,885
1970	4,523	3,348	1,175
1982	3,534	1,973	1,561

Sources: Data for 1910–1970 from Historical Statistics of the United States: Colonial Times to 1970 (U.S. Department of Commerce, Bureau of the Census 1975). Data for 1982 are from Banks and Mills (1983).
[a]Based on last-of-the-month employment averages.
[b]Includes farm operators and members of their families doing farmwork without wages.

CONCLUSIONS

As this brief review suggests, the expansion of the environmental base and particularly the technological base of agriculture has had profound effects on the population base and organizational structure of agriculture in the United States. It has produced an increasingly dualistic agricultural structure that is dependent on an ever-increasing range of complex technologies. It has resulted in a steadily decreasing number of producers and an increasing number of large-scale farming operations. From an ecological perspective, then, these patterns suggest that the evolution of agriculture in the United States can be seen as having largely followed a path of using an extensive land resource base and increasing organizational and technological complexity to adapt, while at the same time decreasing the number of producers and the range of nonfarm communities dependent on these producers.

In sum, the historical patterns of change in agriculture suggest that in order to understand the changing structure of agriculture in the United States and its effects on American society one must examine the environmental, technological, organizational, and demographic factors that affect that structure and carefully trace the interactive effects of the organizational complex containing these factors on the communities and other organizational units dependent on agriculture. It is to the examination of such factors that we now turn our attention.

NOTES

1. The first agricultural census was taken in 1840 as part of the census of population. From 1840 to 1950 an agricultural census was taken as part of the decennial census. A separate mid-decade census of agriculture was conducted in 1925, 1935, and 1945. From 1954 to 1974 a census of agriculture was taken in the years ending in 4 and 9. Then the census was taken in 1978 and 1982 to adjust the reference year to coincide with the economic censuses. After 1982 the census of agriculture reverted to a five-year cycle and will be taken in years ending in 2 and 7 to be coterminous with the economic censuses.

2. Between 1850 and 1982 the census definition of a farm has changed nine times. Consequently, the data used from the various censuses are not directly comparable. These figures are, however, the best available. The 1982 definition describes a farm as any place from which $1,000 or more of agricultural products were sold, or normally would have been sold, during the census year.

3. Ideally, an examination of concentration or any other measure focusing on size would use farm sales as the measure of concentration. Acreage is the other option, but the value of an acre and the amount that can be produced on it vary tremendously from one region of the country to the next (Gardner and Pope 1978). For example, fifty acres would be a large tobacco or strawberry farm, but a very small cattle ranch. However, an acre remains an acre over time, while the value of a dollar varies so much that across time comparisons often become meaningless. Thus, acres are used in the comparisons in this chapter.

4. Broadly defined, a tenant farm is a farm the operator rents rather than owns the land. Typically, three farm tenure categories are utilized: full-owners own all of the land they operate; tenants rent all of the land they operate; and part-owners own part of the land and rent part of the land they operate. Tenants are not a homogeneous class and are generally differentiated on the basis of the degree to which they own and supply the means of production and the amount of control they enjoy over the production process. Cash tenants pay a fixed money rent and provide all nonland inputs and more or less completely determine the manner in which production is carried out. Crop-share and livestock-share tenants return a portion of the animal or vegetable product to the landlord as rent and share with him or her management of the operation and the provision of inputs. Sharecroppers provide only labor for a production process that is almost wholly determined by the landlord, who also supplies all means of production (Kloppenburg and Geisler 1985; Pfeffer 1983). In fact, in many state laws the cropper was officially regarded as a hired worker (Mandle 1983).

The Agricultural Environment

efined ecologically, the concept of environment refers to "all external forces and factors to which an organism or aggregate of organisms is actually or potentially responsive" (Hawley 1950, 12–13). In many respects environment is the most basic of the four dimensions of the ecological complex since it is assumed that the environment is the ultimate source of sustenance for a population (Hawley 1968; Poston et al. 1984). However, very little empirical research in sociological human ecology or in the sociology of agriculture takes the environment directly into account, perhaps because of the breadth of the concept (Dunlap and Martin 1983; Poston et al. 1984). In this regard the environment is the least well-conceptualized variable of the ecological complex (Berry and Kasarda 1977; Hawley 1986).

In attempting to conceptualize the term environment in a theoretically meaningful manner, it is apparent that only those externalities that provide limits or constraints to a population in its acquisition of sustenance should be considered. These constraints may be narrow or broad depending on resource availability and on the technological devices and modes of organization that prevail in a given population (Schnore 1958; Michelson 1976). When these constraints are broad, life may be lived abundantly, but when they are narrow, life-styles and populations are subsequently restricted.

In Chapter 2 it was noted that the number of environmental factors that could be considered is innumerable, but that environmental factors

61

can be conveniently classified into inorganic and organic features. The major differentiating feature of the environment relative to other factors lies in its relative fixity and unalterability over a given period of time.

While making a list of the environmental factors of consequence to agriculture could be a nearly endless process, some factors are obviously more critical than others. For example, successful agricultural production requires the appropriate combination of several inorganic factors including soil, water, and temperature. If these factors are missing or vary too widely, production will either not occur or will be limited to some degree. Although agricultural commodities require all of these essential inorganic resources, the amounts required vary substantially from one commodity to another. For example, wheat can be produced in areas that experience harsh winters and have relatively short growing seasons while citrus fruit cannot, and rice production requires substantially more water than cotton production. Thus, because of these basic environmental constraints, farm production is severely limited in some areas, and certain commodities cannot be effectively produced in other areas.

At the same time several organic features of the environment play an important role in agriculture. The location of metropolitan areas, for example, influences agriculture in many ways. Most obviously, the houses, industries, and highways of an urban area remove land that could potentially be used for agricultural production. In addition, however, urbanization provides numerous part-time job opportunities for farm workers, which may result in higher levels of off-farm employment than in more remote areas. Also, land values are higher in urban areas because of the competing uses of the land. Access to urban markets permits modes of production such as truck farming and dairy farming, and thus such areas are generally characterized by capital-intensive modes of production and by highly intensive land use (Heaton 1980).

From an ecological perspective, then, one would expect that the farm populations in different environments would adapt to their varying conditions with different types of farm structures. From a sociological perspective this is important because the type of farm structure in an area has major consequences for factors of social significance such as social stratification (Smith 1969; Pfeffer 1983; Mann 1984; Mandle 1983), population size, and migration trends (Albrecht and Murdock 1986b; Frisbie and Poston 1975). In this chapter the relationships between several environmental factors and agriculture will be described.

This is done by both presenting an empirical evaluation of the effects of variations in certain environmental variables on the structure of agriculture, and describing two points of intense interaction between the environment and agriculture—the effects of technology on resource availability and its implications for change in the structure of agriculture, and the effects of resource depletion on agricultural productivity. The intent is thus both to demonstrate the impact of environmental factors on agricultural phenomena and to provide a general discussion of the implications of environmental resource use and misuse on agriculture. In each of these areas the elements selected for discussion are only some of the many that could be considered. The intention is not to be inclusive but rather to provide examples of the processes by which the environment influences the structure of agriculture.

EXAMPLES OF THE EFFECTS OF THE ENVIRONMENT ON AGRICULTURE

In this discussion two factors from the inorganic environment (soil and water) and one factor from the organic environment (population density) will be used as examples of how the environment can affect agriculture. We have chosen to examine a limited number in some depth rather than to briefly examine a large number of factors. By limiting the discussion in such a manner it is possible to more fully describe the effects of such factors on farm structure. In discussing each of these environmental factors an attempt is made to show how variations in the environment are related to variations in farm structure. The farm structure variables utilized will include those discussed in Chapter 3 and others.

We are not attempting to argue that environment alone determines agricultural or social development. Such a view, labeled "environmental determinism," has been suggested in the past but is generally disregarded today. The view taken in this text is that the environment provides limits and constraints to development, but numerous other factors are also obviously important in determining the structure of agriculture in the United States.

64   Population Density

Population density is a measure of the resource base of the organic environment. The number of persons that live in each unit of area in an environment reflects the sustenance base of resources in that environment with higher levels of density generally indicating a more developed sustenance base. Population density is empirically defined as the number of persons per square mile. There is tremendous diversity in different parts of the United States in the level of population density. For example, the states with the greatest population density are New Jersey and Rhode Island, both with more than nine hundred people per square mile. Other states with more than two hundred people per square mile include Massachusetts, Connecticut, Maryland, New York, Delaware, Pennsylvania, Ohio, and Illinois. At the opposite extreme Alaska, Montana, Wyoming, and Nevada have fewer than ten people per square mile.

In attempting to discern the relationships between population density and agriculture, county-level data were used (see Albrecht and Murdock [1984] for details on this data set). Correlation coefficients were run between population density and several farm structure measures. Only the forty-eight contiguous states are used because the types of agriculture in Alaska and Hawaii are so different from the rest of the country that meaningful comparisons cannot be made. The results are shown in the first column of Table 4.1. The farm structure variables

Table 4.1. Correlation coefficients between measures of the environment (population density and percentage of total acreage harvested) and farm structure at the county level for the United States ($N = 2,813$)

Farm variables	Population density	Percentage of total acreage harvested
Number of farms	.01	.36*
Average farm size (acres)	−.10*	−.14*
Gross farm sales	−.01	.34*
Gini concentration ratio	.17*	−.58*
Percentage of part-time farms	.15*	−.57*
Percentage family farms	−.09*	−.20*
Percentage partnership farms	.00	.37*
Percentage corporate farms	.15*	−.03
Percentage full-owner farms	.10*	−.61*
Percentage part-owner farms	−.16*	.44*
Percentage tenant farms	.01	.63*
Labor expenses	.40*	−.36*
Vegetable, fruit, and nursery production	.45*	−.26*
Grain production	−.05*	.71*

*Statistically significant at the .01 level.

utilized included measures of the factors discussed in Chapter 3 as well as a few additional factors. The first three farm structure variables shown in Table 4.1 are straightforward. The concentration ratio is a Gini concentration coefficient (Shryock and Siegel 1980). This measure is frequently used to determine the extent to which wealth or other factors are concentrated in a minority of the population and is used here to determine the extent to which gross farm sales are concentrated among the largest farms. The concentration ratio potentially varies from 0 to 1. A value of 0 would mean that the sales from all farms in the county were equal, while a value of 1 would indicate that *all* of the sales came from the largest farm in the county. At the state level concentration ratios ranged from highs of .84 in Florida and .82 in Texas to lows of .51 in North Dakota and .54 in Iowa.

The percentage of part-time farms is the proportion of farms in the county where the farm operator was employed off of the farm for one hundred or more days. The business organization and tenure variables are computed by determining the proportion of the total farms in the county that is in each category. The labor variable is determined by computing the ratio of the total dollars of farm labor expense per gross farm sales. Finally, the vegetable, fruit, and nursery production and grain production variables determine the proportion of the gross farm sales that is from these commodities.

An examination of the first column of Table 4.1 shows that farmers in counties with varying degrees of population density have adapted differently. The relationship between density and both number of farms and gross farm sales is not significant. Thus, both densely populated counties and sparsely populated ones have about equal numbers of farms and similar levels of farm sales. However, differences are apparent for the other variables. The results in Table 4.1 show that farms in densely populated counties tend to be smaller than in sparsely populated counties and densely populated counties have higher levels of farm concentration. In addition, the larger population base in densely populated counties means that there are more opportunities for off-farm work, and as a result there is a greater proportion of farm operators in densely populated counties who are part-time farmers. In examining the business organization and tenure patterns Table 4.1 shows that densely populated counties tend to have a lower proportion of family and full-owner farms and a greater proportion of corporate and part-owner farms. Finally, densely populated counties tend to have farms that are labor intensive

66   and produce a relatively high proportion of vegetables, fruits, and nursery products.

In summary, the results of this analysis show that farmers living in counties with different levels of density have adapted differently to their circumstances resulting in variation in farm structures across counties. Farms in densely populated counties tend to be smaller, more concentrated, and the operators have higher levels of off-farm employment compared to farms in sparsely populated counties. In addition, farms in densely populated counties compared to sparsely populated counties have a greater tendency to be corporate or part-owner farms. In densely populated counties the land is more intensely utilized, and it is more likely to be used to produce crops that have a high value per acre but are very labor intensive.

Obviously, the results of this analysis may be spurious. In other words, the same factors that cause high levels of population density may also cause these variations in farm structure. Additional research is needed to test this point. However, the analysis does support the contention of ecological theory that variations in the environment will result in variations in farm structure.

Soil Type and Quality

This is the first of two factors of the inorganic environment that could influence agriculture that will be explored in this chapter. Soil is an essential element in farm production, but one that is both limited and fragile. The thin layer of soil covering much of the earth (in most places about six inches deep) has always been, is now, and will likely remain the major source of human sustenance (Sampson 1981).

The quality and quantity of soil resources in the United States varies extensively from one part of the country to another. Within the United States there are about 2.25 billion acres of land area. About one-third of the nation's land can be eliminated from consideration as farmland because these lands are either in federal ownership or within urban areas. The vast majority of the land in federal ownership is in the western states and is unsuitable for farming. What remains is about 1.5 billion acres of nonfederal land, which varies extensively in the capability of the soil to support intensive cropping. The United States Department of Agriculture (USDA) has developed a system, known as the Land Capability Classification System, that categorizes land into eight major classes

based on its potential to support crop production without suffering per-   **67**
manent topsoil damage (Soil Conservation Service 1961; 1982). In this
classification system higher values indicate land that can support only
limited crop production because of poor quality soils, steep slopes, or
some other reason. Soils that fall into Classes I through III are commonly referred to as land that is "suitable" for cropland; land in Class IV
is "marginal," and land in Class V through Class VIII is "unsuitable."
Figure 4.1 shows the percentages of rural nonfederal land in each capability class. The figure shows that about 43 percent of the available land
is suitable for cropland, but only 3 percent of this land is sufficient to be
Class I cropland.

The distribution of land suitable for crop production is very un-
evenly dispersed through the country. As shown in Table 4.2, the proportion of nonfederal rural land suitable for crop production varies from a
high of 76 percent in the Corn Belt to a low of 18 percent in the mountain states. These differences are even more extensive when it is consid-

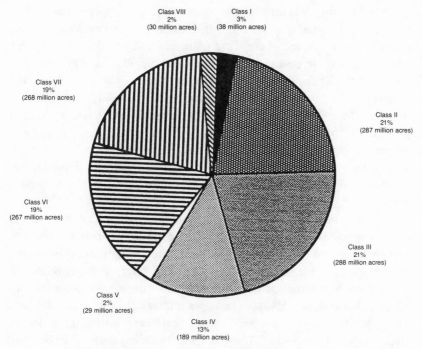

Fig. 4.1. Percentages of rural nonfederal land in each capability
class, 1977 (Soil Conservation Service 1961; 1982).

Table 4.2. Percentages of land in various soil capability classes by USDA farm production regions

| | Land capability classes | | |
Farm production region	I–III Suitable	IV Marginal	V–VIII Unsuitable
Pacific	25	14	61
Mountain	18	12	70
Northern plains	59	11	30
Southern plains	44	13	43
Lake states	59	23	18
Corn Belt	76	10	14
Delta states	55	11	34
Southeast	45	23	32
Appalachian	43	13	44
Northeast	37	10	53

Source: Soil Conservation Service (1961; 1982).

ered that vast amounts of the land most incapable of crop production in the mountain states are in federal ownership and not considered here.

In empirically examining the relationships between soil capability and farm structure, an adequate soil measure is difficult to obtain. Soil type or capability measures at the county level are simply not available. A measure that has been used in other studies is the percentage of the total acreage in harvested cropland (Albrecht and Murdock 1984). This measure appears to be a reasonable indicator of soil capability when it is examined in the context of the capability classes. Thus, nearly all (82 percent) of the Class I land and 65 percent of the Class II land is used as cropland. In comparison, only about 3 percent of the Class V through VIII land is in cropland. Not surprisingly the Corn Belt states of Iowa (66 percent) and Illinois (64 percent) have the largest proportions of their land in harvested cropland, while the mountain states of Nevada, Arizona, and Wyoming have less than 3 percent of their land in harvested cropland.

The second column of Table 4.1 presents correlation coefficients for the percentage of the total acreage in the county in harvested cropland (our measure of soil capabilities) and the various farm structure measures. This table shows that soil capability is very strongly related to the type of farm structure that emerges. Not surprisingly, counties with better soil resources can support a larger number of farms ($r = .36$), and the higher production per acre means that these farms are generally smaller in size ($r = -.14$). There is also a positive relationship between gross farm sales and percentage of the total acreage in harvested cropland ($r = .34$).

Two of the strongest relationships in Table 4.1 are between our **69** measure of soil capability and the concentration ratio and percentage of part-time farms. Counties with greater soil resources have less farm concentration ($r = -.58$), and the ability to make a living from farming results in fewer part-time farms ($r = -.57$) (Albrecht and Murdock 1984). Table 4.1 also shows that counties with better soil resources are characterized by having fewer family and more partnership farms, and having fewer full-owner farms and more part-owner and tenant farms. Counties with extensive soil resources are very heavily dependent on grain production that requires a great deal of land ($r = .71$) with less dependence on the more labor-intensive production of vegetables, fruit, and nursery products. In sum, these results again show that farmers living in different environments have adapted in different ways that have affected the nature of their farm structures.

Water

Water is another element of the inorganic environment that is absolutely essential for successful agricultural production. Approximately three-fourths of the earth's surface is covered with water, yet water remains one of the most severe resource constraints for many agricultural producers. The problem is not that the total amount of water available is limited—this amount is relatively constant—but that the distribution of this water both geographically and temporally is uneven. Some areas consistently have too much water, while other areas have constant problems of water shortages. The temporal distribution of the water supply is also problematic. Too much rainfall or extended periods of drought can both severely limit agricultural production.

Figure 4.2 shows the mean annual precipitation in different divisions of the country. As this map graphically shows, the amount of rainfall received in different parts of the country ranges from over one hundred inches on the Washington coast to less than five inches in southern Nevada and southwest Arizona. Throughout the eastern part of the country and in the Pacific Northwest rainfall is generally sufficient for agricultural production. Thus, other than for an occasional drought or flood, water is not a major constraint for agriculture in these areas. However, the situation is vastly different in the western United States. Moving westward across the Great Plains, the amount of rainfall received diminishes sharply. Between about the 98th meridian and the West

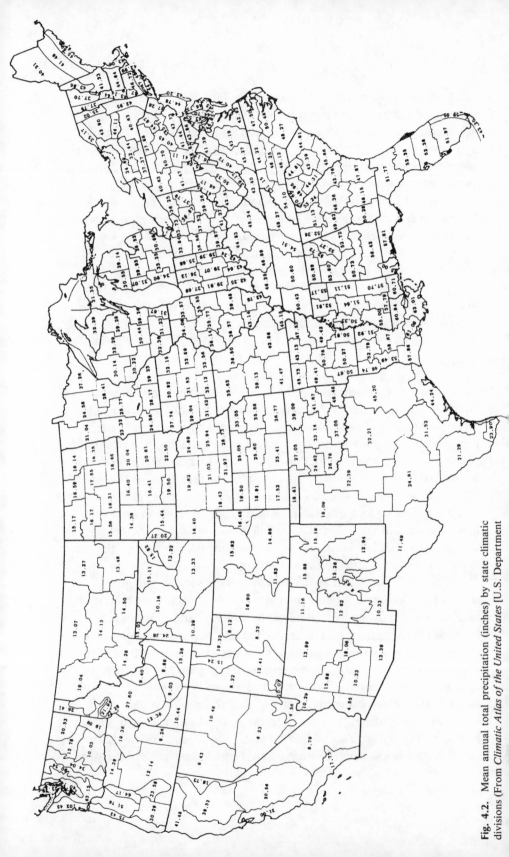

Fig. 4.2. Mean annual total precipitation (inches) by state climatic divisions (From *Climatic Atlas of the United States* [U.S. Department

Coast, natural rainfall will not support the levels of crop production that is possible given the soil and climatic conditions of the region. Consequently, the need for irrigation arises (Whittlesey 1986).

Today about 50 million acres are irrigated in the 17 western states (Frederick and Hanson 1982). There is very little irrigation in the rest of the country. Table 4.3 shows the distribution of this irrigated acreage in the four western USDA farm production regions. As shown, about 60 percent of the irrigated acreage and about 80 percent of the water utilized in the western United States are in the mountain and Pacific states. These mountain and Pacific states are generally more arid, and thus the amount of water utilized per acre is greater. Table 4.3 also shows that most of the water utilized in the plains states is from groundwater sources, while the majority of water used in the mountain and Pacific states is from surface sources.

In much of the West crop production would be virtually impossible without irrigation. For example, in 1982 more than 99.5 percent of the harvested cropland in the states of Arizona and Nevada was irrigated. In other parts of the West and in much of the plains irrigation results in greatly increased production, allows crops to be grown that could not otherwise be, and removes the risks of total crop failure that could occur if there was a lack of rainfall. Table 4.4 shows the enormous difference in productivity that results from irrigation. Corn and cotton yields are more than doubled in the West, while irrigated western crops show yields substantially higher than the same crop grown under nonirrigated conditions in the East. Consequently, in 1980 irrigated agriculture produced 27 percent of the value of the farm crops harvested in the United States on only 12 percent of the harvested acres (Sampson 1981).

Attempting to determine the relationship between rainfall and farm structure is a difficult task. To begin with, adequate rainfall data at the county level are not available, and the diversity between different parts of a state often makes the use of state averages inappropriate. In addition, irrigation in dry areas essentially removes the water constraint and is likely to result in an agricultural structure more similar to the humid East than to the dry West. However, to provide some indication of the influence of rainfall on agriculture, a comparison is made of the eight mountain states (Arizona, New Mexico, Colorado, Utah, Nevada, Wyoming, Idaho, and Montana) with the other forty contiguous states on several farm structure variables. From the information reported in Figure 4.2 the mean annual precipitation for all of the districts in each

Table 4.3. Acres irrigated and acre-feet of water applied in the seventeen western states

Region	Irrigated acres (million)	Percentage	Millions of acre feet						Percentage of water used that is groundwater
			Total water applied	Percentage	Surface water applied	Percentage	Groundwater applied	Percentage	
Northern plains	10.8	21.5	14.3	9.9	3.1	3.5	11.2	20.0	78.3
Southern plains	9.0	17.9	13.9	9.6	2.8	3.2	11.1	19.8	79.9
Mountain	17.1	34.1	65.3	45.3	50.9	57.6	14.5	25.8	22.2
Pacific	13.3	26.5	50.9	35.2	31.6	35.7	19.3	34.4	37.9
Total	50.2	100.0	144.5	100.0	88.4	100.0	56.1	100.0	38.8

Source: Adapted from Frederick and Hanson (1982).

Table 4.4.   Irrigated and dryland yields of selected crops, 1977

Crop	Location	Yield
		(bushels per acre)
Corn	Irrigated West	115.2
	Dryland West	48.3
	East	88.6
Sorghum	Irrigated West	77.4
	Dryland West	45.5
	East	61.4
Wheat	Irrigated West	77.4
	Dryland West	45.5
	East	61.4
		(bales per acre)
Cotton	Irrigated West	1.41
	Dryland West	0.60
	East	1.03

Source: Adapted from Sampson (1981, 157).

state was averaged. Based on this procedure, all eight mountain states had rainfall figures that were less than 16.5 inches per year, and all of the forty other states had rainfall figures greater than this. Thus, it can probably be safely assumed that these are the eight driest states in the country.

Table 4.5 shows data comparing the eight driest states with the forty other states on several farm structure variables. The most obvious difference is on average farm size; in the dry states the average farm is 2,639 acres compared to only 299 acres in the other forty states. The primary reason for this large difference is that most of the farmland in the dry states that cannot be irrigated cannot be used to produce crops.

Table 4.5.   A comparison of the 8 states with the least rainfall with the 40 other states in the contiguous United States on selected farm structure characteristics

Farm structure characteristics	Dry states	West states
Average farm size (acres)	2,639	299
Average sales per farm	$68,498	$42,169
Average Gini concentration ratio	0.73	0.72
Percentage of part-time farms	44	45
Percentage family farms	82	88
Percentage partnership farms	11	9
Percentage corporate farms	7	3
Percentage full-owner farms	58	60
Percentage part-owner farms	30	29
Percentage tenant farms	12	11
Labor expenses	0.07	0.08
Vegetable, fruit, and nursery production	0.05	0.12
Grain production	0.12	0.21
Percentage of total acreage harvested	4.5	21.0

74 Thus, many farm operators in the dry states operate extensive acreages that are used only as range for livestock grazing. Given this use, the per acre value of the farm commodities produced is very low, and farmers must operate an extensive acreage in order to make a living.

A further examination of the data presented in Table 4.5 shows that the differences between the dry states and the wet states on the other variables are not extensive. The average gross sales per farm in the dry states is greater than in the wet states. Also, because of their greater dependence on livestock production, the dry states have a lower proportion of their total sales from both vegetable, fruit, and nursery production, and grain production compared to the states with more rainfall.

In sum, in this section data have been presented which show that farmers living in different environments have adapted by developing farms with different structural characteristics. Variables representing both the organic and the inorganic environments have been shown to affect such characteristics. In the next section a discussion is provided on how changes in important components of the environment result in changes in agricultural structure.

TECHNOLOGICAL DEVELOPMENTS AND RESOURCE AVAILABILITY

The resource base of the inorganic environment does not simply consist of the resources that are present in that ecosystem. In addition to nature the level of technology and the modes of organization also have a major influence on resource availability (Poston et al. 1984; Schnore 1958; Michelson 1976). A resource of value to society may exist in an environment but be of little use to that society because the technology to extract the resource economically from the environment is not available. For example, billions of barrels of oil currently exist in the oil shale formations of Colorado, Utah, and Wyoming. Despite their existence and importance, the technology to make it economically feasible to extract the oil, given current prices, is not available, and consequently the resource is presently not being utilized (Murdock and Leistritz 1979).

A prime example of a case where a technological development made a critical resource available to agriculture occurred with groundwater for irrigation in the Great Plains. Using longitudinal data from the Census of Agriculture and the Census of Population from 1940 to 1980, Al-

brecht and Murdock (1985b, 1986a, 1986b) have explored the demo-   75
graphic and farm structure consequences of technological developments
making water available for irrigated agriculture in the Great Plains. A
brief summary of this research follows.

In many respects the Great Plains is an area ideally suited for agricultural production. Much of the Great Plains is flat, has rich soils and a
sufficient growing season to produce numerous crops. The major deter-
rent to successful agricultural production has been a lack of water (Webb
1936; Kraenzel 1955). Annual rainfall in the Great Plains is well below
the levels received in the East and generally is insufficient for dependable
crop production. Also, with the exception of a few streams, the region is
nearly devoid of surface water (Lawson and Baker 1981).

From early in the settlement period it was well known that much of
the Great Plains was underlain by the extensive groundwater resources
of the Ogallala Aquifer (Gould 1907). Despite the presence of water, the
technology to efficiently pump this water to the surface was not available, so the lack of water remained a major constraint to predictable
levels of production. Most settlers had windmills, but they generally
provided only enough water for household use, to water livestock, and
to possibly irrigate a few rows of garden vegetables.

During the 1930s pumps were developed that made it possible to lift
large amounts of groundwater to the surface for irrigation purposes
(Hughes and Magee 1960; Hughes and Motheral 1950). Soon, thousands
of wells were drilled, millions of acres were placed under irrigation, and
the Ogallala Aquifer became one of the most intensely developed
groundwater resources in the country.

Later technological improvements in irrigation systems have further
improved their utility. Irrigation in the early days meant hours of intensive human labor. After the groundwater was pumped to the surface, it
was immediately set flowing in ditches to the rows of the crop. One then
had to make sure that the proper amount of water was flowing down
each row and maintain the system against erosion, weeds, and rodent
damage. Water was not utilized very efficiently with these open-ditch
furrow irrigation systems. It is estimated that as much as 30 percent of
the water was lost to seepage and evaporation (Green 1973). In addition,
these furrow irrigation systems could not be used in areas characterized
by sandy soils or rolling terrain.

Later, some of the open-ditches were replaced by gated-pipes with
an outlet to each furrow. This helped to reduce the seepage and evapora-

tion losses. However, the major improvement came with the development of the center-pivot sprinkler system in 1952. Center-pivot sprinklers greatly reduced the labor requirements in irrigation agriculture, improved the efficiency by which water could be used and increased the number of acres that could potentially be irrigated. In the Great Plains today millions of acres of sandy or rolling terrain are being irrigated using center-pivot sprinkler systems that could not be irrigated with furrow irrigation systems (Bittinger and Green 1980). Thus, technological developments have made it possible to use groundwater resources for irrigation, and later technological developments have increased both the efficiency of irrigation and the area that could potentially be irrigated.

Having the technology to make water resources available for irrigation provided the impetus for extensive changes in agriculture and consequently in the economic and social structure of the Great Plains. The pumping of groundwater effectively removed a critical ecological constraint and allowed the Great Plains to become one of the most productive farming regions in the nation. This increased agricultural productivity resulted in subsequent population and organizational adaptation. When comparing the development of Great Plains counties between 1940 and 1980, Albrecht and Murdock (1985b, 1986b) found that counties with the water resources available to permit extensive levels of irrigation became substantially different over time when compared with those counties without irrigation. Irrigation has created a system of agriculture that has been more productive and one that has resulted in higher farm incomes than was possible using traditional plains dryland agricultural practices. It has produced a form of agriculture that is more labor intensive and one that has retained profitability on smaller-sized production units. Perhaps most important, the development of irrigation has created a system of agriculture that has been more resistant to farm consolidation, and, as a result, more persons have been able to remain in agriculture. Over the forty-year study period, counties with extensive levels of irrigation development have experienced population increases, while counties with little or no irrigation development have generally experienced population declines. In addition, this more productive agricultural base has resulted in allied and secondary growth. Irrigated agriculture has thus resulted both in more productive and profitable agriculture and in more viable rural communities.

RESOURCE DEPLETION AND AGRICULTURE 77

Just as more and better quality resources from the environment for agriculture result in fewer constraints for farm production, the depletion of resources critical to agriculture can result in more severe constraints and reduced carrying capacity. Resources are threatened in two primary ways—by depletion and by contamination or pollution such that the resources become unusable (Buttel 1982; Poincelot 1986).

In this section an overview is provided of the sociological consequences of the depletion of two major agricultural resources—soil and water. As noted earlier each of these resources is an essential constituent of the environmental resource base of agriculture. Further, each has faced potential depletion in some areas of the United States in recent years (Timmons 1979). In the discussion of each of these resources an overview is provided of the source and extent of the problem. Following this the sociological research on the topic is briefly reviewed. Based on the ecological perspective utilized in this book, our primary concern is with how changes in the availability of these essential resources influence agriculture and society, and the likely future consequences for society of continued change in the availability of these resources.

Soil Erosion

The erosion of our soil resources is like a double-edged sword that both reduces the productivity of cropland while polluting the water and air (Timmons 1979). Both of these effects of soil erosion constitute serious threats to our well-being as a nation. As noted earlier soil is an absolutely essential natural resource, but one that is both limited and fragile.

Producing food and fiber with limited soil erosion is possible but seldom achieved given today's technology. Soil erosion cannot be totally eliminated under any feasible management plan, but it can be reduced to levels that allow the soil to retain productivity. This "tolerable" soil loss might be defined as the maximum rate of annual soil erosion that will permit a high level of crop productivity to be sustained economically and indefinitely. This amount will vary from place to place depending on how fast new topsoil can be formed to replace the soil lost to erosion. Soil formation is a slow, continuous process, with new soil being formed as minerals break down due to chemical and biological processes. When the soil is being eroded faster than it is being formed, it is essentially being "mined" (Sampson 1981). Modern farming practices often result in soil being lost at a rate ten times faster than it can be replenished. Soil losses in the United States from cropland alone amount to about two billion tons annually. In the Corn Belt the production of one bushel of corn currently consumes about two bushels of topsoil (Pimentel et al. 1976). There are places in America where the entire layer of topsoil has been lost in only fifty to a hundred years of cultivation (Sampson 1981).

History clearly demonstrates the consequences of excessive soil erosion. Evidence suggests that the rise of many of the great civilizations of the past has been founded on an extensive natural resource base and, in particular, an extensive base of fertile soil. A base of fertile soil allows surplus farm production, which frees part of the population from agriculture and permits some persons to become artisans, engineers, scientists, writers, artists, and such (Dale and Carter 1955; Lowdermilk 1953). However, with few exceptions humans have not been able to continue a progressive civilization in one locality for more than a few hundred years. This is because the natural resource base (and in particular, the soil base) that permitted the surplus production becomes depleted. As the resource is depleted, surplus production decreases and the civilization declines (Brown 1981). In most cases the more advanced the civilization (technologically), the shorter was its period of progressive existence.

For example, Lowdermilk (1953) found over one hundred dead villages in Syria. These villages now stand on bare rock with the soils completely washed or blown away. Lowdermilk concluded that "if the soils had remained, even though the cities were destroyed and the population dispersed, the area might have repeopled again and the cities rebuilt. But now that the soils are gone, all is gone" (p. 10). Similarly, in Mesopotamia (now Iraq) the rich soils of the Tigris and Euphrates valleys supported some of the world's greatest civilizations. However, through the centuries the soil has been severely eroded and today the land supports less than one-sixth of the population that lived there during its historic peaks. Iraq is now dependent on oil exports, not agriculture, for its wealth (Sampson 1981). Dale and Carter (1955, 15) state:

> Let's not put the blame for the barrenness of these areas on the conquering hordes that repeatedly overran them. True, those con-

querors often sacked and razed the cities, burned the villages, and
slaughtered or drove off the people who populated them. But while
the soil and other resources . . . remained, the cities were usually
rebuilt. It was only after the land was depleted or exhausted that the
fields became barren and the cities remained dead.

In the United States little concern was expressed about soil erosion
until the 1930s when the Dust Bowl phenomena made the problem apparent. Beginning in 1931 and lasting until about 1940 the Great Plains
was devastated by a severe drought. The combination of the breakup of
the native prairie sod, severe drought that killed the soil-holding vegetation, incessant wind, and soils that were subject to wind erosion resulted
in some of the most severe dust storms in United States history (Hurt
1981; Lockeretz 1981). During the 1930s clouds of dust thousands of feet
high rolled across the plains causing total darkness in the middle of the
afternoon, stranding motorists on the highways, and making breathing
difficult. During the most severe storms schools and businesses were
forced to close (Hurt 1981).

At this time a young soil scientist named Hugh Hammond Bennett
was writing and speaking about the perils of soil erosion, but the impact
of his work on policy formation had been limited (Sampson 1981). Then
on May 12, 1934, a major dust storm hit the plains, which was later
described by Bennett as the turning point in the battle to get public
attention focused on the erosion problem.

This particular dust storm blotted out the sun over the nation's
capital, drove grit between the teeth of New Yorkers, and scattered
dust on the decks of ships 200 miles out to sea. I suspect that when
people along the seaboard of the eastern United States began to taste
fresh soil from the plains 2,000 miles away, many of them realized
for the first time that somewhere something had gone wrong with
the land.

It seems to take something like a disaster to awaken people who
have been accustomed to great national prosperity, such as ours, to
the presence of national menace. Although we were slowly coming
to realize that soil erosion was a major national problem, even before that great dust storm, it took that storm to awaken the nation
as a whole to some realization of the menace of erosion (Bennett
1940).

Within a short time of this storm the Soil Conservation Service
(SCS) was created as a permanent agency in the USDA by order of

80   President Franklin D. Roosevelt on March 25, 1935. A month later
Roosevelt signed into law the Soil Conservation Act of 1935 (Public Law
74-46). This law states:

> It is hereby recognized that the wastage of soil and moisture re-
> sources on farm, grazing, and forestlands of the nation, resulting
> from soil erosion, is a menace to the national welfare and that it is
> hereby declared to be the policy of Congress to provide permanently
> for the control and prevention of soil erosion and thereby to pre-
> serve natural resources, control floods, prevent impairment of reser-
> voirs, and maintain the navigability of rivers and harbors, protect
> public health and public lands, and relieve unemployment.

A half century after the passage of the Soil Conservation Act and
the creation of the SCS, in spite of sophisticated technologies and data
systems and $15 billion in federal funds, soil erosion is still a serious
problem in the United States. In fact, the United States is now losing
topsoil at a faster rate than at any time in history including the Dust
Bowl era (Sampson 1981). There are many reasons for this lack of
success in dealing with the soil erosion problem. Soil conservation
measures are expensive to implement, and typically the return on the
investment is not realized for many years. Thus, some studies conclude
that landowners and farm operators are more interested in increasing
their net incomes over a short planning horizon. In particular, tenants
with short-term leases may have short-term planning horizons that moti-
vate them to emphasize immediate income. This problem is further ag-
gravated by the very small profit margin in farming. Small-sized farms
frequently force farmers to exploit the land for a living regardless of the
effects on soil erosion. Finally, some farmers are not fully convinced that
reducing soil erosion is essential for long-term soil productivity (Nowak
and Korsching 1982; Heffernan and Green 1986; Timmons 1979).

The vast majority of the sociological research completed to date on
the soil erosion issue has relied on the adoption-diffusion model (Rogers
1983) and has explored the characteristics of farmers most and least
likely to implement soil conservation techniques (e.g., Bultena and
Hoiberg 1983; Korsching et al. 1983; Napier et al. 1984; Nowak 1983;
Pampel and van Es 1977; Taylor and Miller 1978). This literature is
important because it shows which farmers are and are not utilizing soil
conservation methods and why, and provides a basis for adjusting existing soil conservation policies and programs.

However, major gaps remain in the sociological research on soil erosion and many questions are left unanswered. From an ecological perspective a critical question relates to how the population and social organization of a society adapt to changes in the quality and quantity of critical resources such as soil. The historical evidence discussed earlier and ecological theory suggest that reduced soil quality would result in more severe limits and constraints being placed on agriculture and subsequently a reduced carrying capacity for the land. Declining farm production caused by extensive soil erosion is likely to mean that the size of the farm population that can be supported in an ecosystem will be reduced, and that unless other sustenance activities emerge, total population and economic resources will decline.

As of yet, however, research has not been completed that explores such questions in a modern setting. Research has shown that soil loss reduces crop yields (except legumes) unless liberal amounts of fertilizers are added to replace the nutrients lost from the soil. Soil losses may also reduce the water-holding capacity of the soil and restrict root penetration. Soil erosion thus always increases the costs of production and in severe cases makes it unprofitable to farm (Sampson 1981). While economists have explored the consequences of these increased costs of production for the farm firm (Timmons 1979), the macrolevel organizational and demographic consequences have not been examined. Conducting research on these consequences will be difficult and will require interdisciplinary approaches because they involve biological as well as social dimensions. Obtaining quantitative estimates of the amount of soil lost and the effects of these losses on productivity will be difficult. However, determining how farm populations adapt to changes in soil productivity and the macrolevel consequences of this adaptation is critical to policy and program formation.

Water Scarcity and Depletion

Water is generally referred to as a "flow" resource. This means that it appears on a time-installment basis as it moves through the hydrologic cycle. We can use today's water today or we can store some of it until tomorrow, but we cannot use tomorrow's water until it comes. As such, the water supply cannot be depleted in the sense that soil resources can. However, water supplies can be polluted to the point that they are unusable. Also, much of the groundwater used in agriculture is a "fund" resource like petroleum. If groundwater resources are depleted faster than they can be naturally replenished, then the resource will eventually be gone.

Again history presents graphic evidence of the importance of water resources for agriculture. In ancient Mesopotamia the waters of the Tigris and Euphrates rivers were developed for irrigation with an elaborate system of canals. This region is so arid that dependable crop production is not possible without irrigation. The resulting increase in agricultural productivity from irrigation freed many people from primary production and allowed these societies to flourish. However, the river waters were filled with silt from the overgrazed highlands, and as the water entered the slow-moving canals, the silt settled out and clogged the canals. Keeping the irrigation ditches open was long a chief concern of the people of the region, and the problem was often solved by slave labor. However, if wars or other factors diverted the attention of the people, the irrigation system quickly deteriorated and the food source was threatened. Time and time again, the region experienced periods of mass starvation (Dale and Carter 1955).

As noted earlier, irrigation plays a vital role in American agriculture today, and both surface and groundwater sources for water are critical. Surface water used for irrigation is a flow resource with a limited seasonal supply. In most of the West there is no surplus or unused water. Thus, to add more water to presently irrigated land or develop other irrigated lands would be impossible without decreasing other uses of the water. However, the competitive uses of this water such as industrial, municipal, power generation, recreation, and fisheries are frequently in a position to place a higher economic value on the water than agriculture and thus bid water away (Whittlesey 1986).

In contrast to surface water, groundwater is basically a fund resource with a limited supply available. While most aquifers experience some recharge, the amount varies significantly from formation to formation (Lacewell and Collins 1986). However, throughout the West the mining of groundwater (extracting more than is naturally recharged) exceeds 22 million acre-feet per year (Sloggett 1979). Groundwater irrigation is also heavily dependent on energy resources to pump the underground water to the surface. As the water tables decline, the energy costs of lifting the water to the surface increase. Thus, groundwater mining, energy costs, alternative uses, and the impairment of groundwater quality all pose serious threats to the long-term outlook for irrigation from groundwater in the West (National Water Commission 1973). Some exploratory research has investigated the consequences of groundwater depletion for agriculture. As discussed earlier, technological developments initially made it possible to effectively utilize groundwater for irrigation purposes. In some cases extensive withdrawal resulted in problems of groundwater depletion. Perhaps nowhere is this problem more severe than in the Great Plains.

Years of heavy withdrawal of water from the Ogallala Aquifer resulted in considerable declines in the amount of water available. Of the more than 22 million acre-feet of water that are mined from groundwater sources per year in this country, about 14 million come from the Texas and Oklahoma high-plains areas alone. This is equivalent to the average annual flow of the Colorado River (Frederick and Hanson 1982). In parts of the Texas high plains the water table has already declined by more than 100 feet. These declines in the water table have resulted in reduced irrigation in some areas. For example, in Hockley County, Texas, about 201,000 acres of cropland were irrigated in 1969. By 1978 the number of acres irrigated had decreased to 165,000, and then during the next four years the amount of irrigation declined rapidly; in 1982 only about 99,000 acres of land were irrigated in Hockley County.

Projections show that reduced irrigation and the reimposition of water constraints may have serious implications for the Great Plains (Albrecht and Murdock 1985b). A reversion to dryland agriculture will alter the level of agricultural production and the structure of agriculture and is likely to result in a reduced farm and total population in the area.

In sum, changes in the availability of water resources have major implications for agriculture and agriculturally based communities in the more arid parts of the world. In the western United States water is a major constraining factor for agricultural production. Reductions in the amount of irrigation in the western United States are likely to have major implications for the agriculturally based sections of this region. A substantial amount of research is needed on this issue. Research in the Great Plains has shown irrigation development to have important demographic and farm structure implications as the area adapts to changing environmental constraints. Similar research should be conducted in other parts of the country. Also, future trends should be carefully monitored to see the implications of irrigation declines. Research that could determine and accurately project the demographic, organizational, and social consequences of various levels of irrigation declines could be extremely valuable to policy makers, community leaders, and others.

CONCLUSIONS

In this chapter we have examined the critical role of the environment in shaping the structure of agriculture. As the discussion indicates, the diversity of the environment leads to a corresponding diversity in agricultural structure as farmers adapt their practices to environmental limitations. As with other ecological factors, however, changes in the environment occur both as a result of technological applications and the ways the organizational structures affect it. Thus, as we have noted, irrigation technology has served to expand the production capacity of relatively marginal lands while the intensive and often shortsighted impact of many forms of social organizations have been to deplete the water and soil resources necessary for productive agriculture. In addition, these interrelationships between environmental and other factors have acted to alter the organizational structure of agriculture and to produce the diversity of agriculture apparent throughout the United States.

Although analyses like those described in this chapter point to the need for extensive additional research on the role of environmental factors in the determination of the organizational structure of agriculture, even the results of such preliminary analyses have clear implications for U.S. agriculture. Thus, the history of ecological changes related to agriculture and the environment clearly suggest that agricultural productivity is likely to decline in many parts of the United States unless concerted actions are taken to preserve the soil and more adequately manage the water resources essential to high agricultural productivity. In many of the most agriculturally productive parts of the United States intensive and widespread agriculture production has occurred for only about two hundred years. This is a relatively short period in ecological terms and the long-term changes that have appeared in other agricultural production regions in the past have yet to occur. However, ecological history cautions us that the limits of the environment are real and its resources are not infinite when human social organizations pursue paths detrimental to the resource base.

Equally important is the fact that even limited analysis using an ecological perspective suggests that environmental factors often have pervasive (though not deterministic) influences on other dimensions of the ecological complex. The size of human populations, the nature of its technological base, the organizational structure of its social and sustenance base all influence and are influenced by the environment. Although our knowledge base is insufficient to understand and to trace the implications of the interactive changes of such factors on one another, it is clear that we cannot ignore any of these factors and adequately understand the social world around us including the nature of its agricultural production system. Thus, the ecologist's plea for more concerted attention to environmental factors in the analysis of the structure of agriculture is not to be seen as a subdisciplinary and self-serving interest but a call for a perspective that is essential to the development of more adequate understanding of the complex determinants and implications of changes in the structure of U.S. agriculture.

Technology and Agriculture

Technological changes have impacted agriculture as much as any sector of American society. Technology is generally credited with the phenomenal increase in productivity in American agriculture and with such effects as increases in farm size and the related reduction in farm numbers and reductions in farm labor needs and rural farm populations and with the creation of an increasingly capital-intensive form of agriculture (Berardi and Geisler 1984). In fact, the history of American agriculture can be seen as almost totally reflecting the development and application of technology to agricultural production (Stewart 1979). It is clear, then, that no attempt to describe the present or future structure of U.S. agriculture can be complete without a description of the role of technology in shaping that structure.

In this chapter we examine the role of technology in shaping the structure of U.S. agriculture. Our discussion begins with a presentation of a general ecological interpretation of technology's role in an ecosystem and with a relatively detailed delineation of an ecological differentiation of types of technology and their past and potential future role in shaping the structure of agriculture in the United States. This section provides the ecological basis for the description of the effects of technology on agriculture that are the focus of the remainder of the chapter.

87

88 TECHNOLOGY AND THE ECOLOGICAL STRUCTURE OF AGRICULTURE

The term technology is usually associated with mechanical means of enhancing people's ability to manipulate their environment. Ecologically, however, technology refers not only to mechanical means but also to behavioral means that enhance people's ability to adapt to a changing ecosystem. As such, technology has both engineering as well as social behavioral dimensions, and since even the engineering dimensions are usually aimed at altering the modes of behavior surrounding the production of a given product or service so as to improve the overall level of productivity of the group, technology may be seen as a uniquely "socially oriented" set of processes and behaviors (Duncan 1964).[1]

From an ecological perspective, the impacts of a given type of technology may be seen as resulting from a complex process by which the social organization of a population adapts to the altered environmental factors created by a technology's application. The nature and consequences of the adaptation to a new technology will vary depending on the type of technology, the state of the environment, organization, other technology, and the characteristics of the population at the time the new technology is introduced. Central to this ecological conception is the realization that changes induced by alterations in any one of the dimensions of the ecological complex are affected by the characteristics, the types of interaction, and the forms of interdependence among other parts.[2] To fully discern the likely impacts of a technology, then, it is critical that the likely relationships between the technological form and other parts of the ecological complex be analyzed adequately.

Among the numerous dimensions of such relationships that must be determined, human ecological theory suggests that the types of interdependence that exist between elements of the ecological complex are particularly important (Hawley 1968). The form of interdependence refers to the ways in which elements in an ecosystem relate to one another. This interdependence determines the effects of a newly introduced factor upon the ecosystem and affects the form this factor subsequently takes in adapting to the ecosystem (Hawley 1968). An analysis of the forms of interdependence in an ecosystem is thus instrumental to understanding the magnitude of impacts likely to result from the introduction of a technology into an ecosystem.

Human ecological theory suggests that the key forms of interdependence are commensalistic and symbiotic (Hawley 1950). Commensalistic forms of interdependence involve relationships based on commonality. That is, factors are interrelated on the basis of similar characteristics in each that enhance the abilities of the interrelated factors to survive and exploit the environment. Symbiotic forms of interdependence are based on complementary linkages between interrelated units (Duncan 1964). Factors so related have different characteristics that complement the needs of each other, making their combined characteristics capable of sustaining new and growing populations.

Thus, it seems possible to suggest that one can conceive of new technologies as being related in either symbiotic or commensalistic means to other dimensions of the ecosystem. Although these types of interdependence might occur between technology and any other element of the ecological complex, the form of interdependence between technology and the environment would appear to be especially critical because technology plays a central role in expanding the dimensions of an environment and people's ability to adapt to that environment (Hawley 1950, 1968; Micklin and Choldin 1984). An examination of the impacts of the alternative types of interdependence between technology and the environment is a critical starting point for establishing the impact of technology on the structure of agricultural and other dimensions of society.

Thus, one can examine the effects of technologies that have formed commensalistic relationships with environmental factors (which we refer to as commensalistic technologies) and those that form symbiotic relationships with environmental factors (which we refer to as symbiotic technologies).[3] Commensalistic interdependence between technology and environment will occur when the application of a technological process leads to an accentuation or alteration of already established environmental processes of change. In other words, the technologically based processes are similar to those already evolving in the environment, but the new technology allows the process to be completed more efficiently. Symbiotic interdependence between a technology and the environment involves situations in which the application of the technological process leads to the development of new and complementary processes of change in the environment by which new or previously unavailable resources are made available. So seen, the identification of commensalistic and symbiotic forms of interdependence between technological and environmental processes of change may lead to an increased understanding of the socioeconomic impact of new technologies.

From this perspective, the effects of commensalistic technologies can be seen as allowing existing environmental resource bases to be used in a manner consistent with present use patterns, types of organization, and population bases but to also increase the efficiency of such use. Symbiotic technologies, on the other hand, tend to alter the environmental resource base and related organizations by bringing to bear techniques and practices that make previously unavailable resources, or resources whose use was previously economically unfeasible, available and feasible for use by society. This expansion in resources, in turn, allows for an expansion in population and in the complexity of social organization. Whereas commensalistic technologies tend to increase a population's ability to exploit existing resource bases, symbiotic technologies tend to expand the environmental resource base and the rate of population growth.[4]

The theoretical premises outlined above have particular saliency for understanding the impact of the introduction of different types of agricultural technology. Commensalistic forms of agricultural technology have had major effects on agricultural productivity and efficiency. They include such technology as the tractor and other machinery that increase the work capacity of humans and that have allowed farmers to more efficiently accomplish processes that were already being performed such as cultivation of the soil and harvesting. In fact, the description of such technologies and their impact on the structure of agriculture comprises a major part of the literature on agricultural technology (for example, see Berardi 1981; Hamilton 1939).

Because commensalistic technologies result in increased efficiency in the use of resources, they have tended to result in reduced need for agricultural labor, increased farm size as the amount of acreage that could be farmed by a single farmer, and a decline in the number of farms (Paarlberg 1980). In addition, by reducing the amount of human labor needed on farms, commensalistic technological developments may have made it possible for more farm operators to secure off-farm employment. However, they have had a greater effect on the production unit than on the level of production per unit.

The effects of commensalistic technology are also apparent in other dimensions of the ecological complex. Its effects on population have been extensively documented (Beale 1980) and are evident in the migration of millions of farm and rural people to urban areas in what has been termed the largest voluntary migration in human history (Beale 1979, 1980). Thus extensive use of commensalistic technology has been related to rural nonfarm and rural farm population decline.

Examples of symbiotic technologies in agriculture include biological, chemical, and biotechnological developments, the introduction of hybrid seeds, and irrigation technology (Buttel et al. 1983; Kloppenburg 1984). These technologies have allowed producers to use new or previously unavailable resources. Symbiotic technologies have received less attention than commensalistic ones because they tend to occur less frequently, but as shall be evident in the discussion of biotechnology presented below, when developed, these technologies have the potential to markedly change the organization of U.S. agriculture.

Irrigation technology provides an example of a symbiotic technology. Irrigation technology made the use of previously unavailable water resources feasible and thus greatly increased per acre productivity. In the Great Plains, for example, irrigated land yields from two to six times more per acre than land farmed without irrigation (Casey et al. 1975). As noted earlier, this led to the retention of a larger number of farms in irrigated areas and to a retention of farm and nonfarm population (Albrecht and Murdock 1986b).

The effects of symbiotic technologies have thus been quite different from the effects of commensalistic technologies. By increasing per acre yields, symbiotic technologies make it possible for the farmer to produce enough to maintain a sufficient income on a smaller acreage; and since they are generally more labor intensive than commensalistic technologies, the result is more producers, more population, fewer part-time producers, and increased sales per farm. Symbiotic technologies, then, lead to changes in the structure of agriculture that are different in kind as well as in magnitude from changes resulting from commensalistic technologies.

The ecological perspective outlined above suggests that the relationships between technology and other parts of the ecological complex will determine many of the impacts of such technology on the structure of agriculture. The sections that follow describe the historical impact of agricultural technology and the potential impact likely to occur with future developments in agricultural technology.

92 MAJOR IMPACT OF AGRICULTURAL TECHNOLOGY

The major impact of technology on agriculture has been to reduce the amount of human labor required to produce a given level of output from a given land area by replacing labor and other resources with mechanical technology (commensalistic technology) and the application of nutritive and biological materials (symbiotic technology). The extent to which this process has characterized agriculture in the United States can be seen by examining the data in Tables 5.1–5.5, which are derived from information on productivity for the United States published by the U.S. Department of Agriculture (1986a).

Tables 5.1 and 5.2 indicate some of the types of technology that have been used to bring about productivity increases. These include both standard commensalistic technology such as tractors and trucks and symbiotic technology such as fertilizers. As shown in Table 5.1, the number of tractors increased from 1.5 million in 1940 to 4.6 million in 1985, and tractor horsepower being used for agricultural purposes increased from 42 million to 311 million. As Bertrand (1978) reports, however, even this increase is not as rapid as that revealed when one examines the somewhat longer period of time from 1920 to the present. During this period the number of tractors increased from 246,000 to 4.6 million. Tractor technology has thus increased more than threefold since 1940 and nearly twentyfold since 1920, and the horsepower being applied for agricultural uses has increased nearly eightfold since 1940. Similar increases are evident for other forms of mechanical technology such as trucks, combines, and harvesters. These technologies have largely displaced labor, resulting in producers being able to farm larger production units but also displacing large numbers of farm workers (Berardi and Geisler 1984).

The application of fertilizer has been equally important to the increase in agricultural productivity. Unlike commensalistic technology that decreases the need for labor, the application of these symbiotic forms of technology leads to substantial increases in productivity per acre (see Table 5.5). As shown in Table 5.2, the total tonnage of fertilizers used has increased roughly twentyfold for nitrogen fertilizers, fivefold for phosphate fertilizers, and twelvefold for potash. Biological materials and nutrients have thus been instrumental in the rise in increased production in agriculture.

The extent to which the applications of technology have had com-

Table 5.1. Farm machinery and equipment, United States, 1940–1985

Year	Tractors		Motor trucks	Grain combines[b]	Corn-heads[c]	Pickup balers[d]	Field forage harvesters[e]
	Number[a]	Horsepower					
	Thousands	Millions			Thousands		
1940	1,567	42	1,047	190	110	N/A	N/A
1945	2,354	61	1,490	375	168	42	20
1950	3,394	93	2,207	714	456	196	81
1955	4,345	126	2,675	980	688	448	202
1960	4,688	153	2,834	1,042	792	680	291
1965	4,787	176	3,030	910	690	751	316
1970	4,619	203	2,984	790	635	708	304
1975	4,469	222	3,032	524	615	667	255
1980[f]	4,752	304	3,344	652	701	756	293
1985[g]	4,676	311	3,380	645	684	800	285

Source: U.S. Department of Agriculture (1986a, 30).

[a]Includes wheel- and crawler-type tractors; does not include steam and garden.

[b]Data for 1975 and after are for self-propelled combines only.

[c]Includes corn pickers and picker shellers.

[d]Does not include balers producing bales weighing more than 200 pounds.

[e]Data for 1976 and after do not include flail-type forage harvesters.

[f]U.S. totals for 1978 and after are not directly comparable with totals for 1974 or earlier census years because they include state-level data from farm operators represented on the census mailing list plus estimates from the direct enumeration sample for farms not represented on the mailing list. As a result, figures for nearly all categories are somewhat higher than they would be using the earlier base. The 1974 U.S. data include only operations represented on the mailing list. Estimates are pegged to census-year data for all noncensus years before 1978.

[g]Preliminary.

N/A = not available.

Table 5.2. Fertilizer: Primary plant nutrients and liming materials used, United States and Puerto Rico, 1940–1984

	Primary plant nutrients[b]								Liming materials[c]	
	Quantity (1,000 tons)				Index (1977 = 100)				Quantity (1,000 tons)	Index (1977 = 100)
Year[a]	Nitrogen	Phos- phate[d]	Potash[e]	Total[f]	Nitrogen	Phos- phate	Potash	Total (all types)		
1940	419	912	435	1,766	4	16	8	8	14,406	46
1945	641	1,439	752	2,832	6	26	13	13	23,055	74
1950	1,005	1,950	1,103	4,058	9	35	19	18	29,842	95
1955	1,960	2,284	1,865	6,109	18	41	32	28	20,659	66
1960	2,738	2,572	2,153	7,463	26	46	37	34	22,614	72
1965	4,639	3,513	2,835	10,987	44	62	49	50	28,075	90
1970	7,459	4,574	4,035	16,068	70	81	69	73	25,901	83
1975	8,608	4,511	4,453	17,572	81	80	76	80	31,128	99
1980	11,407	5,432	6,245	23,084	107	97	107	104	34,402	110
1984[g]	11,146	4,929	5,809	21,884	105	88	100	99	N/A	N/A

Source: U.S. Department of Agriculture (1986a, 26).
[a]Calendar year for 1939–1949. Fertilizer year ending June 30 for 1950–1984.
[b]Includes 50 states and Puerto Rico.
[c]Includes 48 states only.
[d]To convert P_2O_5 to P multiply P_2O_5 by 0.43642.
[e]To convert K_2O to K multiply K_2O by 0.83016.
[f]Includes material for nonfarm use.
[g]Preliminary.
N/A = not available.

mensalistic effects on the structure of agriculture is evident in the reduction of the number of hours required for farm work shown in Tables 5.3 and 5.4. Thus, the number of hours devoted to livestock production has decreased from about 7 billion in 1939 to about 1 billion hours in 1984 (a reduction of 86 percent), and the total number of hours for crop production have been reduced from 10.4 billion to 2.3 billion (a reduction of 78 percent) from 1940 to 1984, while the total number of hours for all types of farm work has been reduced from 20.5 billion to 3.7 billion, a reduction of 82 percent. Finally, the dual impacts of technology in reducing the labor required on the farm while at the same time increasing overall productivity are evident in the data in Table 5.4. As shown in this table, although farm employment has decreased from 11.0 to 3.5 million from 1940 to 1984, the average farm worker supplied food for 77.3 persons in 1984 compared to 10.7 in 1940. In sum, employment in agriculture decreased 68 percent while productivity per worker increased by nearly 700 percent from 1940 to 1984. It is evident, then, that commensalistic forms of technology have had pervasive effects on the human labor component of agricultural production.

The data in Table 5.5 show some of the effects that symbiotic technologies have had on agricultural production. The data in this table indicate that the amount of harvested cropland has remained relatively stable over the past forty-five years but that productivity per acre has more than doubled. The number of acres in harvested cropland increased from 331 million acres in 1940 to 337 million in 1984, an increase of only 6 million acres, while the index of production per acre has increased from 53 to 111 during the same period of time. It is evident, then, that the land resource or environmental base has remained relatively stable while its productivity has increased dramatically, suggesting the magnitude of effects associated with the application of symbiotic technology to an environmental resource base.

An examination of the data in Tables 5.1–5.5 clearly indicates that agricultural productivity has been markedly increased by the application of both commensalistic and symbiotic technology. This has enabled U.S. farmers to produce an abundance of food at a relatively low price for American consumers as well as to create a substantial base of commodity products for export (Knutson et al. 1983). In a sense, then, technology has produced impacts that have been positively adaptive for the aggregate of Americans.

What has been positive for consumers in the United States as a

Table 5.3. Labor: Total hours used for farmwork by enterprise groups, United States, 1940–1984

Year	All farmwork[c]	Livestock and livestock products[a]				Crops[b]									
		All	Meat animals	Milk cows	Poultry	All	Feed grains	Hay and forage	Food grains	Vege- tables	Fruits and nuts	Sugar crops	Cotton	Tobacco	Oil crops
						Million Hours									
1940	20,472	7,023	1,309	3,495	1,008	10,378	2,709	1,262	517	803	734	181	2,414	626	256
1945	18,838	7,045	1,438	3,365	1,294	8,967	2,240	1,083	496	804	670	170	1,583	824	307
1950	15,137	5,548	1,451	2,749	1,161	6,922	1,484	695	327	643	619	135	1,298	745	199
1955	12,808	4,948	1,498	2,422	840	6,012	1,154	671	253	521	536	88	1,235	710	175
1960	9,795	3,826	1,307	1,745	593	4,590	784	524	188	438	531	71	831	549	164
1965	7,335	2,969	1,107	1,250	444	3,416	502	410	176	407	454	85	482	468	203
1970	5,896	2,344	997	817	373	2,788	425	339	152	359	452	74	244	308	205
1975	4,975	1,701	731	568	251	2,630	377	287	222	355	472	77	105	286	219
1980	4,281	1,285	547	382	210	2,443	338	244	215	314	496	60	81	218	248
1984[d]	3,745	1,008	432	257	176	2,253	324	219	191	342	443	57	55	174	218

Source: U.S. Department of Agriculture (1986a).

[a]Livestock and livestock products in each group include horses and mules (excluded); clipped wool, mohair, and (for 1950 to date) honey and beeswax; cattle and calves, sheep and lambs, and hogs; butter and butterfat, wholesale and retail milk, and milk consumed on farms; and chickens and eggs, commercial broilers and turkeys.

[b]Crops in each group include: hayseeds, pasture seeds, and cover-crop seeds, and some miscellaneous crop production (farm gardens were excluded after 1964); corn for grain, oats, barley, and sorghum grain; all hay, sorghum forage, corn silage, and (for 1950 to date) sorghum silage; all wheat, rye, and rice (buckwheat excluded after 1964); potatoes, sweet potatoes, dry edible beans, dry field peas, truck crops for processing, and truck crops for fresh market; fruits, berries, and tree nuts (citrus production is on year of harvest, 1960 to date; earlier years on year of bloom); sugar beets, sugarcane for sugar and seed, sugarcane syrup, and maple syrup; and soybeans, peanuts or nuts, cottonseed, flaxseed, and (for 1950 to 1964) tungnuts and peanuts hogged.

[c]Includes labor used on crops, livestock, and overhead. After 1964, labor used for horses and mules and farm gardens was excluded.

[d]Preliminary.

96

Table 5.4. Persons supplied farm products by one farm worker, United States, 1940–1984

Year	Persons supplied per farm worker Total	Persons supplied per farm worker At home	Persons supplied per farm worker Abroad	Total farm employment[a] (millions)	Total United States population, July 1 (millions)
1940	10.7	10.3	0.4	11.0	132.1
1945	14.6	12.9	1.7	10.0	139.9
1950	15.5	13.8	1.7	9.9	151.7
1955	19.5	17.3	2.2	8.4	165.3
1960	25.8	22.3	3.5	7.1	180.8
1965	37.0	30.8	6.2	5.6	194.4
1970	47.9	40.6	7.3	4.5	205.1
1975	58.3	44.2	14.1	4.3	216.0
1980	75.7	52.3	23.4	3.7	227.7
1984[b]	77.3	57.3	20.0	3.5	236.7

Source: U.S. Department of Agriculture (1986a).
Note: Includes the farm worker; thus in 1940, the average farm worker supplied her or himself and 9.7 other persons.
[a]Includes farm operators, unpaid family workers, and hired workers.
[b]Preliminary.

Table 5.5. Cropland used for crops and index of crop production per acre, United States, 1940–1984

Year	Cropland harvested[a]	Crop failure	Cultivated summer fallow	Total	Index (1977 = 100)[b]	Index of crop production per acre (1977 = 100)
	Million acres					
1940	331	16	21	368	97	53
1945	345	9	18	372	98	57
1950	336	12	29	377	100	59
1955	333	16	29	378	100	63
1960	317	6	32	355	94	77
1965	292	6	38	336	89	85
1970	289	5	38	332	88	88
1975	330	6	31	367	97	96
1980	342	10	30	382	101	100
1984[c]	337	6	30	373	99	111

Source: U.S. Department of Agriculture (1986a).
[a]Land from which one or more crops were harvested.
[b]Computed from unrounded data.
[c]Preliminary.

97

98   whole has not necessarily been positive for many agricultural producers. In fact, as noted in earlier chapters, for many producers technological change has resulted in their being forced from agriculture. Because of this the impact of technology on agriculture has been both positive and negative.

Whereas many scholars doing societalwide analysis and many agricultural scientists (Stewart 1979; Zahara and Johnson 1979) have pointed to the aggregate good brought about by the application of technology in agriculture, other analysts (Hightower 1973; Friedland et al. 1981; Busch and Lacy 1983; Poincelot 1986) have suggested that agricultural technology has led to the demise of millions of family farms and to the loss of employment for farm laborers, has been developed for the largest producers at the expense of smaller producers, has led to less nutritious and desirable products for consumers and to a type of agriculture that is input-intensive and destructive of the long-term productivity of the land. These latter sources see the impact as at least, in part, a product of the organizational structure of agricultural research and extension in the United States, charging that agricultural research is controlled and oriented to assisting capital-intensive agricultural enterprises that are sufficiently large to make use of economies of scale (Busch and Lacy 1983). They further argue that the impact of technology should be assessed prior to its widespread application to agriculture.

An additional body of scholars (Copp et al. 1983; Dillingham and Sly 1966; Bertrand et al. 1956; Bertrand, 1958; Martin and Havlicek 1977) suggest that the impact of technology has been both good and bad. Technology appears to have had mixed effects, increasing production and reducing exposure to the dirtier and more dangerous farm tasks, but at the same time creating new accident hazards and displacing farm laborers. In addition, however, these researchers point to the difficulty encountered in establishing a clear causal relationship between technology and impact, either positive or negative. Although technological impact obviously exists, the isolation of the unique effects of given types of technology is in many cases extremely difficult. Additional research to establish the positive and negative impacts of technology is essential.

ROLE OF TECHNOLOGY IN THE FUTURE OF U.S. AGRICULTURE

As the discussion above indicates, technology has had a profound effect on U.S. agriculture in this century, creating perhaps the most productive food and fiber production system in the world but at the same time reducing the number of farms and farm workers to a fraction of those who were involved at the beginning of this century. As dramatic as such changes have been, the future impact of agricultural technology may be even more extensive. The development and application of new biotechnologies to agriculture provides an excellent example of the potential effects of future technologies, and we use it here as an example of both the likely rapid pace of future technological change and to further explicate the utility of a human ecological framework for explaining that change. The fact that biotechnology will be one major source of change in agriculture, however, should not lead us to forget that other forms of technological change (e.g., further applications of computer technology) will also have major effects on agriculture.

The use of biotechnologies in agriculture and medicine has been referred to as the fourth major scientific revolution of this century, comparable in impact to what has occurred as a result of unlocking the secrets of the atom, escaping earth's gravity, and the information revolution brought about by the development of the digital computer (Clarke 1986). It has also been estimated that the worldwide market for biotechnology related to agriculture and food processing could reach $100 billion per year by the year 2000 (Harlander and Garner 1986). It is essential, then, both to describe some of the likely forms of such technology that may affect agriculture and some of the potential effects of such technology on the structure of agriculture.

Biotechnology promises to have significant impacts on nearly all aspects of U.S. and world agriculture. Among the impacts of biotechnology are such potential innovations as the use of biotechnology to increase the speed and the accuracy of wine and cheese fermentation processes, the enhancement of artificial sweeteners, and the alteration of food products to change their caloric and flavor characteristics (Lund 1986; Harlander and Garner 1986). Other applications include the use of soil microbes to treat chemical wastes and control fungi and other factors that endanger plant productivity (Kearney 1986; Papavizas and Loper 1986), the breeding of farm animals with desirable characteristics

100   (such as lower fat contents in beef carcasses) (Seidel 1986), the production of multiple offspring from a single embryo and selection of the preferred sex of the offspring (e.g., females for dairy cattle, males for sheep and beef cattle production) (Johnson 1986), increased milk production of dairy cattle (Smith and Bauman 1986), the treatment of animal diseases such as diarrhea, shipping fever, brucellosis, and cancer (Argenzio 1986), increased efficiency of production of vaccines, and increased accuracy of diagnosis of diseases (Snyder 1986). Additional plant applications include increasing the ability of plants to photosynthesize, improving nitrogen fixation (Martin 1986), improving the stalk or leaf quality of plants, increasing the speed of plant growth (Dilworth 1986), increasing resistance to plant diseases (Beachy 1986), and producing plants that are disease resistant and tolerant of extreme temperature and rainfall variation (Blum 1986). Still other applications include altering insect species biologically to prevent infestation of key agricultural crops and thus reduce the level of insecticide and pesticide use (Adams 1986).

Although such uses of biotechnology promise to increase agricultural productivity substantially, the social and economic implications are less apparent and are the subject of a substantial debate. In large part, the concerns related to biotechnology involve four major substantive issues.

1. The characteristics of those producers likely to adopt such technology most rapidly
2. The effects of differentials in adoption on the structure of agriculture in the United States and on regional variations in the structure of agriculture
3. The structure of the biotechnology research enterprise
4. The environmental dangers involved in the release of new biotechnological products

Initial assessments of the impact of biotechnology in agriculture have pointed to some startling impacts for producers. A study of the implications of the bovine growth hormone for the dairy industry in New York (Kalter et al. 1985), for example, has suggested that milk production could increase from 10 to 40 percent per cow with daily use of the hormone and that adoption rates would exceed 50 percent in the first year and would eventually reach 60 to 85 percent. Although early adopters would experience positive economic returns, the analysis indicated that increased production would lead to a 20 to 50 percent decline in the number of dairy farms and to a reduction in milk prices, and that early adopters would likely be those managing relatively large herds (Kalter et al. 1985). In addition, the analysis suggested that unless the milk price support system was changed, it could lead to a significant increase in cost to the public for this system. In like manner, a study conducted under the sponsorship of the Office of Technology Assessment (Office of Technology Assessment 1986) suggests that the impact of biotechnology will likely lead to further reductions in the number of middle-sized farms and that biotechnology will be most rapidly adopted by larger producers and have diverse regional effects that could lead to large shifts in the location of agricultural production for specific commodities.

Other concerns have been expressed related to the implications of the structure of biotechnological research for the public interest (Buttel 1985; Buttel et al. 1983). Biotechnological research involves a substantial interface between private firms and public and private universities. These arrangements create the possibility of conflict of interest between public and private rights related to such research products, cause concern related to who will be able to afford some products, and raise issues concerning public subsidization for private research as publicly funded laboratories and scientists come to be used to develop patented products.

Still other concerns relate to the ethical and environmental consequences of such research (Curry 1986). Such concerns relate to the extent to which it is in our province to manipulate biological elements and the extent to which sufficient knowledge exists to ensure that newly developed biotechnological products can be released with adequate knowledge of their environmental and social effects. Although regulations for the control of such research have been developed by the National Institutes of Health, the U.S. Department of Agriculture, and other agencies, concerns have resulted in suits by environmental organizations such as the Foundation on Economic Trends (FOET) against the Department of Health, Education, and Welfare, and the National Institutes of Health to block the release of substances such as the ice nucleation bacteria in California. Opponents argue that an environmental impact assessment must be completed prior to the release of such a substance into the environment. The results of cases resolved to date suggest that regulations for laboratory development of experimental products are suffi-

102 ciently strict to protect the public, but that it is necessary to conduct an environmental impact statement prior to the release of a product into the environment (Curry 1986).

Defenders of more rapid development of biotechnology argue that existing safeguards are sufficient to protect the environment (Harlander and Garner 1986). They suggest that the negative social and economic impacts of biotechnological products have been exaggerated for such products as bovine growth hormone because of overestimates of the rate of production increase and the rate of adoption. Furthermore, they claim the impacts are much more neutral in relation to the size of production units than is sometimes claimed (Jorgenson 1986). They warn that biotechnology is a key focus of international competition and that delays in development of products in the United States will lead to the United States losing its competitive position in agriculture as it has in such areas as steel and automobile production (Jorgenson 1986). Finally, they point out that this research involves a continuation of people's long-standing role in selecting specific biological organisms for development rather than a new role in the management of the biological and chemical environment (Jorgenson 1986; Harlander and Garner 1986).

The debate related to biotechnology is likely to continue as new technologies are developed. What is perhaps most noteworthy about this debate is not the relative merits of the opposing arguments for or against biotechnology but the fact that such a debate is occurring. Past applications of agricultural technology have been conducted with little concern for the long-term consequences of such technology on the structure of agriculture, the environment, or other aspects of American society. The existence of such a debate is a clear indication that agriculture is increasingly perceived to be a societywide rather than merely a rural and producer arena for concern.

What will the impact of biotechnology and other forms of technology be on agriculture? The use of the ecological perspective may provide additional insight related to the future role of technologies in altering the structure of agriculture. Most existing analyses of the social impact of biotechnology (Buttel et al. 1983; Kalter et al. 1985; Kloppenburg 1984) suggest that biotechnology will be most beneficial to large producers and result in an additional decline in the number of intermediate-sized farms. The ecological perspective, however, suggests that if public or other funding were used to reduce the cost of transferring such technologies so that small producers could utilize them, biotechnological developments (as symbiotic forms of technology) could in fact lead to a retention of the number of smaller farms. Using such technologies, producers with smaller acreages and smaller numbers of livestock could produce levels of income capable of making smaller farms economically viable. If such a situation prevailed biotechnology might lead to a slowdown or even to a partial reversal of the trend (toward a smaller number of larger farms) that has prevailed during most of this century.

The use of the ecological perspective, in fact, suggests that many of the new forms of agricultural technology likely to prevail could have similar effects as symbiotic forms of technology in society as a whole. Thus, symbiotic technological developments (e.g., the microchip) often have commensalistic forms of technology applied to produce them more efficiently. Rather than remaining products available to only the wealthy, they become objects of mass production. If agricultural technologies, even when produced by private enterprises, follow a similar pattern the revolution in agricultural technology presently underway might lead to a markedly different structure of agriculture than previously anticipated. The trends toward corporate agriculture and large-scale agriculture might be inhibited rather than expedited by the revolution. Although this is a bold (and some may say naive) interpretation, it clearly demonstrates the ways in which an ecological approach to the analysis of technological impact provides new premises worthy of empirical examination.

Finally, the use of an ecological perspective also suggests the need for several new avenues of research. In relation to agriculture there is clearly a need for further ecologically based historical analysis of the impacts of different forms of technology. These would be similar to past studies (see Friedland and Barton 1975; Friedland et al. 1981; and Perkinson and Hoover 1984) but would have an ecological emphasis.

In addition, the potential utility of the ecological perspective suggests that other ecological principles and concepts should be examined as they relate to the impact of technology in agriculture. Thus, the effects of alternative forms of adaptation (e.g., somatic vs. genetic), of different levels of differentiation, of different types of sustenance activities, and of other ecological concepts should be examined as they relate to agricultural technology and the impacts of such technology. Although ecological analyses exist that provide a general overview of the role of technology in such processes as urbanization (Berry and Kasarda 1977), population growth (Matras 1973), and energy use (Odum and Odum

104   1976), such analysis has been largely restricted to examination of broad-based rather than individual forms of technology. Further extension of the ecological perspective or technological impacts in agriculture is thus essential.

Technology has clearly played a major role in shaping the structure of U.S. agriculture. Technology has increased the productivity of the American producer but at the same time has led to a reduction in the need for agricultural labor and to a decline in the number of farms. The impact of future technology will have equally profound effects. Monitoring the impact of new technology is thus likely to remain a major task for those interested in the sociology of agriculture. The use of theoretical perspectives such as that of human ecology is essential to ensure that we can accurately describe the past impact of technology and gain the insight necessary to anticipate the effects of future forms of technology on the structure of agriculture in the United States.

NOTES

1. Most sociological examinations of the role of technology in agriculture have been inadequate, however. They have tended to provide either retrospective historical descriptions of the general effects of agricultural technology on society (e.g., Berardi 1981; Berardi and Geisler 1984; Donaldson and McInerney 1973; Friedland 1973; Hamilton 1939; Quaintance 1904) or to explore the social impact of individual technologies such as the tomato harvesting machine (Schmitz and Seckler 1970), lettuce harvesting mechanization (Friedland et al. 1981), and tobacco harvesting machines (Berardi 1981; Perkinson and Hoover 1984). Those few examinations of technological development and application have tended to focus on either the adoption of technology (Rogers 1983) or on establishing the socioeconomic consequences of these technologies (Goss 1979).

Relatively few attempts have been made to develop theoretical bases for explaining the past impacts and projecting the future impacts of technology on agriculture. Although some attempts have been made to examine technology from the perspectives of systems theory (Bertrand 1958), conflict theory (Friedland et al. 1981), and critical theory (Busch and Lacy 1983; Buttel and Newby 1980), these have largely been restricted to describing the historical impact of technology rather than to developing truly explanatory models of technology.

2. Even the resource base is capable of undergoing some alteration. Ciriacy-Wantrup (1952, 28), for example, notes:

> The concept "resource" presupposes . . . certain technological means at the disposal of the agent and certain institutions (laws, customs, and so on) of the society in which it operates. . . . A resource, therefore, is a highly rela-

tive concept changing with the ends-means scheme—that is with the planning agent, with his objective, with the state of technology, and with existing social institutions.

3. Recently, other researchers have also noted that the consequences of a technology may vary depending on the type of technology. Dorner (1983) has, in fact, identified two forms of technology that he refers to as laborsaving and yield increasing.

Throughout this discussion it is important to note that although the effects of such technologies are emphasized, it is the forms of interdependence that are commensalistic or symbiotic (not the technologies) and that the differences in interdependence are assumed to produce the differences in effects that are hypothesized.

Symbiotic and commensalistic forms of interdependence have traditionally been seen as resulting from the nature of the relationships between the characteristics of interrelated elements or organisms. When the use of these concepts of interdependence is extended from relationships between organisms to relationships between ecological components such as the POET variables, the definitions of symbiotic and commensalistic must also be extended. Thus, although the concepts of commensalistic and symbiotic relationships have usually been seen as applying to the forms of interdependence between different species of organisms (Hawley 1950), recent expansions of the ecological framework to the analysis of relationships between organizations (Hannan and Freeman 1977; Kasarda and Bidwell 1984) have tended to see such concepts as being applicable to individual organisms. The necessary extension is that of extending the concepts of symbiotic and commensalistic interrelationships from the nature of the relationships between the characteristics of the interrelated elements to the nature of the processes through which one element interacts with another. Such an extension clearly reflects the ecological emphasis that analyses should be centered on discerning the patterns (organization) of activity constellations (processes) in an ecosystem (Duncan 1964).

4. Considerable historical evidence can be brought to bear to support such a perspective on technology. Thus, many of the major historical patterns in the development of modern western social organization reflect the simultaneous development of technologies, some of which formed commensalistic and others that formed symbiotic relationships with existing resource use processes. The rapid growth of the world's population can be seen as the result of an ecological process in which symbiotic technologies played a lead role (Matras 1973). The curtailment of infectious diseases through the use of public sanitation and other methods has been the major cause of declining mortality in the world and resultant population increase (Preston 1976). Such technologies directly altered the environment through the introduction of processes for the use of beneficial organisms and substances that formed symbiotic relationships with various types of destructive (at least to humans) organisms.

The growth of the social organizational process referred to as urbanization (Hauser and Schnore 1965) reflects both commensalistic and symbiotic forms of technology. On the one hand, the development of new breeds of domesticated livestock and new plant varieties symbiotically extended the resource base of agriculture and allowed it to support an ever-larger urban population base.

These larger population concentrations, in turn, took on unique social organizational characteristics (Wirth 1939). Urbanization, however, also expanded as a result of the development of commensalistic technologies such as more efficient means of transportation and communication. These allowed existing organizational functions to be performed more effectively and existing resources to be exploited more efficiently.

Nonfarm Organizations and Agriculture

Defined ecologically, organization "is assumed to be a property of the population that has evolved and is sustained in the process of adaptation of the population to its environment" (Duncan and Schnore 1959, 136). It is that "system of relations among interdependent parts through which a population adapts to an environment" (Boland 1966, 1). A basic objective of modern sociological human ecology theory is to account for the organizational forms that arise in social systems as their populations adapt to varying environmental constraints, technological developments, or demographic transitions (Kasarda and Bidwell 1984).

Within the sociology of agriculture organizational variation can be dealt with in two major ways. First, the organizational variations and characteristics of the farm unit or aggregate of farm units can be described. These characteristics can then be seen as reflecting the ways farm operators adapt to an ever-changing but always restricted environment. Thus, farm size, business organization, tenure arrangements, the amount of off-farm employment, and numerous other factors can be seen as organizational characteristics of the farm that have been adapted to deal with a changing environment. In this regard, changes in technology, the environment, or any other aspect of the ecological complex would consequently be reflected in organizational adjustments by the farm. Chapter 3 dealt with some of the historical changes in the organizational structure of American farming, and Chapters 4 and 5 explored

107

108   how environment and technology (and changes therein) are reflected in agricultural structure and change.

A second approach for dealing with organizations in the sociology of agriculture, and the approach utilized in this chapter, is to examine some of the many nonfarm organizations that influence agriculture. It is obvious that numerous organizations outside of the farm unit itself have emerged over time and play a critical role in the development of agriculture and changes therein. At one time this was not the case as farming and agriculture in the United States were largely synonymous. Farmers provided most of their own production inputs such as fertilizer, seeds, and labor. In addition, farmers stored, processed, and distributed their agricultural products themselves. Farming techniques were generally passed from father to son with little change from generation to generation (Green 1984).

Over the years a variety of organizational entities have emerged that play a vital role in the total food production system and greatly influence how individual farm operators adapt to their environment. Government funded researchers have developed a variety of products that have greatly increased the efficiency of agricultural production; federal farm policies influence farmers' decisions about what to produce and the prices they will receive for their products; the increased capitalization of agriculture has resulted in an extensive increase in farm credit; and a number of large agribusiness firms have emerged that now provide farmers with most of their input items such as fuel, feed, and fertilizer and also store, process, and distribute the products. In addition, numerous farm organizations, commodity groups, and cooperatives now play an important role in farmers' decisions and in influencing farm policy.

It is important that such organizations be described because while the rapid development and the current level of production and efficiency achieved in American agriculture is partially a result of an extensive natural resource base and partially a result of major technological breakthroughs, the present condition of American agriculture would not be possible without the support of these nonfarm organizations. These organizations have provided farmers with a series of new technological developments and production methods, the necessary infrastructure to get the products to market, relevant information, credit, viable markets, and numerous other factors that improve the efficiency and productivity of American agriculture. Thus, while some countries are endowed with plentiful resources for agricultural production and could utilize the same

technologies that American farmers employ, farmers in these countries **109**
generally lack the organizational support and infrastructure enjoyed by
American farmers. Consequently the productivity of their farms is less,
nutritional quality of their products is lower, and costs to consumers are
relatively higher. Finally, the role such organizations play in allowing
agricultural producers to deal with the political realities of agricultural
policy must be recognized.

Viewed ecologically, nonfarm organizations serve largely to moderate the relationship between the farm organization and the environment.
They have tended to play one of two major roles in this regard. They
have been used either to directly moderate the relationship between the
environment and the farm organization or to increase the ability of the
farm organization to adapt to changes in the environment. Included
among the first types of organizations are those that have attempted to
directly provide the sustenance items essential to the survival of operators. Included among this type of organization are those that provide the
financing essential to operate a farm organization and agribusiness firms
that provide linkages between farm operators' resource needs and producers, on the one hand, and act as intermediate processors between
producers and consumers on the other. The second type of organizations
are those that have attempted to provide operators with the ability to
influence other political and economic institutions affecting farm operations and those that have sought to allow producers to organize into
forms (such as cooperatives) that allow them to more effectively and
efficiently obtain the sustenance items necessary to survive. Whereas the
latter represent commensalistic organizations (not unlike the trade organizations that exist in nearly all industries and agribusiness firms) and
play symbiotic roles (not unlike the wholesaling sectors of other basic
extractive industries) the organizations that have sought to directly assist
agriculture have few counterparts in other industries. They appear to
reflect societal recognition of the ultimate importance of the food producing sustenance function. In sum, then, nonfarm organizations play
key ecological roles in the structure of agriculture.

The purpose of this chapter is to describe the role of some of these
nonfarm organizations in the historical development and current structure of American agriculture. Four major types of organizations will be
described: government, financial and economic institutions, agribusiness
firms, and organizations that represent farmers. Government, financial
and economic institutions, and agribusiness firms are examples of or-

ganizations that seek to directly intervene between either the environment and the farm organization (i.e., government and financial institutions) or between the farm organization and consumers (agribusiness firms). The final organizational form, farmers' organizations, includes those which have attempted to supplement the adaptive abilities of producers.

The purpose of this chapter is not to provide an in-depth discussion of these nonfarm organizations. Other researchers have accomplished this task and their works are cited herein. Rather, our purpose is to provide a general overview and show how these organizations are important in the sociology of agriculture.

GOVERNMENT

In the United States today the role of the federal government appears to be ubiquitous. The government is deeply involved in the development and execution of land policies, in the support of technological advances through research and development, in the building of social and physical infrastructure (e.g., universities, roads, and railroads), in the formulation and execution of immigration and trade policies, and in the development and structure of agricultural markets. Such extensive involvement of the government in agriculture has not always been the case, however. In this section a historical overview of government involvement in American agriculture will be presented. This will include a discussion of some of the major agricultural policies of today and their influence on American agriculture.

Historical Evolution of Government Involvement in U.S. Agriculture

Through time, the nature of government involvement in agriculture has varied widely. For the most part the government's role in agriculture has increased with the passage of time. Figure 6.1 depicts some of the major government policies that have influenced agricultural development. This figure, adapted largely from the work of Paarlberg (1980), divides government involvement in agriculture into four time periods. It shows that with the onset of each new period the government has kept the functions it was performing and then added to them. The first period is prior to the Civil War, the second period is from 1862 to 1933, the **111** third period from 1933 to 1965, and the fourth period extends from the mid-1960s to the present.

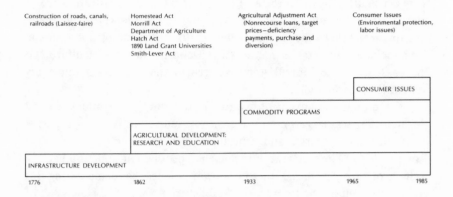

Fig. 6.1. Historical evolution of federal government involvement in U.S. agriculture (adapted from Paarlberg 1980).

Infrastructure Development

As shown in Figure 6.1, during the first period (prior to the Civil War) the role of government in agriculture largely consisted of the construction of canals, railroads, and roads to get farm products to market (Armbruster et al. 1983). During this pre–Civil War era governments in much of the western world, and in the English-speaking nations in particular, sought to interfere in the economic and social life of individual citizens as little as possible, and thus government involvement in other areas was discouraged (Cochrane 1979). But because having a dependable and productive food sector is critical to any society, societies historically have not been willing to depend solely on the marketplace to produce the desired ends. Eventually such intervention began in the United States.

Agricultural Development: Research and Education

In 1862, at the height of the Civil War, came the U.S. government's first major deviation from a laissez-faire policy in agriculture. The leaders of this policy initiative were Abraham Lincoln and his new Republican party. While the southern vote and most other adversaries were absent, they were able to push major changes through Congress. One important policy passed at this time was the Homestead Act of 1862. This act made it possible for a settler, after paying a registration fee of $10 to $25 and residing on and working 160 acres of land for five years, to gain clear title to the land (Tweeten 1970). Other important events in 1862 included the establishment of the Department of Agriculture and the passage of the Morrill Act that created the land grant university system (Robinson 1983).

Government involvement in agriculture from this beginning in 1862 through 1933 was largely concerned with agricultural development, especially through research and education (Hoiberg and Bultena 1981; Rohrer 1970). The goals were to increase production and stabilize the welfare of farm families. Other important policies that came during this era largely built on the foundation established in 1862. The Hatch Act of 1887 provided federal funds for research at agricultural experiment stations associated with land grant colleges. In 1890 the land grant concept was extended to black colleges in the South. The organizational base for the threefold mission of today's land grant system was completed in 1914 with passage of the Smith-Lever Act, which provided federal funds for agricultural extension (Robinson 1983).

This policy initiative has had impressive results. Experiment stations developed new agricultural sciences and the extension service disseminated this science to the farmers, which immensely increased the efficiency of agricultural production as well as the total supply of food and fiber products. Although the intent of this legislation was to serve the farmers, perhaps consumers benefited more than anyone from the low costs that emerged for food and fiber products. Agricultural development through research, education, and extension remains an important aspect of the government's involvement in agriculture today.

Commodity Programs

Prior to the 1930s reliance on the marketplace was basically unchallenged as the arena for most market decisions in agriculture. However, with the onset of the Great Depression farmers were benefiting from decades of investment in research and development and were capable of producing far in excess of demand. Surplus associated with collapsing

markets from the Great Depression led to a rapid decline in farm prices. **113**
For example, the price of a bushel of wheat, which had reached $2.48 in
1917, fell to $.34 in 1931 (Svobida 1940). Total net income in agriculture
fell from $6.3 billion in 1929 to $1.9 billion in 1932 (Paarlberg 1980).

By the early 1930s the problem of low farm incomes had become so
severe that public intervention was deemed necessary for the survival of
the agricultural industry. The policy agenda of research and education
was incapable of dealing with the problems of the Great Depression. It
was at this time that the passage of the Agricultural Adjustment Act of
1933 became one of the most significant landmarks in the development
of American farm policy. By initiating the era of the commodity programs this act marked the beginning of direct government intervention
in agricultural markets and decision making. Although the specifics
change with time, the commodity programs that began in 1933 continue
to be the heart of agricultural policy in the 1980s (Paarlberg 1980).

The major idea behind the commodity programs was to limit output
in order to increase the price per unit and thereby raise the net income of
farmers. Three primary tools were utilized and continue to be used pe-
riodically even today. The first of these tools is "nonrecourse loans."
Under this program a farmer obtains a loan at an established level on the
amount of his wheat, feed grains, cotton, sugar, wool, tobacco, or honey
that he or she pledges as security. The loan rate can be adjusted up or
down by the government depending on whether it wants to encourage or
discourage production. A high rate will result in increased production,
while a lower rate will reduce the amount of the commodity produced.
The loan is typically due within a year. The farmer has two options to
repay the loan. First, the farmer can sell the crop, pay off the loan with
interest, and keep any profit. The farmer will choose this option if the
market price is higher than the loan level. If the market price is below the
loan rate, the farmer will choose the second alternative, which is to
deliver the commodity to the government and have the loan canceled.
The intentions of the government when obtaining a commodity are to
reduce the amount in the marketplace, which will consequently result in
higher prices.

Because of this program the government has, at times of continued
low commodity prices, acquired huge surpluses of grain or other commodities. Table 6.1 shows the amounts of various price-supported commodities that the government has owned at various times since the commodity programs were instigated. Obviously, the amount owned by the

Table 6.1. Agricultural commodities owned by the government as of December 31 for selected years

| Year | Commodity and amount owned | | | |
	Corn (million bushels)	Sorghum (million bushels)	Wheat (million bushels)	Cotton (thousand bales)
1940	176	**	**	6,185
1945	**	**	77	3,218
1950	399	25	271	98
1955	984	26	889	8,014
1960	1,471	557	1,133	5,028
1965	530	493	572	10,155
1970	215	163	283	2,077
1975	**	**	**	**
1980	254	44	203	**
1984	296	106	419	**
1985	389	131	517	**
1986	968	292	864	**

Source: U.S. Department of Agriculture (1985b).
** = A small amount.

government has varied greatly over the years depending largely on prices. When prices are low (such as during the 1960s and 1980s), large surpluses are obtained. However, when the market price of the commodity gets higher, the government-owned surpluses are released into the market, which then tends to depress prices for that product but also reduces government surpluses (such as during the early 1970s). The loan rate effectively sets the minimum price for a commodity and acts as a stabilizing force. By doing this the loans reduce the risks faced by producers and consequently lead to the increased production of the commodity. A high loan rate can also price U.S. commodities out of the world market (Johnson et al. 1985b; Knutson et al. 1986; Paarlberg 1980).

The second tool utilized by the commodity programs is "target prices." Target prices do not directly influence the market price of a commodity, although they do indirectly affect prices by influencing the production decisions made by farmers. Under this program the government establishes a target price for each commodity. If the market price falls below the target price farmers receive deficiency payments from the government based on the difference. If the market price is above the target price the farmer sells for the higher market price and owes the government nothing.

Deficiency payments are not automatically available to all farmers. To receive them farmers are required to participate in supply management programs such as acreage reduction programs. Typically, farmers **115** are paid the target price for a percentage of their normal yield on the acreage held out of production (Paarlberg 1980; Tweeten 1970). The Payment-In-Kind (PIK) program of 1983 was a tool of this type. Under the PIK program farmers were paid in kind a percentage of their normal yield in return for reducing acreage. The PIK program was instituted to reduce the available stocks of grain and cotton, to strengthen market prices, and to lower government costs for storage and deficiency payments (Johnson et al. 1985b). Target price programs do reduce production and by reducing acreage they consequently result in higher prices. However, these programs may also result in large treasury outlays. Table 6.2 shows the amount of money that farmers have received from the government over the years and the proportion this represents of total agricultural cash receipts. This table makes it apparent that government payments to farmers vary substantially from year to year. In 1984 alone more than $8.4 billion were given in direct payment to farmers from the government as part of the commodity programs. A comparison of tables 6.1 and 6.2 also indicates that the amount of the various commodities owned by the government is related to government payments. In years when commodity prices are low (such as 1970 or 1984) farmers receive large deficiency payments and are also likely to turn extensive amounts of their commodities over to the government in payment of their nonrecursive loans. However, when commodity prices are high (such as in

Table 6.2. Agricultural cash receipts for selected years

Year	Farm marketings	Government payments	Total cash receipts	Government payments as a percentage of total
		Million dollars		
1935	7,120	573	7,693	7.4
1940	8,382	723	9,105	7.9
1945	21,663	742	22,405	3.3
1950	28,461	283	28,744	1.0
1955	29,490	229	29,719	0.8
1960	34,154	702	34,856	2.0
1965	39,350	2,463	41,813	2.0
1970	50,509	3,717	54,226	6.9
1975	88,902	807	89,709	0.9
1980	139,760	1,286	141,046	0.9
1984	141,835	8,430	150,265	5.6
1985	142,103	7,704	149,807	5.1

Source: U.S. Department of Agriculture (1985b).

116 1975), farmers use regular market channels and are not compelled to participate in government programs.

In Table 6.3 data are presented that show the amount of government payments to farmers received by state in 1984 and the proportion these payments represent of total cash receipts. This table shows that the total government payments received and the proportion these payments make of the total agricultural cash receipts varies extensively from one state to another. In two states, Texas and Iowa, government payments to farmers amounted to more than $700 million in 1984. This was more than the total farm cash receipts in fourteen states. North Dakota (15.4 percent) and Montana (14.4 percent) were the two states that received the largest proportion of their total agricultural cash receipts from government payments. In contrast, Alaska, Connecticut, Florida, Hawaii, Maine, Massachusetts, and Rhode Island had less than 1 percent of their total cash receipts in government payments. Generally, government payments were greatest in the Midwest where farmers depend heavily on crops that are a part of the government programs.

In some instances the effectiveness of the target price program is reduced by slippage. Slippage is that portion of reduced acreage that does not result in correspondingly lower production because the poorest land is removed from production (Knutson et al. 1986). For example, a center-pivot sprinkler irrigation system is typically intended to go on a 160-acre plot of land. As the sprinkler system rotates in a circle around the center-pivot, it cannot reach the corners and usually only about 125 to 130 of the 160 acres are irrigated. The 30 to 35 acres that are in the corners would then be used in an acreage reduction program. The removal of these acres from production has little affect on overall commodity production.

The third major feature of the commodity programs for which the groundwork was established in 1933 is "purchase and diversion." This method is sometimes used to provide assistance to the producers of perishables such as dairy products, fruits, and vegetables. The government purchases these products, which reduces the amount moving through the commercial market and thus increases the price. These government-acquired products are then diverted outside the regular market channels through donations here and abroad and through the school lunch programs (Paarlberg 1980; Johnson et al. 1985b).

As with the other farm programs, the purchase and diversion program has become very expensive. For example, during the 1980s the

Table 6.3. Agricultural cash receipts by state, 1984

State	Farm marketings	Government payments	Total cash receipts	Government payments as a percentage of total
	Thousand dollars			
Alabama	2,188,949	57,052	2,246,001	2.5
Alaska	24,949	181	24,988	0.7
Arizona	1,521,420	118,385	1,639,805	7.2
Arkansas	3,336,038	209,567	3,545,605	5.9
California	14,184,886	335,259	14,520,145	2.3
Colorado	3,352,115	153,592	3,505,707	4.4
Connecticut	359,117	2,814	361,931	0.8
Delaware	520,448	5,201	525,649	1.0
Florida	4,587,029	40,728	4,627,757	0.9
Georgia	3,587,474	79,286	3,666,760	2.2
Hawaii	616,719	607	617,326	0.1
Idaho	2,288,457	132,464	2,420,921	5.5
Illinois	6,737,927	543,241	7,281,168	7.5
Indiana	3,923,846	308,846	4,232,692	7.3
Iowa	9,312,296	742,763	10,055,059	7.4
Kansas	5,947,492	573,878	6,521,370	8.8
Kentucky	2,652,148	96,670	2,748,818	3.5
Louisiana	1,527,492	121,464	1,648,956	7.4
Maine	455,831	4,339	460,170	0.9
Maryland	1,153,998	23,773	1,177,771	2.0
Massachusetts	382,934	3,106	386,040	0.8
Michigan	2,776,998	167,669	2,944,667	5.7
Minnesota	6,242,368	529,908	6,772,276	7.8
Mississippi	2,167,923	164,478	2,332,401	7.1
Missouri	3,728,517	224,626	3,953,143	5.7
Montana	1,419,444	239,609	1,659,053	14.4
Nebraska	7,081,666	532,981	7,614,647	7.0
Nevada	252,330	4,489	256,819	1.7
New Hampshire	108,888	1,690	110,578	1.5
New Jersey	505,310	7,303	512,613	1.4
New Mexico	988,725	49,183	1,037,908	4.7
New York	2,705,420	63,690	2,769,110	2.3
North Carolina	4,125,398	71,884	4,197,282	1.7
North Dakota	2,544,164	463,245	3,007,409	15.4
Ohio	3,610,698	232,204	3,842,902	6.0
Oklahoma	2,562,466	309,379	2,871,845	10.8
Oregon	1,791,783	76,100	1,867,883	4.1
Pennsylvania	3,165,530	80,658	3,246,188	2.5
Rhode Island	61,533	205	61,738	0.3
South Carolina	1,135,815	45,164	1,180,979	3.8
South Dakota	2,888,784	231,348	3,210,132	7.2
Tennessee	1,984,557	76,561	2,061,118	3.7
Texas	9,682,653	782,441	10,465,094	7.5
Utah	580,060	28,026	608,086	4.6
Vermont	399,948	8,450	408,398	2.1
Virginia	1,794,440	45,989	1,840,429	2.5
Washington	2,932,502	171,002	3,103,504	5.5
West Virginia	225,632	5,807	231,439	2.5
Wisconsin	5,135,838	237,814	5,373,652	4.4
Wyoming	573,851	25,251	599,102	4.2
U.S. Total	141,834,664	8,430,370	150,265,034	5.6

Source: U.S. Department of Agriculture (1985b).

118   costs of the dairy portion of this program exceeded $2 billion annually and the government was purchasing over 10 percent of the total milk supply. To deal with this massive overproduction the government attempted a dairy buyout program in 1986 in which farmers were paid to slaughter or export their cows and discontinue milking operations for at least five years. This diversion program was not especially effective at reducing production, considering the costs of the program. Participation was highest in those areas already experiencing decreasing production, and nonparticipants reacted by increasing production. There is also evidence of an extensive amount of cow trading to circumvent the intent of the program. Just as the least productive acres tend to end up in the acreage reduction programs, it was the least productive cows that were slaughtered as part of the dairy buyout. A participating farmer would trade his best cows for his nonparticipating neighbors' poor cows. Thus, although there were fewer cows, there was not a corresponding decrease in production. Controlling such practices proved nearly impossible, because while acres cannot move at night, cows can (Knutson et al. 1986).

To a large extent the commodity programs established in 1933 are still practiced today. There are variations to deal with changing conditions, but the large-scale government intervention in the agricultural market that began in 1933 continues at the present time (Fig. 6.1). Now every four years a new farm bill is passed that establishes loan rates, target prices, acreage reduction levels, and such for the various commodities. As of this writing the last farm bill was passed in 1985. Although the commodity programs are a vital part of agriculture today, they are not without controversy. Numerous criticisms have been leveled against the programs in general, as well as the specifics of the programs. For example, the ink was barely dry on the 1985 farm bill when proposals began to emerge for its modification. Each adjustment results in some people benefiting and others being hurt, depending on the location of the individual in the agricultural system (Knutson et al. 1987). Despite the controversy the commodity programs are likely to remain and be a vital part of American agriculture into the foreseeable future.

Consumer Issues

Figure 6.1 also shows that in addition to the commodity programs, government involvement in U.S. agriculture today is also impacted by a variety of consumer issues such as consumer safety and nutrition, environmental issues, and labor issues. Government concern with such **119** issues began in the mid-1960s, and there is no evidence of a decline in such involvement. Rural people in general and farmers in particular are now a very small minority of the total U.S. population. Consequently, issues raised by the urban majority have begun to appear on the agricultural forum and the farm bloc is no longer in a position to resist their implementation of programs (Paarlberg 1980). Some of the issues that have emerged include:

• *Consumer Safety and Nutrition.* As a result of the efforts of consumer advocates, the meat inspection process has been tightened, food items are now labeled with the nutritional content, food is dated to show its freshness, and efforts continue to remove certain chemicals and additives from food.

• *Environmental Issues.* As a result of the environmental movement, several major pieces of legislation were passed that have a direct bearing on agriculture. These include the Federal Air Quality Act of 1970, which was intended to reduce air pollution. Agriculture, which was previously excluded from pollution laws, lost its exemption. On January 1, 1973, DDT was banned by the EPA, and numerous other agricultural chemicals have since been banned. The Federal Water Pollution Control Act as amended in 1972 was intended to clean up rivers and lakes, and this included an effort to control nonpoint pollution of which farm runoff is a major source.

• *Labor.* Initially, agriculture in this country was exempt from a whole set of laws related to hired labor including child labor laws, working conditions, minimum wages, workmen's compensation, collective bargaining, and unemployment insurance. Recently the situation has changed. Minimum wage laws now apply to agriculture, and California and Hawaii provide collective bargaining rights to farm workers.

In sum, government involvement in agriculture has greatly increased over the years, and the consequences of this involvement are extensive. There is no doubt government involvement in agriculture will continue to be extensive into the foreseeable future. But while government involvement is likely to remain, it will not be without debate. It has long been a source of major controversy (Hightower 1973), and an important source of contention is the immense cost of farm programs. During the 1986 crop year, for example, government costs for the whole range of farm programs approached $30 billion (Knutson et al. 1987). Another major criticism is that government-supported farm programs have provided greater benefits to some categories of farmers than others. Those benefiting the most have historically been the larger farms producing commodities covered by the government farm programs. It has been found that over 90 percent of the farm program benefits go to the farms that are larger than the median (Paarlberg 1980). In addition, some argue that the benefits of the state agricultural experiment stations and extension services are more likely to be received by the operators of the larger-sized farm units (Busch and Lacy 1983). It has been argued that such inequitable distribution has enhanced the trend towards larger farm size. Further, by placing many small farms at an economic disadvantage the government is partially but directly responsible for numerous farm foreclosures and the vast out-migration of farm people.

Proponents of government involvement counter by arguing that farm people are at an economic disadvantage relative to the rest of the U.S. population, that the government is needed to assure agricultural stability, and that the government is needed to counteract agriculture's chronic tendency to overproduce (Paarlberg 1980). The future political resolutions of this debate will be critical, and policy decisions by the government will continue to have a major influence on agriculture for years to come.

FINANCIAL AND ECONOMIC INSTITUTIONS

Of the many changes that have occurred in agriculture in recent decades, increased reliance on capital and credit are two of the most important. In traditional agriculture there was little need for the assistance of financial organizations. The major input into agriculture was labor, which was primarily provided by the family. There were few capital inputs that farmers had to purchase. Many farmland transactions took place within the family, which again meant there was often little need for outside credit. For example, prior to World War I more than 75 percent of the credit in agriculture came from private individuals (Raup 1978).

Today the situation in agriculture is vastly different. Technological developments (as discussed in Chapter 4) and government policies (discussed earlier in this chapter) have resulted in farmers increasing produc-

tion through greater capital inputs (Goss et al. 1980). In 1870, for exam- **121**
ple, 65 percent of the inputs into agricultural production consisted of
labor and 17 percent were capital. One century later labor accounted for
only 16 percent of the inputs, while capital accounted for 62 percent
(Cochrane 1979; Green 1984). With this increased dependence on capital
inputs, access to credit to purchase these inputs and the cost of credit
have become important concerns in agriculture. Further, the amount of
money involved in many farmland transactions has become so great that
they are beyond the capacity of most individuals to finance. In addition,
with reduced opportunities to remain in agriculture, many farmland
transactions involve nonfamily members. Consequently, the financial
organizations that provide credit play an increasingly important role in
American agriculture today. In this section data showing the importance
of credit in U.S. agriculture will be presented. This will be followed by a
brief discussion of the major financial organizations providing credit to
farmers. Finally, the farm crisis of the 1980s will be described as an
example showing the importance of these financial institutions in agriculture.

Credit and U.S. Agriculture

In Table 6.4 data are presented that show total assets and debts in
agriculture from 1969 to 1985 and give some indication of the importance of credit in American agriculture today. This table shows that debt
levels in agriculture in the 1980s were approximately $200 billion.
Slightly more than one-half of these debts was for real estate, with the
remainder being for machinery, the purchase of livestock, and operating
loans. Total debt levels in agriculture more than quadrupled between
1969 and 1985. Part of this increase was due to inflation but part of it
reflects farmers' growing reliance on credit. Debt levels reached a peak
of $203.7 billion in 1982 and have declined slightly since that time.

Table 6.4 also shows total agricultural assets from 1969 to 1985. It is
evident that the majority of farm assets (72.5 percent in 1985) are for
farmland and farm structures. Agricultural assets reached a peak value
of over $1 trillion in 1981 and have declined rather rapidly since that
time to $771.4 billion in 1985 (a decline of 23.3 percent). The value of
agricultural land and buildings reached a peak of $780.2 billion in 1981
and declined to $559.6 billion in 1985 (a decline of 28.3 percent). These
declines are even more substantial in certain areas of the country, reach-

Table 6.4. Farm assets and debts as of December 31, 1969–1985 (excludes farm households)

Year	Assets (billion dollars)				Debts (billion dollars)			
	Total	Land and buildings	Livestock, machinery, and stored crops	Financial assets	Total	Land and buildings	Livestock, machinery, and crops	Ratio of debts to assets
1969	270.5	194.2	62.7	13.6	48.9	26.2	22.7	18.1
1970	280.2	201.2	64.5	14.5	50.5	27.4	23.1	18.0
1971	303.0	216.4	71.2	15.4	55.3	29.1	26.2	18.3
1972	341.4	241.8	83.0	16.6	60.2	31.7	28.5	17.6
1973	418.9	297.1	103.8	18.0	68.1	35.8	32.3	16.3
1974	442.2	326.9	97.1	18.2	76.0	40.6	35.4	17.2
1975	510.1	381.0	108.7	20.4	85.2	45.2	40.0	16.7
1976	590.4	453.5	114.2	22.7	97.0	50.4	46.6	16.4
1977	656.6	507.6	126.6	22.4	114.9	58.0	56.9	17.5
1978	783.7	600.7	157.5	25.5	131.9	65.6	66.3	16.8
1979	918.1	704.2	185.7	28.2	155.2	78.5	76.7	16.9
1980	1,003.2	779.2	193.9	30.1	170.4	87.9	82.5	17.0
1981	1,005.2	780.2	192.6	32.4	189.0	97.3	91.7	18.8
1982	977.8	745.6	197.2	35.0	203.7	101.2	102.5	20.8
1983	956.5	736.1	183.8	36.6	202.5	103.7	98.8	21.2
1984	856.0	639.6	178.4	38.1	198.7	102.9	96.0	23.2
1985	771.4	559.6	175.2	36.1	192.1	97.3	94.8	24.8

Source: U.S. Department of Agiculture (1985b).

ing 59 percent in Iowa and Nebraska in early 1986 (Brooks et al. 1986). **123**
This rapid decline in the value of agricultural assets has resulted in a steady increase in the average debt-to-asset ratio of American farmers since the early 1980s, reaching 24.8 percent in 1985. This increasing debt-to-asset ratio has been partially responsible for a growing financial crisis in American agriculture during the 1980s.

Additional evidence of the increased reliance of farmers on credit is apparent from Table 6.5. This table presents information on the value of land and buildings in agriculture (including farm households), the value of farm real estate debt for these land and buildings, and an index number of the average value per acre for farm land and buildings. This table shows that from 1940 to 1981 there was a nearly constant increase in the value of agricultural land and buildings. In contrast, farm debts for land and buildings decreased throughout the 1940s. In 1940 real estate debt amounted to 19.6 percent of the value of real estate assets, while in 1950 debt was only 7.4 percent of the value of real estate assets in agriculture. Since 1950 debt levels for real estate have steadily increased until the 1980s when they stabilized. Since 1981 the value of land and buildings in agriculture has steadily declined from $843.7 billion in 1981 to $603.0 billion in 1985 (a decline of 28.5 percent). The index number of the average value per acre for land and buildings in agriculture (based on 1977) increased from 14 in 1950 to a peak of 158 in 1981, and then declined to 112 in 1986. This substantially more expensive farmland is partly responsible for farmers' increased reliance on commercial credit.

Financial Institutions in U.S. Agriculture

Given the extensive dependence of modern U.S. agriculture on credit, it is important to briefly review who is providing this credit. Information on the major organizations providing credit to farmers is provided in Table 6.6. This table shows that the three biggest agricultural creditors include the farm credit system (31.8 percent), commercial banks (23.9 percent), and individuals and others (22.7 percent). Other important financial institutions include the Farmers Home Administration (11.9 percent), life insurance companies (5.8 percent), and the Commodity Credit Corporation (3.9 percent).

Table 6.5. Farm real estate (land and buildings): Value of farmland and buildings, farm real estate debt, and index numbers of average value per acre (includes farm households)

Year	Value of land and buildings (million dollars)	Farm real estate debt for land and buildings (million dollars)	Index number of average value per acre for land and buildings (1977 = 100)
1940	33,636	6,586	—
1941	34,400	6,494	—
1942	37,547	6,376	—
1943	41,604	5,956	—
1944	48,200	5,396	—
1945	53,884	4,941	—
1946	61,046	4,760	—
1947	68,463	4,987	—
1948	73,664	5,064	—
1949	76,623	5,288	—
1950	75,255	5,579	14
1951	86,586	6,112	16
1952	95,078	6,662	18
1953	96,535	7,241	18
1954	95,038	7,740	18
1955	98,172	8,245	19
1956	102,934	9,012	19
1957	110,422	9,822	21
1958	115,934	10,382	22
1959	124,393	11,091	23
1960	129,929	12,082	24
1961	131,752	12,820	25
1962	137,956	13,899	26
1963	143,834	15,168	27
1964	152,121	16,804	29
1965	160,942	18,894	31
1966	178,663	21,187	33
1967	188,529	23,077	35
1968	199,099	25,142	38
1969	208,572	27,396	40
1970	215,042	30,346	42
1971	222,324	32,192	43
1972	238,656	35,094	47
1973	266,241	39,527	53
1974	326,569	44,705	66
1975	358,638	49,682	75
1976	417,150	55,268	86
1977	496,376	63,458	100
1978	554,967	71,610	109
1979	652,693	85,599	125
1980	748,202	95,764	145
1981	843,657	105,801	158
1982	843,304	110,026	157
1983	804,765	112,622	148
1984	793,946	111,637	146
1985	687,008	105,400	128
1986	602,959	N/A	112

Source: U.S. Department of Agriculture (1985b).
N/A = not available.

Table 6.6. Distribution of farm debt by lender, January 1, 1985

Lender	Real estate %	Nonreal estate %	Total %
	Type of Debt		
Commercial Banks	4.8	19.1	23.9
Farm credit system	22.8	9.0	31.8
Federal land banks	22.8	—	22.8
Production credit associations	—	8.6	8.6
Federal intermediate credit banks[a]	—	0.4	0.4
Farmers Home Administration	4.7	7.2	11.9
Life insurance companies	5.8	—	5.8
Individuals and others[b]	14.1	8.6	22.7
Commodity Credit Corporation	—	3.9	3.9
Total	52.3	47.7	100.0

Source: U.S. Department of Agriculture (1985a).
Note: Preliminary. Due to rounding, subcategories may not add to totals.
[a]Financial institutions other than PCAs that obtain funds from the FICBs.
[b]Includes Small Business Administration.
— = not applicable.

Commercial Banks. The commercial banks have long represented an important source of credit to farm operators (Table 6.6). A majority of the commercial banks in the United States are located in communities with populations of less than ten thousand. For many such banks in agriculturally based rural areas, agricultural loans represent a major part of their portfolios. Even some of the larger banks in urban areas provide some credit to agriculture.

From the farmer's point of view commercial banks have several advantages over other agricultural creditors. First, they provide prompt credit with a minimum of red tape; second, they are readily accessible, and third, they provide checking and other banking services within the local community (Nelson and Murray 1967). Consequently, commercial banks represent farmers' most important credit source for intermediate-term loans (such as those for machinery and equipment) and short-term loans (such as those for operating expenses). Commercial banks also provide some credit for long-term real estate loans. However, many rural banks lack the backing to provide large real estate loans, and often they are unable to match the terms offered by other lenders.

Since commercial bankers represent the gate through which many farmers must go in order to purchase farm capital and technological innovations, they are now in an important position of power in U.S. agriculture and play a major role in determining who is able to adopt

126   such technologies and innovations (Green 1984; McIntosh and Zey-Ferrell 1986). At one time, rural banks generally had few worries in making loans to farmers. Often the banker and the farmer knew each other personally, and farmland was excellent collateral. Today the directors— who often are not from the local area—of many rural banks require written evidence that the farmer is in a position to repay the loan. In addition, declining land values have depleted many farmers' primary source of collateral. As a result, many farmers now face difficulty in getting a loan, which is necessary for them to obtain technology as well as operating expenses (McIntosh and Zey-Ferrell 1986).

The Farm Credit System. From early in our nation's history the demand for more adequate credit in agriculture was an enduring concern. The continuing needs for land and livestock were supplemented by a growing need for capital. The existing credit facilities were accustomed to financing urban businesses that had a faster turnover and displayed little interest in lengthening their loan terms to accommodate the slower turnover in agriculture. In addition, such credit facilities were used for regular payments, while agricultural incomes were more uneven both during the year and from year to year. Further, some farmers occasionally experienced years where they had a total crop failure.

Farmers' campaigns for improved credit climaxed during the last years of the nineteenth century and were an important platform of many of the farm organizations of the day. These efforts finally achieved some success when the Federal Farm Loan Act of 1916 was passed and signed by President Woodrow Wilson. Although not providing direct government credit, as some farmers had demanded, this act laid the groundwork for farmers to build a credit system of their own to deal with the unique needs of agriculture. The Federal Farm Loan Act created twelve land banks to serve the different regions of the country. These land banks were authorized to make long-term real estate loans to farmers. Through the system, farmers pooled their credit needs and obtained funds by the sale of bonds. The federal government provided the initial capital, but this has long since been paid off. As shown in Table 6.6, the federal land banks now represent the most important source of real estate credit to farmers (Nelson and Murray 1967; Stokes 1973).

A severe farm depression in the early 1920s made obvious the gap between the long-term real estate loans provided by the land banks and the short-term credit supplied by commercial banks. Consequently, the federal intermediate credit banks were created in 1923. These credit banks do not loan directly to farmers but are "wholesalers" of credit. As such they are authorized to discount loans for, and make loans to lending institutions that finance the credit needs of farmers. They were designed to help farmers obtain loans for longer periods than those typically available from commercial banks (American Institute of Banking 1969; Nelson and Murray 1967).

During the Great Depression the stressed financial conditions of many farmers made it difficult for them to obtain even short-term credit from commercial banks. As a part of the Roosevelt administration's overall farm plan, the Farm Credit Act of 1933 created a system of production credit associations (PCA). This act also created the Farm Credit Administration to bring the supervision of these various parts of the farm credit system under one unit. Each production credit association is an individual corporation chartered by the Farm Credit Administration. The production credit system has a mixed ownership with part of the capital being owned by the federal government and part by the farmers who own stock in the system. The government capital is gradually being retired and eventually the system will be entirely farmer owned. The PCAs are authorized to provide production and short-term loans to farmers including those for family living expenses. As such they provide direct competition to commercial banks in rural areas. PCA loans are made with special consideration to when the farmer's income will become available (American Institute of Banking 1969; Nelson and Murray 1967).

Farmers Home Administration. The Farmers Home Administration is a government lending agency established in 1946 that operates within the U.S. Department of Agriculture. While the farm credit system had been initiated by the government as a means whereby farmers could obtain credit suited to their needs through cooperative action, there was still a demand for direct government loans. Many beginning farmers and those with limited resources were unable to qualify for loans from either commercial sources or from the farm credit system. Thus, the primary function of the Farmers Home Administration is to make loans to these selected farmers who are unable to obtain commercial credit. The Farmers Home Administration also has the charge to make loans to improve rural communities and to alleviate rural poverty. The Farmers Home Administration makes both short- and long-term loans to meet emergency situations and to help disadvantaged farmers acquire, enlarge, or develop farms. They are also authorized to make loans for erecting or improving farm residences and buildings. In 1985 11.9 percent of the total farm debt in the United States was held by the Farmers Home Administration.

Commodity Credit Corporation. The Commodity Credit Corporation (CCC) is a government agency within the U.S. Department of Agriculture. It is the agency that administers the commodity programs described earlier in this chapter and is involved in farm lending through nonrecursive loans. About 4 percent of the total farm debt was held by the CCC in 1985.

Life Insurance Companies. Life insurance companies have become some of the largest financial institutions in the world and constitute an important source of long-term mortgage credit for farmers (holding 5.8 percent of the total farm debt in 1985). Historically, life insurance companies have sought low-risk investments to protect their policyholders. Because of steadily increasing values for farmland, agricultural real estate loans were considered to be such low-risk loans. Traditionally, insurance companies concentrated their farm lending in major agricultural regions and most of their loans were relatively large. For example, in 1979 life insurance companies were the major source of real estate credit for farms with gross sales of $500,000 or more (Barry 1984). The recent decline in farmland values and the financial insecurity of agriculture in general may result in the reduced participation of life insurance companies in agricultural lending in the near future.

Individuals and Others. Historically, private individuals were the major source of farm credit. For example, prior to World War I individuals supplied about three-fourths of the credit to agriculture (Raup 1978). Recently, their dominance has declined with the capitalization of agriculture, government farm programs, and the use of conventional private sources of financing. Often the seller of a farm cannot find a buyer with sufficient backing to obtain a loan for the entire purchase **129** price of the farm. In these cases the seller is often willing to accept partial payment, taking a mortgage for the balance. This more often occurs when the buyer and seller are acquainted. Also, many farm transfers occur within a family, and many of these are financed by the seller. Such transactions were more common in the past, but they still represent an important part of the credit in U.S. agriculture today.

Importance of Farm Financial Institutions in U.S. Agriculture: The Example of the Farm Crisis of the 1980s

The extreme importance of the role played by financial institutions in American agriculture as well as the interdependence between such institutions and the structure of agriculture is exemplified by an examination of the role of farm financial factors in the farm crisis of the 1980s. This farm crisis is the result of a complex series of events including declining land values, high interest rates, and low commodity prices. Ecologically, changes in the financial institutions that deal with agriculture can be expected to result in major adjustments by farmers since the two are so extensively intertwined. Further, the farm crisis should affect different segments of the farm sector differently depending on the various relationships with financial institutions.

Since 1981 farmers' collateral has been dwindling with rapidly declining land values. After four decades of continuous increases in farmland values the speculation that such trends would continue resulted in land values being bid to levels far above what the productive potential of the land would warrant. Coupled with eroding assets during the 1980s, the debt levels that some farmers assumed were no longer sustainable. Farmers whose financial solvency depended on continuously rising land values or who pursued an aggressive expansion strategy were pushed toward insolvency (United States Department of Agriculture 1984a).

A second reason for the farm crisis of the 1980s is the record high interest rates that were prevalent during the early 1980s. Throughout the 1970s farmers had responded to accelerating inflation by borrowing heavily to invest in new capital equipment, to adopt new production technologies, and to purchase increasingly expensive farmland. Farmers attempting to pay back the loans made during this period of high interest had a very substantial financial burden.

Another factor leading to the farm crisis is the relatively low com-

130 modity prices that have been prevalent during most of the 1980s. Commodity prices during the 1980s were substantially lower than they had been just a few years earlier. These low prices have resulted in farmers' incomes declining considerably. Table 6.7 shows index numbers of the prices paid and the prices received by farmers from 1970 to 1986 (based on 1977 values). The index values of prices paid by farmers are computed by determining the total costs for farm inputs for each year and then comparing each year with costs for 1977, which have been set to equal 100. Similarly, the index of prices received by farmers is calculated by determining the prices farmers received for their products and then comparing to prices in 1977, which have been set to equal 100. This table shows that during the 1970s farmers' costs were relatively lower than prices received, while during the 1980s costs were relatively higher than prices received. The ratio of prices received to costs was 77 in 1986, which is the lowest it had been since before 1970.

The reasons for the lower commodity prices during the 1980s are very complex. However, much of the differences can be explained by the basic economic principles of supply and demand. During the 1970s extensive agricultural exports, including those to the Soviet Union, depleted government grain reserves and increased demand for farm prod-

Table 6.7. Index numbers of prices paid and received by farmers (1977 = 100)

Year	Index number of prices paid by farmers (costs)	Index number of prices received by farmers	Ratio of prices received to prices paid (100 = Prices received equal to prices paid)
1970	55	60	109
1971	58	62	107
1972	62	69	111
1973	71	98	138
1974	81	105	130
1975	89	101	113
1976	95	102	107
1977	100	100	100
1978	108	115	106
1979	123	132	107
1980	138	134	97
1981	150	139	93
1982	157	133	85
1983	160	134	84
1984	164	142	87
1985	163	128	79
1986	159	123	77

Source: U.S. Department of Agriculture (1985b).

ucts. This resulted in higher prices, which in turn led farmers to increase production. The 1980s has largely been a period of high production with reduced worldwide demand. In addition, government enforced embargoes in connection with a strong American dollar that made the farm products of other countries more attractive to importing nations have also been partially responsible for the lower demand for farm products.

The result of this series of events is that American farmers are now facing their most severe financial crisis since the Great Depression, and an unprecedented proportion of farmers are likely to be forced to leave farming in the next few years (Bultena et al. 1986; Murdock et al. 1986). Research on the farm crisis has found that farmers with certain characteristics are substantially more likely than other farmers to experience financial stress. Specifically, it has been found that farmers who are younger, better educated, operate larger farms, rent a larger proportion of their farmland, and use more recommended farming practices are more likely than other farmers to experience financial stress as a result of the farm crisis. Many of these farmers recently entered agriculture or pursued a policy of farm expansion during the 1970s, only to find that the conditions of the 1980s made it impossible for them to meet their financial obligations. In contrast, other farmers are relatively well insulated from the farm crisis including those who are older, well established, relatively debt-free, and employed in off-farm jobs that cushion them from the fluctuations in farm income (Albrecht et al. 1987a; Bultena et al. 1986; Leholm et al. 1985; Murdock et al. 1985, 1986).

Researchers are also finding that the deteriorating financial conditions of many farmers are having negative consequences for agriculturally dependent rural communities (Doeksen 1987; Murdock et al. 1987). The businesses in such communities are finding that their clientele is becoming fewer in number and many of them are reducing their family living expenses and postponing capital purchases because of the farm crisis. Further, it appears that the farm crisis is having important consequences for the lives of farm families. As a result of the farm crisis, many families are experiencing psychological stress, depression, and marital problems (Albrecht et al. 1987b; Hargrove 1986; Heffernan and Heffernan 1986).

The farm crisis has also had important implications for the financial institutions that provide credit to farmers (Green 1984; McIntosh and Zey-Ferrell 1986). As farmers experience financial stress, they transmit it, to some extent, to farm lenders through loan delinquency and loan

132   losses. As farmers' asset values decline, lenders have less adequate security for new or existing loans. If too high a proportion of the portfolio of a lender becomes nonperforming loans, then the lender will face serious financial difficulty (United States Department of Agriculture 1985a).

It is now apparent that those lenders who are heavily dependent on agricultural loans face major financial problems. A very high proportion of the outstanding farm debts are owed by farmers who are highly leveraged. In 1984, 23.7 percent of the farm debt was owed by farmers with debt-to-asset ratios over 70 percent, while an additional 32.5 percent was owed by farmers with debt-to-asset ratios between 40 and 70 percent (United States Department of Agriculture 1985a). This has resulted in much higher rates of loan failure. With increased loan failures agricultural lenders have become increasingly concerned about farm loan defaults and delinquencies. Many farm lenders have tightened credit requirements and more overdue accounts are being foreclosed. This has made it increasingly difficult for many farmers to obtain basic operating funds as well as loans to adopt new agricultural innovations (McIntosh and Zey-Ferrell 1986).

When examining individual agricultural lenders, the indications of financial stress are evident. Many commercial banks in agricultural areas are now facing severe financial problems. Table 6.8 presents data showing the total number of banks that have failed from 1981 through the first quarter of 1987, and the number of these that are agricultural banks (defined as a bank where 25 percent or more of the loans are agricultural). This table vividly shows the development of the farm crisis as

Table 6.8.   Total number of banks failing and number of banks failing where 25 percent of the loans are agricultural from 1981 to 1987

Year	Total bank failures	Agricultural bank failures[a]	Percentage of banks failing that are agricultural banks
1981	10	1	10.0
1982	42	7	16.7
1983	48	6	12.5
1984	79	26	32.9
1985	120	60	50.0
1986	136	56	41.2
1987	203	59	29.1

Source: Data obtained from the annual reports of the FDIC.
[a]Agricultural banks are defined as banks where 25 percent or more of the loans are agricultural. In 1987, 27 percent of the banks insured by FDIC were agricultural banks by this definition.

the number of agricultural banks that failed increased from one in 1981   **133**
to sixty in 1985. Table 6.8 also indicates that the farm crisis had not
subsided as of 1987 because fifty-nine agricultural banks failed during
that year. In addition, the farm crisis has adversely affected the farm
credit system. The growing economic stress first became apparent
among the PCAs, but later also affected the federal land banks. In both
cases the number of delinquent loans has increased greatly, and a number of PCAs have been liquidated (United States Department of Agriculture 1985a).

In sum, agriculture is obviously very closely interrelated with financial institutions, and changes in the financial sector have major implications for agriculture. At the same time, changes in agriculture have important consequences for these financial and economic institutions. The
nature of this interrelationship has been vividly illustrated in the recent
farm crisis, which is likely to be an important factor in the changes that
occur in American agriculture during the next few years.

From an ecological perspective the relevance of the study of financial organizations for agriculture as discussed in this section is evident.
Because of the close interrelationship of agriculture to these organizations, financial and economic changes are going to result in major adaptations in agriculture, and changes in agriculture will affect the market
for agricultural financing. Thus, changes in farmland values and interest
rates are going to have important implications for farm operators, and
changes in commodity prices will have consequences for lenders involved
in agricultural loans. These changes will not affect all segments of the
agricultural industry equally, and thus it is likely that some farm financial institutions will find that a large proportion of their traditional
market of producers may have been forced to leave farming.

AGRIBUSINESS FIRMS

Agribusiness is a term used to describe the commercial activities
related to the food industry. Typically, production at the farm sector is
omitted when discussing agribusiness. Agribusiness thus includes the
business firms from whom farmers buy their inputs and to whom they
sell their products. In a traditional agricultural system agribusiness as
defined here would not exist or would exist on a much smaller scale. In
traditional agriculture the farmer would provide all of his or her own

134 inputs (most of which would be labor) and then take his or her product to the market and distribute it directly to the consumer. In this manner the farmer would receive virtually 100 percent of the money that consumers spend on food. Such a system is not used in a modern society based on a highly complex division of labor.

Size and Importance of Agribusiness in the United States

Agribusiness has become a major industry in the United States. This includes both those who provide farmers with their inputs and those who process, transport, and distribute the commodities once they leave the farm. The farm input suppliers compose a sizeable financial unit. In 1981, for example, the total sales of manufacturing input suppliers to the farm sector totaled $74.1 billion. Farm input suppliers can be categorized into four groups including (1) the feed manufacturing industry, (2) the fertilizer industry, (3) the agricultural chemical industry, and (4) the farm machinery and equipment industry (Penson et al. 1986).

The majority of marketed farm output is utilized as input by the food manufacturers and retailers, the other side of the agribusiness industry. These firms are then the suppliers of food to the American consumer. Table 6.9 shows that Americans spend an average of about 16 percent of their disposable personal income for food. Only housing expenditures consume a larger proportion of our income. Food expenditures surpassed those for transportation, medical, and other areas (Shepherd and Futrell 1982). Despite the vast size of the American food industry, Americans spend a relatively small proportion of their disposable income on food. In Table 6.10 data are presented that compare the United States with selected other countries in the world on the propor-

Table 6.9. Expenditures of disposable income, 1979

Item	%
Housing	27.7
Food	16.4
Transportation	13.0
Medical	8.8
Clothes	6.1
Other expenditures	23.1
Savings	4.5
Total	100.0

Source: Adapted from Shepherd and Futrell (1982).

Table 6.10. World comparison among selected countries of proportion of after-tax income spent on food

Country	%
United States	16
West Germany	17
Netherlands	21
Sweden	21
Canada	22
Belgium	23
United Kingdom	23
South Africa	23
Finland	25
France	26
Denmark	28
Malta	31
Korea	52
Philippines	62

Source: Adapted from Shepherd and Futrell (1982).

tion of disposable income spent on food. As is apparent in this table, Americans spend a smaller proportion of their income on food than persons in most other countries in the world (Shepherd and Futrell 1982).

The proportion of the food dollar that the U.S. farmer receives varies extensively by commodity. Table 6.11 presents data showing the farm value as a percentage of the retail cost for a variety of food products from 1970 to 1984. In 1984 the farm value as a percentage of the

Table 6.11. Farm value as a percentage of retail cost for various food products, 1970–1984

Year	Bakery and cereal products	Meat	Dairy	Poultry and eggs	Fresh fruits and vegetables	Processed fruits and vegetables
1970	16	53	48	53	30	19
1971	16	52	47	51	32	18
1972	17	56	48	52	31	19
1973	22	60	50	63	34	19
1974	24	54	49	60	33	22
1975	19	57	49	61	33	21
1976	15	51	52	60	31	20
1977	12	53	50	59	31	18
1978	13	54	51	61	31	25
1979	14	52	52	59	29	23
1980	14	51	52	58	26	23
1981	13	49	51	58	29	23
1982	11	50	50	55	28	20
1983	11	48	49	57	26	19
1984	11	49	48	59	29	20

Source: U.S. Department of Agriculture (1985b).

136   retail cost ranged from a high of 59 percent for poultry and eggs to a low of 11 percent for bakery and cereal products. The reason for this vast difference is that poultry and eggs require little processing, while bakery and cereal products are extensively processed before they are provided to the consumer. Generally, the greater the amount of processing, the lower the proportion of the total cost that is comprised of the farm value. Thus, the farmer receives about half of the consumer dollar for meat and dairy products and only a small part of the total expenditures for fresh fruits and vegetables and processed fruits and vegetables. Also apparent from Table 6.10 is the fact that the proportion of the consumer dollar that farmers receive varies extensively from year to year. For the limited time period shown in the table, the farmers' share was greatest for most products in 1973 and 1974 when farm commodity prices were at a relatively high level, and were at their lowest in the mid-1980s.

Table 6.12 provides data on the total food expenditures from 1970 to 1986 by cost categories. This table shows that food expenditures in the United States increased from $110.6 billion in 1970 to $361.1 billion in 1986. Much of this increase was due to inflation and part of it was due to

Table 6.12.   Civilian expenditures for U.S. produced farm foods by cost category, 1970–1986

Year	Total food expenditures	Farm value	Marketing bill	Farm value as a percentage of total expenditures
		Billion dollars		
1970	110.6	35.5	75.1	32.1
1971	114.6	36.2	78.5	31.6
1972	122.2	39.8	82.4	32.6
1973	138.8	51.7	87.1	37.2
1974	154.6	56.4	98.2	36.5
1975	167.0	55.6	111.4	33.3
1976	183.0	58.3	125.0	31.9
1977	190.9	58.2	132.7	30.5
1978	216.9	69.5	147.4	32.0
1979	245.3	79.2	166.1	32.3
1980	264.4	81.7	182.7	30.9
1981	287.7	83.2	204.5	28.9
1982	298.9	83.7	215.2	28.0
1983	315.0	84.9	230.2	27.0
1984	332.0	89.5	242.7	27.0
1985	345.4	88.3	257.1	25.6
1986[a]	361.1	89.0	272.1	24.6

Source: U.S. Department of Agriculture (1985b).
[a]Data were obtained by telephone from USDA officials prior to their release in printed form.

the fact that the size of the population of consumers was larger. To **137** provide some indication of the size of the agribusiness industry in the United States, Table 6.12 shows that in 1986 the marketing bill reached $272.1 billion. These total food expenditures are shown for the farm value of the products and the marketing bill, which includes the costs involved in processing, packaging, and distributing the products. For the time period shown the farm value has generally amounted to about 30 percent of the total food expenditures, while the marketing bill has comprised the other 70 percent. However, the farm value as a percentage of the total food expenditures has varied extensively over the years examined. The farm value reached a high of 37.2 percent in 1973 and dropped to a low of 24.6 percent in 1986. The farm value as a percentage of total expenditures steadily declined from 1979 through 1986. Despite these variations corporate profits in agribusiness have remained at about 6 percent during this time period.

Concerns with Agribusiness

In addition to their large size and obvious importance in the American economy, many other important concerns surround agribusiness in the United States today. Perhaps the most prevalent are concerns about the extensive amount of concentration in the food manufacturing sector of the agribusiness industry and concerns about vertical integration.

In the United States over two million farmers produce agricultural commodities. These farmers obtain their inputs and sell their products to a relatively small number of suppliers and food manufacturers who process, package, and distribute them. The food manufacturers then sell their products to hundreds of thousands of food distributors, who in turn supply millions of households. Partly because of their small numbers, these agribusiness firms occupy a powerful position in the U.S. food system (Marion 1986). This situation is intensified because of the total number of food manufacturers; a handful of the largest control much of the market. This has led to charges of monopoly, to claims that manufacturers manipulate prices, squeeze out competing firms, engage in market sharing, and, as a result, extract exorbitant profits at the expense of both farmers and consumers (Hightower 1975; Paarlberg 1980; Schulman 1981). The extent to which concentration exists, then, is seen as the key determinant of agribusiness influence.

In examining the extent of concentration among agribusiness firms

138 several potential measures may be used. One measure, the total number of firms involved, tells us little about competitive conditions unless this number is very small. In 1982 there were about 17,000 companies that were primarily classified in food manufacturing. Most of these firms were very small. Over one-half had fewer than 10 employees, and over 90 percent had fewer than 100 employees. The number of companies in the individual food industries varied greatly, ranging from 9 manufacturers of chewing gum to 1,863 wholesale bakers (Marion 1986). Similarly, during the early 1980s there were some 6,500 feed manufacturing firms in the United States (Penson et al. 1986).

Competitive conditions are better measured by the four-firm concentration ratio (CR4) than by the number of companies. This ratio measures the proportion of sales that are made by the four largest firms in an industry. In 1977, 9 of 98 food and tobacco product classes had a CR4 rating of over 80 percent. On the other hand, 41 product classes had a CR4 rating below 40 percent (Connor et al. 1985). The CR4 measure shows extensive concentration among the farm input suppliers. For example, 80 percent of the tractors, 83 percent of the combines, and 57 percent of the pesticides were produced by the 4 largest firms in each industry.

Another important measure is aggregate concentration, which measures the market share controlled by the largest companies (such as the top 100 or 500) in a segment of the economy. In 1977 the top 100 food manufacturers' share of the total market amounted to about 53 percent, which is very large considering that there were over 17,000 total firms. Concentration was especially high among the 20 largest food manufacturing firms. In 1977 the market share of these 20 firms was about equal to that of the next 80 largest firms and was considerably larger than the combined shares of the 101st to 500th largest firms (Connor et al. 1985). This trend toward increased concentration has likely continued since 1977 because in recent years several leading food manufacturing companies have been involved in a number of large mergers. This includes the largest nonoil merger in history (to that time) when Philip Morris acquired General Foods, which created the largest U.S. consumer products company (Marion 1986).

Of the four broad categories of farm input suppliers, three are categorized by extensive concentration. The major exception is the feed manufacturing industry, where there are about 6,500 firms, and concentration seems to be a concern in only a few isolated regions (Hamm

1979). The fertilizer industry is fairly competitive but less so than the **139** feed manufacturing industry. To some extent, the fertilizer industry is characterized by conglomerate firms (such as petroleum producers and chemical companies) that produce a wide variety of products in addition to agricultural fertilizers. The agricultural chemical industry is extensively concentrated and is also dominated by conglomerates that produce a wide variety of products. A prime example of these conglomerates is DuPont, which manufactures a variety of nonfarm-oriented products, such as paint, in addition to their line of agricultural chemicals (Penson et al. 1986). The farm machinery and equipment industry is very concentrated as a few large companies (such as John Deere, International Harvester, and Ford) dominate the market (Hamm 1979).

Despite these high levels of concentration in agribusiness, the centralization of control over decision making may be even greater than these measures indicate. It has been argued that the true level of concentration is even higher because the largest firms are linked to each other in a network of overlapping stockholdings, directors, financial ties, and other business contacts (Caswell 1984; Schulman 1981). Obviously, trends in agribusiness concentration should be monitored, and the extent to which this concentration influences the effectiveness and performance of the U.S. food system needs to be determined.

A second issue of concern relative to agribusiness in the United States is vertical integration. Vertical integration by food manufacturers occurs when a single firm obtains ownership or control over successive stages of the food system. In agriculture this has become an issue of concern when a farm input supplier or a food manufacturing industry gains control over production at the farm level. An example of vertical integration in agriculture is what has occurred in the poultry industry. Heffernan (1982b) notes that at one time most diversified family farms in the United States had a flock of chickens. In addition, nearly all rural communities had several hatcheries and feed stores from which chicks and feed could be purchased, and a farmer usually had access to many firms that could purchase the broilers and/or eggs the farmer produced.

The situation in the poultry industry today is vastly different. The suppliers of chicks and feed, as well as those who process and distribute poultry products, have become integrated into a small number of firms. The poultry producer signs a contract with an integrating firm and relinquishes all major decision-making responsibilities. Those who do not sign such a contract simply do not have a market for their products

140 (Heffernan 1982b). Thus, agribusiness firms have extensive control over production at the farm level.

Similar examples of this type of vertical integration have been reported in the fruit and vegetable industry, the hog industry, and others (Friedland et al. 1981; Molnar and Korsching 1983). Such trends obviously have important consequences for the number of farms and the independence of these farms in the United States and thus should be monitored and be a topic of additional research efforts.

FARM ORGANIZATIONS AND COLLECTIVE BARGAINING

From the discussion on agribusiness it is apparent that farmers are at an economic disadvantage relative to the persons or firms from whom they buy their inputs and sell their products. There are several reasons that farmers are in this disadvantaged position. The first is that farmers are more numerous than those with whom they buy and sell. This makes it extremely difficult for farmers to work cooperatively. In addition, farmers, even the very large farms, operate on a much smaller scale than the firms they deal with. Consequently, individual farmers are not in a position to appreciably influence the agricultural market. This generally means that farmers are price takers and not price setters. A third factor is that farmers, on the average, are less well informed than those they deal with. Finally, farmers are less able to control or differentiate their output or production. That is, agribusiness firms can use various product names or packaging to differentiate their product, while the wheat grown by one farmer is virtually impossible to differentiate from the wheat grown by another farmer (Roy 1970).

The market structure of agriculture relative to the food manufacturing industries has been termed an oligopsony where there are few buyers and many sellers. This is opposed to an oligopoly where there are many buyers and a few sellers (e.g., the automobile industry). In agriculture the farm input suppliers represent an oligopoly to farmers. In an effort to deal with their position of relative disadvantage in the marketplace, farmers have made numerous attempts to organize and collectively bargain for better prices over the years. These efforts have generally consisted of two major approaches. The first consists of farmers organizing in an effort to influence public policy, consumer choices, and the marketing decisions of individual farmers, while the second is an attempt to develop cooperatives where groups of farmers coordinate their buying and selling efforts in order to get a better price for their products or to pay a lower price for their inputs. In this section both of these types of organizations representing farmers will be briefly described.

Farm Organizations

There are two major types of farm organizations that are intended to represent farm people and give them a united voice in the formulation of farm policy, help them influence consumer choices, and influence the marketing decisions of individual farmers. These include the general farm organizations and the commodity groups. In the paragraphs that follow, each of these types of organizations representing farmers will be described.

General Farm Organizations. Regardless of how much wealth the speculators, landlords, money lenders, merchants, and transportation agencies have gained from the production of agricultural products, the income of the actual farmer has historically been far below the average of the rest of the population. Farming has been a way of life not a road to material wealth. During the great wars of American history increased demand has led to rising prices in the short term. Invariably this has been followed by a period when money was scarce and prices were low (Shannon 1957).

Numerous times throughout American history farmers have attempted to organize themselves and protest what they considered to be unfair conditions or practices. At other times farmers have organized in an attempt to influence prices or public policy. Typically, when conditions for farmers deteriorate, interest and membership in farm organizations increase, only to decline when conditions improve. Some of the better-known early farmers' movements included Bacon's Revolt (1676), Shays's Rebellion (1786), and the Whiskey Insurrection (1794). The period from 1870 to 1900 was perhaps the era of greatest political strength for organizations of farmers. Following the Civil War a depreciating dollar made it very difficult for farmers to meet their debts. This was associated with relatively low prices for farm commodities, high costs

142   for farm inputs, scarce money, tight credit, high interest rates, and excessive transportation charges. As the economic conditions of farmers deteriorated, numerous farm organizations emerged. The largest and most influential of these was the Patrons of Husbandry, otherwise known as the Grange.

The Grange was first organized in 1867 by Oliver H. Kelley in Washington, D.C. The Grange was initially a secret, nonpolitical society that admitted both men and women. Its purpose was to work for the betterment of the social, educational, and economic conditions of farmers through cooperative enterprises. The Grange attracted few members in its early years, but as economic conditions in agriculture worsened through the 1870s, farmers joined in droves hoping that the organization could save them from bankruptcy and foreclosure. By 1875 the Grange had 858,000 members (Shannon 1957). During the 1870s the National Grange was influential in getting the legislatures in several states to pass laws regulating railroad fares and freight rates. It was also instrumental in the passage of the Interstate Commerce Act in 1887, which gave the federal government the right to regulate interstate traffic. During that time the railroads represented a near monopoly for transporting farm products, and the farm community was concerned that they were able to charge exorbitant prices. The Grange and other farm organizations of the time were also instrumental in getting rural free mail delivery and the Hatch Act of 1887, which initiated state agricultural experiment stations.

The Farmers Alliance was another important farm organization of the late nineteenth century. The Alliance was the basis for the Populist movement and the emergence of the People's party. In 1892 the People's party had a strong candidate for president of the United States; it won eight congressional seats, three governorships, and innumerable other state and county offices (Howe 1986; McConnell 1969).

Today there are several major general farm organizations. The general farm organizations include among their members those producers with many interests usually living in different parts of the country. The organizations carry out a broad range of business activities and services for their members, and their legislative efforts cover a variety of issues dealing with food and agriculture (Guither 1980).

The general farm organizations still represent an important force in shaping farm policy today. Because farmers represent such a small share of the total population, the farm organizations are no longer in a position to have much influence on issues outside of agriculture. While a **143** number of general farm organizations exist today, only four play a major role at the national level. These include the National Grange, the National Farmers Union, the American Farm Bureau Federation, and the National Farmers Organization. The first three are relatively old organizations while the NFO began during the recession of the mid-1950s and has emerged as a fourth major national organization. The National Farmers Organization also differs from the others in that it has a major thrust toward collective bargaining. The NFO encourages farmers to retain their membership in other organizations but to join NFO to price their products. It encourages farmers to join together in marketing their products and attempts to negotiate contracts with processors for their members. Each organization maintains a Washington office and employs registered lobbyists (Guither 1980). Table 6.13 provides summary information about these four general farm organizations.

The primary niche that the four major general farm organizations occupy today is one of employing lobbyists and attempting to influence public policy and other decisions that affect farmers. They work toward securing favorable loan rates and target prices, implementing programs to assist the family farm, and providing educational materials for their members. Often the organizations will all agree with one another on an issue and work towards its implementation, but there are also many areas of disagreement. Although the general farm organizations continue to exert an important influence on policy formation and are likely to continue to do so in the future (Hadwiger and Browne 1978), they have been replaced by the commodity groups as the major source of power in the implementation of farm policy. With the enactment of the Agricultural Adjustment Act of 1933, farmers were guaranteed minimum price levels. This caused insecurities about the marketplace to be reduced and emphasis to be placed on the price levels of the various commodities. Such issues are best dealt with by the commodity groups.

Commodity Groups. As opposed to the general farm organizations, the commodity groups are organized to meet special needs and provide services to those who produce a specific commodity or agricultural product. While the general farm organizations have a broad range of policy resolutions on a variety of topics affecting farming and living conditions

Table 6.13. Major general farm organizations, 1979

Organization	Year Founded	Membership (1979)	Funding	Number of registered Washington lobbyists
American Farm Bureau Federation	1919	3,198,631	Membership dues and fees for direct services	11
National Farmers Organization	1955	40,000 (est.)	Membership dues and fees for direct services	1
National Farmers Union	1902	260,000	Membership dues, fees for direct services, Green Thumb Program	6
National Grange	1867	500,000	Membership dues	3

Source: Adapted from Guither (1980).

in rural areas, the commodity groups are usually concerned with only one or a few limited issues that directly affect their product. By focusing their efforts on only a few issues the commodity groups have become among the most effective lobbyists in the country today (Browne 1982). Also, since they represent the producers of only one commodity, membership in these commodity groups tends to be more geographically concentrated.

The enactment of agricultural policy has been isolated (to a large degree) from interference by outsiders but is rent with internal divisions. These internal divisions are best exemplified by the battles among the various interest groups. For example, cattle farmers are subjected to losses when the grain producers win higher prices (Browne 1982). In this example, cattle farmers have found that they are better represented by an organization representing only cattle farmers, while grain producers found the same to be true of their grain producing organizations, rather than the general farm organizations. At any given time during the 1980s, from 90 to 120 commodity groups are likely to be active in Washington (Browne 1982) and as a result the competition among such groups is common.

Generally, the commodity groups with the greatest power represent the most important commodities (in terms of dollars of sales) such as cotton, corn, wheat, cattle, and dairy. Each of these major commodities are represented by more than one commodity group. However, in some cases a dominant group unifies support in that commodity area. Such dominant groups include the National Milk Producers Federation, the National Cotton Council, and the National Association of Wheat Growers. In other commodities greater diversity has resulted in some long-term disagreements. For example, the differences between range cattlemen and feedlot farmers who fatten animals the final few months before marketing have resulted in a strained relationship between the National Cattlemen's Association and the National Livestock Feeders Association (Browne 1982).

Legislative activity is usually only a small part of the programs offered by the commodity groups. Other services may include information through newsletters or magazines, annual conventions, trade shows, market development to expand demand for products, and specific export marketing services to facilitate shipments to overseas locations (Guither 1980). Often members of the commodity groups may also be members of one or more of the general farm organizations.

146   Some of the more important and well-known commodity groups include the National Cattlemen's Association, the National Wool Growers Association, the National Corn Growers Association, the National Association of Wheat Growers, the American Soybean Association, the Grain Sorghum Producers Association, the National Milk Producers Federation, and the National Cotton Council.

Farmer Cooperatives

Cooperative endeavors of various types have been practiced among farmers since pioneer days. Early settlers frequently exchanged labor with their neighbors, and whole communities pitched in to help newcomers get established. Many of the difficult farm tasks such as barn raising, stump pulling, and cornhusking were accomplished through neighborly cooperation (Scroggs 1957). Later, expensive farm machinery such as threshing machines were often purchased by groups of farmers who would share the machine and assist one another in getting the work done.

As the productivity of American agriculture increased as a result of westward expansion and technological developments, economic forces pressed farmers toward greater and more formal cooperative endeavors. Even during the nineteenth century overproduction was common, and often the eastern market price for wheat, corn, and oats was less than the transportation costs of moving these commodities from the Midwest. Farmers often accused the middleman of being the cause of low prices, and some cooperative endeavors were made to avoid these persons. During the early 1800s several dairy cooperatives were initiated that typically consisted of cheese factories. These cooperatives would pool the milk produced by farmer members, process the milk into cheese or butter, and then market these products directly. Marketing cooperatives for several other farm commodities soon followed (Scroggs 1957). During the later decades of the nineteenth century the National Grange and the Farmers Alliance carried out a number of cooperative activities for their members. Orders for supplies were lumped together, and volume deals were made with jobbers and manufacturers at savings over the usual retail prices. In addition, farm products were pooled for shipment to the large markets in order to obtain better prices (McConnell 1969; Scroggs 1957).

In 1900 the U.S. Department of Agriculture reported that 1,167 marketing cooperatives were active in the United States with about four-fifths of these being cooperative cheese factories or creameries (Scroggs 1957). From the turn of the century until about 1920 the role of cooperatives in U.S. agriculture remained rather stable. The year 1920 opened in a state of postwar agricultural prosperity. However, by the end of the year this prosperity had vanished and farmers were confronted by one of the worst agricultural depressions in history. Faced with low and rapidly declining farm prices, farmers' reliance on cooperatives increased greatly and farmers viewed marketing cooperatives as a means of restoring farm prosperity. The depression in agriculture also encouraged the American Farm Bureau Federation, which had been formed in 1919, to promote cooperatives (Knapp 1973).

The cooperative movement received a major boost when the Capper-Volstead Cooperative Marketing Act was signed into law February 18, 1922, by President Warren Harding. This act freed farm cooperatives from federal antitrust laws and declared that they were not in restraint of trade. In the few years prior to the Capper-Volstead Act, several milk marketing cooperatives had been harassed by legal actions (Knapp 1973). This act provides that farmers have a right to enter into agreements with other farmers (integrate horizontally) in order to integrate vertically without violating antitrust legislation. The act is analogous to labor legislation that allows workers to enter into agreements to form labor unions. Both were designed to create greater equality in the distribution of income (Walsh 1978).

Farmer cooperatives of today act as an off-farm extension of the farm firms that allow farm operators to extend themselves vertically to one or more stages in the marketing channel. The intent of cooperatives is to enable farmers (who are numerous and small) to join together in an effort to deal more effectively with the agribusiness firms they interact with (who are relatively few and large). By combining the efforts of numerous individual businesses, cooperatives attempt to provide the benefits of a large-scale organization to the individual farm operators (Torgerson 1977).

Cooperatives play an important role in U.S. agriculture today. The data presented in Table 6.14 show that the volume of business dealt with by cooperatives increased substantially from 1950 to 1980 (from $8.1 billion to $66.3 billion). During this time the aggregate share of the agricultural market that cooperatives handled also increased. The majority of the business conducted by cooperatives today is handled by

Table 6.14. Cooperative business volume and market share statistics for selected years

Year	Aggregate net business volume (billion dollars)	Market share percentage Marketing	Farm supply
1950	8.1	17.0	14.1
1955	9.8	22.1	15.3
1960	12.4	23.8	15.3
1965	15.6	25.5	16.0
1970	20.6	26.0	15.6
1975	40.0	31.1	18.0
1980	66.3	31.4	19.8

Source: U.S. Department of Agriculture (1984b).

marketing cooperatives, which are primarily concerned with providing a market for agricultural products. Table 6.14 shows that in 1980 marketing cooperatives handled about one-third of the gross agricultural sales in the United States, which is up from about 17 percent in 1950. In contrast, the supply cooperatives that provide inputs to farmers handled about 20 percent of the total farm business in 1980 compared to 14 percent in 1950.

Table 6.15 presents data showing the farm-level share of the market handled by both marketing and supply cooperatives for a variety of specific commodities and farm supplies. For marketing cooperatives the dairy cooperatives have historically accounted for more gross sales than

Table 6.15. Farm level share of the market handled by farmer cooperative, 1974–1975

Functional area	Number of cooperatives handling	Percentage of cash farm receipts
Product marketed		
Cotton and products	494	26
Dairy products	631	75
Fruits and vegetables	436	25
Grain and soybeans	2,540	40
Livestock and products	572	10
Poultry products	167	9
Other	164	35
Farm supplies purchased		
Feed	3,744	18
Seed	3,553	16
Fertilizer and lime	3,865	30
Petroleum	2,624	35
Farm chemicals	3,328	29
Other supplies	4,224	10

Source: Adapted from Torgerson (1978).

cooperatives dealing with any other commodity. The table shows that 75 **149** percent of the dairy products were marketed through cooperatives in 1974–75. Only for rice and dairy products do cooperatives traditionally account for more than one-half of the total cash farm receipts (Schmelzer and Campbell 1978). The commodities with the lowest proportions marketed through cooperatives included poultry products (9 percent) and livestock and livestock products (10 percent). For the supply cooperatives the data show that the product with both the largest total dollar volume and the largest proportion being marketed through cooperatives is petroleum.

While cooperatives are likely to remain as an important factor in U.S. agriculture, they have in recent years been besieged by an unprecedented series of criticisms. Several large dairy cooperatives were defendants in antitrust cases. The antitrust exempt status and hence the legality of the activities of the National Broiler Marketing Association and Central California Lettuce Growers Cooperative were both challenged in the courts. Further, the extent to which large cooperatives have become similar to large corporations and are no longer controlled by and responsive to their producer members has become a concern (Marion 1978). Thus, it appears that research related to cooperative issues needs to be an important concern in the future.

SUMMARY AND CONCLUSIONS

In this chapter several organizations that operate outside the farm unit itself but have an important influence on the individual farm have been described. Each of these organizations has played an important role in the past development and current structure of American agriculture. Further, as agriculture becomes more interwoven into the mainstream of the economy and society, the extent of these influences is likely to increase.

The role of the federal government in agriculture has increased immensely over the years. Today federal farm policy influences all aspects of farming and farm life. Future farm policy decisions will have a major influence on agricultural structure and change. Also, the role of credit in agriculture has grown in recent decades. As a consequence, financial and economic institutions play a key function in the development and change of American agriculture. In future years changes that occur in financial

150   institutions are likely to have major implications for U.S. agriculture.

Agribusiness firms are other nonfarm organizations that are playing an increasingly important role in U.S. agriculture. These firms provide inputs to farmers and purchase the commodities that farmers produce. Recently some have expressed concern about the increased concentration and vertical integration in agribusiness and the influence that these trends will have on farm structure and the independence of farm families. Also, a variety of organizations representing farmers have played and will continue to play an important role in the development and change of American agriculture.

Given the historical and ecological importance of nonfarm organizations in shaping the nature of the ecosystem in which farm organizations operate, additional research on the roles and on the effectiveness of nonfarm organizations in shaping the ecosystem is essential. It is critical to understand the linkages and forms of interdependence between nonfarm organizations and elements of the structure of agriculture so that we may determine if intervention in the agricultural-environment relationship will be effective and so that the effectiveness of agricultural policy will be improved. Establishing such relationships is important both in advancing our state of knowledge regarding the structure of agriculture and in improving our knowledge of the utility and forms of interventions that might be used to affect the welfare of producers. Research related to the interrelationships between nonfarm organizations and the structure of agriculture will thus remain both a conceptually and pragmatically important area of research in the years to come.

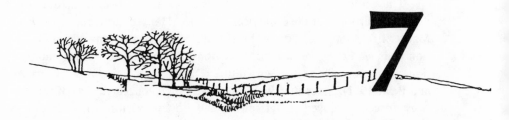

The Population Structure
of Rural America

The population component of the ecological complex (Duncan and Schnore 1959; Hauser and Duncan 1959; Duncan 1964) is treated in various ways in ecological analyses. Some ecologists treat it as a noncausative factor (Sly and Tayman 1977) that serves only to designate the unit of analysis in ecological studies; others examine its influences on numerous structural and other ecological factors (Micklin and Choldin 1984). However perceived, the populations of rural areas affect and reflect changes in agricultural structure (Albrecht and Murdock 1986b; Albrecht 1986). In this chapter, we examine the major demographic characteristics of rural areas in the United States. This analysis involves an extensive examination of differences between rural and urban and rural farm and rural nonfarm populations on key demographic and socioeconomic characteristics. We begin by tracing the conceptual linkages between the ecological concept of population and characteristics of the structure of U.S. agriculture. This section is followed by a description and a presentation of extensive data on the historic patterns of change in rural farm populations compared to those in urban and rural nonfarm populations. The final section of the chapter formulates generalizations about past and likely future ecologically based patterns of population change in rural areas.

151

152 POPULATION ECOLOGY AND THE STRUCTURE OF U.S. AGRICULTURE

The ecological basis for the analysis of population structure is described throughout the ecological literature (Hauser and Duncan 1959; Matras 1973) and is evident in historical and recent patterns of population change. Pervasive historical relationships prevail between population change and changes in agriculture (Duncan and Reiss 1956; Brown and Beale 1981). Since the 1940s, areas with high concentrations of their work forces employed in agriculture have lost population (Brown and Beale 1981). In fact, even during the period of renewed rural population growth that came to be known as the nonmetropolitan population turnaround, counties with economic bases dependent on agriculture continued to lose population (Albrecht 1986; Bender et al. 1985). For most counties, employment in agriculture has been a major predictor of continued population decline because agricultural technology has replaced the need for agricultural labor and economies of scale have led to increasing farm consolidation.

The conceptual linkages between population change and farm structural change are evident not only in relation to population size, however, but also in relation to each of the major demographic dimensions, that is, to changes in population size, distribution, and composition and to the demographic processes of fertility, mortality, and migration. Thus, the population size of an area is largely a reflection of the ecological carrying capacity of an environment augmented and supplemented by technological factors (Duncan 1959). This carrying capacity is most commonly described in terms of the type of economic activity or activities (industrial base) in an area. For areas in the United States that are economically dependent on agriculture, population densities are generally low. However, such densities also depend upon the productive capacity of the environment, the ability of the ecosystem to support multiple forms of sustenance bases, and the types of technological supplementation of the environmental base that have occurred. For example, in states such as Illinois, Indiana, Iowa and other midwestern states, the land is very fertile and the weather patterns are generally conducive to consistently high productivity. In areas with such high per acre productivity, farm sizes are relatively small and the rural farm population relatively extensive. At the same time, these areas support a diverse range of other economic activities that make the proportion of the population who live on farms relatively small. In the northern Great Plains of the United States, although the environment is less conducive to high productivity than in the Midwest (e.g., the weather is less consistently conducive to high levels of productivity), the farm population is smaller but forms a higher proportion of the total population because few alternative ecological sustenance bases exist. In yet other places such as the southern Great Plains, farm populations are relatively large and farm sizes relatively small, but this is because of the application of irrigation technology that has substantially increased the agricultural carrying capacity of the land (Albrecht and Murdock 1986a). In sum, the interrelationships between population size and the ecological bases of an area are complex and determined by multiple factors reflecting both agricultural and nonagricultural bases of activity.

Similarly, the distribution of population, particularly the distribution of the farm population that is distinctly tied to agriculture, varies with the ecological factors described above. The agricultural productivity of the environmental base, its supplementation by technology, and other competing uses for environmental resources affect the distribution of the population among rural areas in the United States (Albrecht and Murdock 1986b). In addition, the organizational base of agriculture may have lasting effects on rural populations. Thus, the plantation system of crop production that prevailed in the South resulted in a large rural minority population whose numbers remained large until recent decades (Hickey and Hickey 1987).

The composition of the population (that is, its age, race/ethnicity, type of household, and other characteristics) also reflects and affects the ecosystem of an area. Many rural areas, for example, have relatively old populations. This characteristic has resulted, in part, from the fact that technological advances have reduced the need for agricultural labor and made the cultivation of larger-sized farms possible. Excessive labor is most easily removed by the displacement of persons who have reached maturity but have not yet entered the labor force—that is, young post–high school adults. The massive out-migration of a majority of young adults for several decades has resulted in the older age structures evident in many rural areas.

The racial/ethnic composition of rural populations is largely reflective of initial patterns of settlement and the organizational forms of agriculture that historically prevailed in different areas. Black rural populations, for example, have been concentrated in the South due to the

154   slave system that once existed to support plantation agriculture. This system was, of course, itself a reflection of the environmental base of the area and the world economic markets for textiles.

The larger household and family sizes in rural areas can be seen as reflecting an initial ecologically compatible goal of having larger-sized families to share in the labor-intensive tasks of agricultural production. Social organizational norms resulting from such needs established cultural expectations that have persisted to create a pattern of consistently higher fertility and resulting larger family size in rural than in urban areas.

Other demographic processes such as historical mortality differences between rural and urban populations can be explained largely as a result of differentials in rural populations' access to the system of health care, the relatively high accident levels associated with agricultural production, the older age distribution of the rural population, as well as the socioeconomic conditions of the rural farm population (largely reflecting their ability to derive a living from the environment and the productivity of that environment). Migration, as alluded to earlier, has been a major factor reflecting changes in the economic and technological bases of agriculturally dependent rural ecosystems and has, in turn, altered the composition of rural populations.

Population size, distribution, and composition affect the structure of agriculture in yet additional ways. The population base of an area determines the types of services than can be provided. This influences which services are available to support agricultural and other forms of economic development. The levels and forms of public services available for farm and nonfarm residents reflect, at least in part, the population base of the ecosystem.

In sum, the population structure of agriculturally dependent rural areas reflect and affect the structural base of agriculture. The size of populations in rural areas have increased or declined with changes in agricultural technology and vary with differences in the productive base of resources in the environment. Demographic processes and composition reflect such environmental bases as well as the initial organizational base of agriculture. Population bases, in turn, provide the basis for rural service provision, and their size and distribution affects the types of services that can be provided in rural areas to support agriculture. Population change and population processes are thus processes affecting agricultural ecosystems. Therefore, an understanding of the population bases of rural areas is essential to understanding the ecological processes affecting the structure of U.S. agriculture.

DEMOGRAPHIC AND SOCIOECONOMIC CHARACTERISTICS OF RURAL POPULATIONS IN THE UNITED STATES

In this section the characteristics of the rural farm population are compared to other components of the U.S. population. The intent is to provide the reader with a better understanding of the population base that affects and is being affected by changes in the structure of agriculture in the United States.

Demographic Characteristics of Rural Populations in the United States

Table 7.1 presents an historical view of changes in the size of the farm population from 1930 to 1985. As an examination of the data in this table indicates, the farm population changed dramatically from 1930 to 1985. The farm population declined by over 25 million persons during that period, declining from nearly 25 percent of the total U.S.

Table 7.1. Change in the farm population of the United States, 1930–1985

Year	Population	Change from previous year %	Portion of U.S. poulation %
1930	30,529,000	–	24.9
1940	30,547,000	0.1	23.2
1950	23,048,000	−24.5	15.3
1960	15,635,000	−32.2	8.7
1970	9,712,000	−27.7	4.8
1980	6,051,000	−37.7	2.7
1981	5,850,000	−3.3	2.6
1982	5,682,000	−3.8	2.4
1983	5,787,000	1.8	2.5
1984	5,754,000	−0.6	2.4
1985	5,355,000	−6.9	2.2
Total change	−25,174,000	−82.5	

Source: Adapted from Kalbacher and DeAre (1986).

population in 1930 to 2.2 percent in 1985. Thus, while the U.S. population was nearly doubling (from 122 million in 1930 to 238 million in 1985), the farm population declined by over 82 percent. This decline has been both large and continuous with each decade since 1940 witnessing nearly a 25 percent decline in the farm population and with an average of nearly 500,000 persons leaving the farm each year from 1930 to 1985. During the 1980s (from 1980 to 1985) the total decline exceeded 11 percent and suggest that the rate of decline increased as a result of the farm crisis (Murdock et al. 1986). If such trends are intact from 1985 to 1990 the 1980s will have experienced a decline in the farm population exceeding 20 percent.

Tables 7.2 and 7.3 indicate that rural farm population decline has occurred despite growth in the total population and in the nonfarm component of the rural population. Thus, the rural nonfarm population has shown steady growth (from 23 million in 1930 to 53 million in 1980) and increased its share of the rural population (from 44 percent in 1930 to 91 percent in 1980). As a result, while the rural nonfarm population was 20 percent smaller than the rural farm population in 1930, by 1980 the rural nonfarm population was nearly ten times larger than the rural farm population.

The age structure of the rural farm population for 1950, 1960, 1970, and 1980 is shown in Table 7.4. An examination of these data indicates that the age structure of the rural farm population is a bipolar one. For each of the decennial years the rural farm population had a higher percentage of its population in the age groups of less-than-20 and 65-and-over than other population groups. On the other hand, the rural farm population shows the obvious effects of heavy out-migration of young adults with rural farm populations showing much smaller percentages of adults in the young and middle adult ages, particularly in the 20–34 age group. As a result of such patterns, rural farm populations tend to have high youth and old age dependency ratios (i.e., proportions of persons under 19 and over 65 compared to the number 20 to 64). Thus, as shown in Table 7.5, the youth and old age dependency ratios in rural farm populations have consistently exceeded those for urban populations, and the old age dependency ratio in the rural farm population has been higher than that for the rural nonfarm population since 1960. The rural farm population then is a population with an age composition indicative of the long-term adjustments of a population in an ecosystem that has required decreasing amounts of human labor inputs.

Table 7.2. Population and percentage of population in the United States by urban, rural, rural farm, and rural nonfarm residence, 1930–1980

Year	Total population	Population				Percentage of population			
		Urban	Rural	Rural farm	Rural nonfarm	Urban	Rural	Rural farm	Rural nonfarm
1930	122,775,046	68,954,823	53,820,223	30,157,513	23,662,710	56.2	43.8	24.5	19.3
1940	131,669,275	74,423,702	57,245,573	30,216,188	27,029,385	56.5	43.5	22.9	20.6
1950[a]	150,697,361	96,467,686	54,229,675	23,048,350	31,181,325	64.0	36.0	15.3	20.7
1960[b]	178,466,732	124,714,055	53,752,677	13,431,791	40,320,886	69.9	30.1	7.5	22.6
1970	203,212,877	149,334,020	53,878,857	10,588,534	43,290,323	73.5	26.5	5.2	21.3
1980[c]	226,545,805	167,054,638	59,491,167	5,617,903	53,873,264	73.7	26.3	2.5	23.8

Source: Data were obtained from the *U.S. Census of Population and Housing* (U.S. Department of Commerce, Bureau of the Census 1930–1980).

[a]1950 census definitions of urban-rural and rural farm and nonfarm.
[b]1960 census definitions of urban-rural and rural farm and nonfarm.
[c]1980 census definitions of urban-rural and rural farm and nonfarm.

Table 7.3. Percentage of change in population in the United States by urban, rural, rural farm, and rural nonfarm residence, 1930–1980

Period of change	Percentage of change in population				
	Total change	Urban	Rural	Rural farm	Rural nonfarm
1930–1940	7.2	7.9	6.4	0.2	14.2
1940–1950	14.5	29.6	−5.3	−23.7	15.4
1950–1960	18.4	29.3	−0.9	−41.7	29.3
1960–1970	13.9	19.7	0.2	−21.2	7.4
1970–1980	11.5	11.9	10.4	−46.9	24.4
1930–1980	84.5	142.3	10.5	−81.4	127.7

Source: U.S. Census of Population and Housing (U.S. Department of Commerce, Bureau of the Census 1930–1980).

Table 7.4. U.S. population by age groups by urban, rural, rural farm, and rural nonfarm residence: 1950–1980

Age	Urban Number	%	Rural Number	%	Rural farm Number	%	Rural nonfarm Number	%
U.S. Population: 1950								
<20	29,555,314	30.6	21,543,808	39.7	9,768,841	42.4	11,774,967	37.8
20–34	23,947,825	24.8	11,293,270	20.8	4,154,410	18.0	7,118,860	22.9
35–49	20,607,533	21.4	9,913,291	18.3	4,198,757	18.2	5,714,534	18.3
50–64	14,530,735	15.1	7,036,048	13.0	3,175,826	13.8	3,860,222	12.3
65+	7,826,279	8.1	4,443,258	8.2	1,750,516	7.6	2,692,742	8.7
Total	96,467,686	100.0	54,229,675	100.0	23,048,350	100.0	31,161,325	100.0
U.S Population: 1960								
<20	46,259,061	37.0	22,454,388	41.7	5,639,032	41.9	16,815,356	41.8
20–34	24,089,444	19.4	9,328,279	17.4	1,794,272	13.3	7,534,007	18.7
35–49	25,019,263	20.0	9,789,368	18.2	2,554,344	18.9	7,266,130	18.1
50–64	18,030,631	14.5	7,291,704	13.6	2,217,781	16.5	5,073,923	12.6
65+	11,315,656	9.1	4,858,243	9.1	1,256,037	9.4	3,601,799	8.8
Total	124,714,055	100.0	53,721,982	100.0	13,461,466	100.0	40,291,215	100.0
U.S Population: 1970								
<20	55,611,580	37.3	21,597,069	40.0	4,123,393	39.0	17,473,676	40.3
20–34	31,611,878	20.9	9,738,938	18.1	1,465,132	13.8	8,273,806	19.2
35–49	26,081,746	17.4	9,134,308	17.0	1,895,805	17.9	7,238,503	16.8
50–64	21,759,848	14.6	7,975,636	14.8	1,991,900	18.8	5,983,736	13.7
65+	14,668,968	9.8	5,432,906	10.1	1,112,304	10.5	4,320,602	10.0
Total	149,734,020	100.0	53,878,857	100.0	10,588,534	100.0	43,290,323	100.0
U.S Population: 1980								
<20	51,952,508	31.1	20,463,796	34.4	1,797,696	32.1	18,666,100	34.7
20–34	44,775,946	26.8	13,699,242	22.9	958,958	17.0	12,740,284	23.6
35–49	26,498,063	15.8	10,164,417	17.1	1,004,835	17.9	9,159,582	17.0
50–64	24,827,355	14.9	8,666,092	14.7	1,144,380	20.3	7,521,712	14.0
65+	19,000,766	11.4	6,497,617	10.9	712,034	12.7	5,785,583	10.7
Total	167,054,638	100.0	59,491,164	100.0	5,617,903	100.0	53,873,261	100.0

Table 7.5. Youth and old age dependency ratios for the United States by urban, rural, rural farm, and rural nonfarm residence, 1950–1980

	Youth dependency ratio				Old age dependency ratio			
Year	Urban	Rural	Rural farm	Rural nonfarm	Urban	Rural	Rural farm	Rural nonfarm
1950	50.0	76.3	84.7	70.5	13.2	15.7	15.2	16.1
1960	68.9	84.9	86.2	84.5	16.9	18.4	19.2	18.1
1970	70.3	80.4	77.0	81.3	18.6	20.2	20.8	20.1
1980	54.2	62.9	57.8	63.4	19.8	20.0	22.9	19.7

Source: *U.S. Census of Population and Housing* (U.S. Department of Commerce, Bureau of the Census 1950–1980).

The sex composition of the rural farm population also differs from that of other groups. Table 7.6 provides data on the population by sex in the urban, rural, rural farm, and rural nonfarm populations for 1950, 1960, 1970, and 1980. The data in this table clearly show rural farm populations to have a disproportionate number of males. For each of the four decades the rural farm population was over 51 percent male, compared to the urban population that was roughly 48 percent male. The rural nonfarm population has shown a pattern of gradual change resembling the rural farm population in terms of its male percentage in 1950 and 1960 but developing patterns very similar to the urban population by 1970. The rural farm population is thus a population that is different from urban and rural nonfarm populations in both its sex and its age composition.

An examination of the data in Table 7.7 indicates that the rural farm population also differs from other population groups in terms of its racial and ethnic composition. As a result of a rapid decline in its nonwhite population base, the rural farm population had only 111,000 blacks in 1980. From 1950 to 1980 the black population on farms declined by over 3 million persons, a decline of more than 96 percent. Whereas the rural farm population was more than 13 percent black in 1950, by 1980 less than 2 percent of its population was black. In 1950 the percentage of the rural farm population that was black exceeded that in the urban or rural nonfarm populations, but by 1980 the proportion of the rural farm population that was black was only one-sixth of the proportion of the urban population that was black and one-third of the proportion of the rural nonfarm population that was black. The rural farm population has become an increasingly homogeneous population in terms of its racial and ethnic composition.

Rural farm populations have traditionally had high rates of fertility.

Table 7.6. Population, percentage of population, and percentage change in population by sex by urban, rural, rural farm, and rural nonfarm residence for the United States, 1950–1980

Time period	Male				Female			
	Urban	Rural	Rural farm	Rural nonfarm	Urban	Rural	Rural farm	Rural nonfarm
1950	46,891,782	27,941,457	12,078,610	15,862,847	49,575,904	26,288,218	10,969,740	15,318,478
1960	60,422,911	27,414,129	6,978,998	20,435,131	64,291,144	26,338,552	6,482,468	19,856,084
1970	71,945,716	26,944,799	5,403,796	21,541,003	77,388,304	26,934,058	5,184,738	21,749,320
1980	80,292,291	29,760,870	2,918,219	26,842,651	86,758,701	29,733,943	2,699,684	27,034,259
Percentage 1950	48.6	51.5	52.4	50.9	51.4	48.5	47.6	49.1
Percentage 1960	48.4	51.0	52.0	50.7	51.6	49.0	48.0	49.3
Percentage 1970	48.2	50.0	51.0	49.8	51.8	50.0	49.0	50.2
Percentage 1980	48.1	50.0	51.9	49.8	51.9	50.0	48.1	50.2
Change 1950–1960	28.9	−1.9	−42.2	28.8	29.7	0.2	−40.9	29.6
Change 1960–1970	19.1	−1.7	−22.6	5.4	20.4	2.3	−20.0	9.5
Change 1970–1980	11.6	10.5	−29.1	24.6	12.1	10.4	−47.9	24.3
Change 1950–1980	71.2	6.5	−75.8	69.2	75.0	13.1	−75.4	76.5

Source: U.S. Census of Population and Housing (U.S. Department of Commerce, Bureau of the Census 1950–1980).

Table 7.7. Population, percentage of population, and percentage change in population by race/ethnicity by urban, rural, rural farm, and rural nonfarm residence for the United States, 1950–1980

Time period	Urban			Rural			Rural farm			Rural nonfarm		
	White	Black	Other	White	Black	Other	White	Black	Other	White	Black	Other
1950	86,756,435	9,392,608	318,643	48,185,593	5,649,678	394,404	19,715,254	3,158,301	174,795	28,470,339	2,491,377	219,609
1960	110,216,317	13,785,782	711,956	48,244,382	5,051,285	457,014	11,873,087	1,481,971	106,408	36,371,295	3,569,314	350,606
1970	129,069,749	18,338,421	1,925,850	49,037,441	4,211,394	630,022	9,816,142	674,420	97,972	39,221,299	3,526,974	532,050
1980	134,948,026	22,583,845	9,622,767	54,086,986	3,898,504	1,505,677	5,432,353	111,107	74,443	48,654,633	3,787,397	1,431,234
Percentage 1950	89.9	9.8	0.3	88.9	10.4	0.7	85.5	13.7	0.8	91.3	8.0	0.7
Percentage 1960	88.4	11.1	0.5	89.8	9.4	0.8	88.4	11.0	0.6	90.2	8.9	0.9
Percentage 1970	86.4	12.3	1.3	91.0	7.8	1.2	92.7	6.4	0.9	90.6	8.2	1.2
Percentage 1980	80.8	13.5	5.7	90.0	6.6	2.5	96.7	2.0	1.3	90.3	7.0	2.7
Change 1950–1960	27.0	46.8	123.4	0.1	−10.6	15.9	−39.8	−53.1	−39.1	27.8	43.3	59.7
Change 1960–1970	17.1	33.0	170.5	1.6	−16.6	37.9	−17.3	−54.5	−7.9	7.8	−0.9	51.8
Change 1970–1980	4.6	23.2	400.0	10.3	−7.4	138.9	−44.7	−83.5	−24.0	24.1	7.1	169.0
Change 1950–1980	55.5	140.4	2919.9	12.2	−31.0	281.8	−72.4	−96.5	−57.4	70.9	52.0	551.7

Source: U.S. Census of Population and Housing (U.S. Department of Commerce, Bureau of the Census 1950–1980).

As an examination of the data in Table 7.8 suggests, however, rural farm **161** fertility, though still higher than that in other populations, has decreased over the past decades. Whereas the number of children ever born in rural farm populations exceeded that in urban populations by more than 70 percent in 1950, by 1980 the ratio for rural farm populations was roughly 30 percent higher than that in the urban population. In addition, although rural farm fertility was nearly 20 percent higher than that of the rural nonfarm population in 1950, by 1980 the two differed by less than 5 percent.

Mortality in rural areas has consistently been higher than that in urban areas, and numerous scholars have noted the persistence of this differential (Roemer 1976; Navarro 1976; Wright and Lick 1986). Unfortunately, data are not available on mortality patterns for rural farm and rural nonfarm populations. Table 7.9, however, provides data that show crude death rates for populations in counties with different-sized populations. These data taken from a recent analysis by Clifford et al. (1986) suggest that mortality remains substantially higher (over 16 percent higher in 1980) in rural than in urban areas. These differences are apparently largely due to differences in the population composition of rural and urban populations. As shown in Table 7.10, when rates in rural areas are standardized by age, race, and sex, rural mortality is little different from urban mortality and, in fact, may be lower for white females in rural counties than for nonwhite females and other groups. As with several other demographic characteristics discussed in this chapter, mortality in rural areas appears to be increasingly similar to that in urban areas.

Perhaps no recent pattern of population change in rural areas has received greater attention than the rural population turnaround. The population turnaround is the pattern of net in-migration to nonmetropolitan areas from metropolitan areas that occurred in the 1970s after decades of rural population decline involving net losses of migrants from rural areas to urban areas (Brown and Beale 1981). As was the case with mortality, migration data are not available separately for rural farm and nonfarm populations. The data in Table 7.11 clearly show both the historical patterns of migration between nonmetropolitan-metropolitan areas, the dramatic change in such patterns during the 1970s, and the recent return to historical patterns. Thus, although nonmetropolitan areas gained more than 1.3 million persons due to out-migration from metropolitan areas during the period from 1975 to 1980, since 1982–83

Table 7.8. Number of children ever born and children ever born per 1,000 women by age of women by urban, rural, rural farm, and rural nonfarm residence for the United States, 1950–1980

Children born per 1,000 women

		Urban				Rural			
			Age groups				Age groups		
Year		Total	15–24	25–34	35–44	Total	15–24	25–34	35–44
1950	Number of children ever born	28,133,925	2,830,530	12,087,648	13,215,747	19,654,657	2,120,220	8,031,130	9,503,307
	Ratio	1,215	386	1,432	1,792	1,769	537	2,123	2,813
1960	Number of children ever born	42,588,315	4,414,740	17,785,746	20,387,829	20,441,047	2,121,441	8,262,205	10,057,401
	Ratio	1,637	514	2,104	2,269	2,029	602	2,585	3,001
1970	Number of children ever born	48,871,807	4,588,275	19,260,633	25,022,899	19,728,773	1,834,255	7,847,648	10,046,870
	Ratio	1,533	337	2,035	2,840	1,880	434	2,442	3,291
1980	Number of children ever born	48,881,650	4,836,249	19,714,387	24,331,014	19,956,014	1,834,118	7,962,076	10,159,820
	Ratio	1,228	300	1,391	2,561	1,526	372	1,740	2,849

		Rural farm				Rural nonfarm			
			Age groups				Age groups		
Year		Total	15–24	25–34	35–44	Total	15–24	25–34	35–44
1950	Number of children ever born	8,687,448	801,120	3,279,693	4,606,635	10,966,209	1,319,100	4,750,437	4,896,672
	Ratio	2,074	572	2,378	3,269	1,733	566	2,337	2,494
1960	Number of children ever born	4,898,603	372,436	1,738,066	2,788,101	15,542,444	1,749,005	6,524,139	7,269,300
	Ratio	2,133	443	2,798	3,337	1,999	652	2,534	2,889
1970	Number of children ever born	3,657,373	237,149	1,272,379	2,147,845	16,071,400	1,597,106	6,575,269	7,899,025
	Ratio	1,946	309	2,567	3,479	1,865	461	2,419	3,244
1980	Number of children ever born	1,658,759	98,606	557,464	1,002,689	18,297,255	1,735,512	7,404,612	9,157,131
	Ratio	1,595	237	1,911	3,021	1,520	384	1,728	2,832

Source: U.S. Census of Population and Housing (U.S. Department of Commerce, Bureau of the Census 1950–1980).

Table 7.9. Crude death rates by residence for the continental United States, 1970, 1975, and 1980

Year	Residence[a] Most urban counties							Most rural counties		Rural/urban difference (percentage)[b]
	1	2	3	4	5	6	7	8	9	
1970	9.11	8.71	8.77	9.88	11.11	10.40	9.85	11.42	11.68	+23.9
1975	8.63	8.44	8.30	9.19	10.34	9.65	9.18	10.70	10.87	+21.2
1980	8.49	8.39	8.08	8.86	9.82	9.12	8.76	10.09	10.20	+16.4

Source: Adapted from Clifford et al. (1986).

Note: Crude death rates are 3-year averages centered on 1970 and 1975; the 1980 rates are 2-year averages for 1979 and 1980.

[a]The residence categories are: (1) core or fringe metropolitan counties with 1 million or more population, (2) metropolitan counties with 500,000 to 999,999 population, (3) metropolitan counties with 50,000 to 499,999 population, (4) nonmetropolitan, adjacent counties with the largest urban place 10,000+, (5) nonmetropolitan, adjacent counties with the largest place 2,500 to 9,999, (6) nonmetropolitan, adjacent counties with the largest place less than 2,500, (7) nonmetropolitan, nonadjacent counties with the largest place 10,000+, (8) nonmetropolitan, nonadjacent counties with the largest place 2,500 to 9,999, (9) nonmetropolitan, nonadjacent counties with the largest place less than 2,500.

[b]The rural/urban percentage difference is calculated by dividing the average difference between the 3 most rural counties (categories 7–9) and the 3 metropolitan counties (categories 1–3) by the average of the metropolitan counties.

163

Table 7.10. Age-adjusted death rates by sex, race, and residence for the continental United States, 1970, 1975, and 1980

Year and race group	Residence[a]									Rural/urban difference (percentage)[b]	White/ nonwhite difference (percentage)[c]
	Most urban counties						Most rural counties				
	1	2	3	4	5	6	7	8	9		
Males											
1970: White	11.89	11.85	11.77	12.01	12.02	11.87	12.19	12.15	11.78	1.7	22.6
1970: Nonwhite	14.81	13.82	15.00	14.85	14.75	13.50	15.68	15.51	13.92	3.4	
1975: White	10.77	10.90	10.82	10.96	11.07	10.97	11.18	11.33	10.89	2.8	22.0
1975: Nonwhite	13.11	12.88	13.35	13.52	13.48	12.82	14.17	14.24	13.11	8.3	
1980: White	10.02	10.06	9.86	9.99	10.10	10.04	10.20	10.25	9.91	1.4	25.7
1980: Nonwhite	12.24	12.28	12.60	12.68	12.84	12.40	13.25	13.20	12.17	4.0	
Females											
1970: White	7.14	6.93	6.87	7.08	6.90	6.87	6.97	6.97	6.84	-0.8	38.0
1970: Nonwhite	9.40	8.96	9.95	9.80	9.41	8.92	10.38	10.14	9.35	5.4	
1975: White	6.33	6.21	6.13	6.17	6.13	6.13	6.19	6.17	6.04	-1.5	33.1
1975: Nonwhite	7.90	8.03	8.32	8.57	8.17	7.87	8.74	8.52	7.77	3.2	
1980: White	5.88	5.78	5.66	5.70	5.58	5.56	5.64	5.59	5.45	-3.7	31.7
1980: Nonwhite	7.30	7.35	7.60	7.43	7.48	7.23	7.73	7.69	7.13	1.4	

Source: Adapted from Clifford et al. (1986).

Note: Adjusted using the 1970 U.S. population as the standard.

[a] See Table 7.9 for detailed description of residence categories.

[b] The rural/urban percentage difference is calculated by dividing the average difference between the 3 most rural counties (categories 7–9) and the 3 metropolitan counties (categories 1–3) by the average age-adjusted rate of the metropolitan counties.

[c] The white/nonwhite percentage difference is merely the average difference between the 2 groups expressed as a percentage of the white average for all residence categories.

Table 7.11.   Migration in metropolitan and nonmetropolitan counties, 1965–1984 (numbers in thousands)

County group/ period	Inmigrants	Outmigrants	Net migrants
Metropolitan counties			
1965–1970	5,457	5,809	−352
1970–1975	5,127	6,721	−1,594
1975–1980	5,993	7,337	−1,344
1980–1981	2,156	2,350	−194
1981–1982	2,217	2,366	−149
1982–1983	2,088	2,066	22
1983–1984	2,609	2,258	351
Nonmetropolitan counties			
1965–1970	5,809	5,457	352
1970–1975	6,721	5,127	1,594
1975–1980	7,337	5,993	1,344
1980–1981	2,350	2,156	194
1981–1982	2,366	2,217	149
1982–1983	2,066	2,088	−22
1983–1984	2,258	2,609	−351

Source: U.S. Department of Commerce, Bureau of the Census (1981; 1983; 1984b; 1986).

the historical pattern of net out-migration from nonmetropolitan areas to metropolitan areas is evident. It appears that the migration turn-around may have been a relatively short-lived phenomenon (Richter 1985). In fact, data for 1980 to 1985 show metropolitan areas had a population increase of 5.9 percent while nonmetropolitan areas increased by only 3.7 percent (Engels 1986). In addition, although no data are available for rural farm populations, analyses of patterns in counties with large percentages of their labor forces employed in agriculture (Richter 1985; Bender et al. 1985) suggest that areas dominated by agriculture never shared in the turnaround patterns of net migration. These authors suggest that the turnaround was largely a rural nonfarm phenomenon. In sum, then, it appears that the historical Table 7.11 pattern of net out-migration from rural farming populations to urban populations is still occurring.

Taken together, Tables 7.1 through 7.11 provide an overview of the demographic characteristics of the rural farm population compared to other residence groups. An evaluation of the data in these tables suggests that the rural farm population has declined to roughly one-sixth of its 1930 size, is increasingly concentrated in younger and older age groups, is increasingly racially and ethnically homogeneous, is disproportionately male, retains a level of fertility that exceeds that in other popula-

166 tions, has mortality patterns that are reflective of its aged population base, and has shown a historical pattern of continued net out-migration. It is a population that reflects its unique patterns of ecological adaptation. Its young adult age groups have been depleted due to the heavy out-migration of young adults who are no longer needed to provide the agricultural labor made superfluous by agricultural technology. Its non-white population has been depleted as a result of being composed largely of nonowners of land during a period in which expansion in land ownership was the key to survival. In sum, then, the rural farm population has been required to make dramatic adaptations to the rapidly changing circumstances in agriculture-based ecosystems.

Socioeconomic Characteristics of Rural Populations in the United States

In this section the socioeconomic characteristics of the rural farm population are examined in comparison to the urban, rural, and rural nonfarm population components. The characteristics include employment by industry, occupation, and education. This section describes the changing patterns of sustenance activities in rural farm populations and the implications of these patterns for the social and economic conditions of rural farm populations.

Tables 7.12 and 7.13 show employment by industry in rural farm and other population components for 1950 and 1980. The results in these tables point to a clear evolution in the sustenance base of rural farm populations. Whereas over 70 percent of the labor force in rural farm populations in 1950 was engaged in agriculture, forestry, and fishing, by 1980 less than one-half of the labor force living on farms was employed in this area. On the other hand, by 1980, nearly 25 percent of the rural farm population was employed in services (including professional services) and nearly 12 percent was engaged in manufacturing. Urban populations show even a more rapid transition to service-based economies and reductions in manufacturing employment. Rural nonfarm populations display patterns similar to those in urban populations. Rural nonfarm populations experienced a shift towards manufacturing-based economies during the 1950s and 1960s, followed by a reduction in manufacturing employment after 1970 and a rapid increase in employment in service industries. It is important to note, however, that the percentage of the labor force engaged in manufacturing in rural nonfarm areas in

Labor force

Industry	Number	% of total	Urban %	Rural %	Rural farm %	Rural nonfarm %
Agriculture, forestry, fisheries	7,005,403	11.7	1.1	35.4	70.4	8.6
Mining	929,152	1.5	0.8	3.2	1.3	4.6
Construction	3,439,924	5.7	5.6	6.1	3.1	8.4
Manufacturing	14,575,692	24.2	27.2	17.6	9.3	24.0
Transportation, communication, and utilities	4,368,302	7.3	8.4	4.8	2.0	7.0
Wholesale trade	1,975,817	3.3	4.0	1.8	0.8	2.5
Retail trade	8,571,752	14.3	16.3	9.7	3.5	14.4
Finance, insurance, and real estate	1,916,220	3.2	4.1	1.2	0.5	1.8
Services	5,453,937	9.1	10.3	6.3	2.6	9.1
Professional services	9,349,096	15.6	17.4	11.3	5.3	15.8
Public administration	2,488,778	4.1	4.8	2.6	1.2	3.8
Total	60,074,073	100.0	41,533,255	18,540,818	8,040,796	10,500,022

Source: U.S. Census of Population and Housing (U.S. Department of Commerce, Bureau of the Census 1950).

Table 7.13. Labor force by industry and urban, rural, rural farm, and rural nonfarm residence for the United States, 1980

			Labor force			
Industry	Number	% of total	Urban %	Rural %	Rural farm %	Rural nonfarm %
Agriculture, forestry, fisheries	2,913,589	2.5	0.9	7.6	41.1	3.8
Mining	1,028,178	0.9	0.6	1.7	0.8	1.8
Construction	5,739,598	4.9	4.4	6.5	4.0	6.8
Manufacturing	21,914,754	18.7	17.7	21.7	11.9	22.8
Transportation, communication, and utilities	7,087,455	6.0	6.1	5.7	3.5	6.0
Wholesale trade	4,217,232	3.6	3.7	3.2	2.7	3.3
Retail trade	15,716,694	13.4	13.8	12.0	6.9	12.6
Finance, insurance, and real estate	5,898,059	5.0	5.6	3.3	2.2	3.4
Services	27,976,330	23.7	25.0	20.0	13.7	20.7
Professional services	19,811,819	16.9	17.6	14.6	10.8	15.0
Public administration	5,147,466	4.4	4.6	3.7	2.4	3.8
Total	117,451,174	100.0	89,497,838	27,953,336	2,772,134	25,181,202

Source: U.S. Census of Population and Housing (U.S. Department of Commerce, Bureau of the Census 1980).

168   1980 exceeded that in urban areas and that manufacturing was the most significant employer in rural nonfarm areas.

Finally, the changing size of the labor force among the different population components is also important to note. Whereas the size of the rural farm labor force was declining from more than 8 million in 1950 to 2.7 million by 1980, the labor force in urban areas was increasing from 41.5 million to 89.5 million and that in rural nonfarm areas from 10.5 million to 25.1 million. In addition, although the rural farm labor force declined by over 64 percent in the 30 years from 1950 to 1980, this decline was not sufficient to maintain the dominance of agriculture in the rural farm economy. The number of rural farm residents employed in agriculture declined by 80 percent (from 5.7 million in 1950 to 1.1 million in 1980). Between 1970 and 1980, the number of persons engaged in agriculture in rural farm areas declined from 1.5 million to 1.1 million, a decline of nearly 24 percent, but total employment in the rural farm population decreased by even more — 31 percent. The data on industry in Tables 7.12 and 7.13 thus suggest that the sustenance base of agriculture has not been able to support its human resource base. As a result, even among rural farm populations there has been a clear evolution in the structure of sustenance bases away from extractive and towards service-based industrial economies.

Tables 7.14 and 7.15 display data on occupational patterns in rural farm and other populations for 1950 and 1980. In general, these data verify the patterns shown for the industrial data. Whereas over 70 percent of the rural farm labor force in 1950 was employed as farm operators/managers or farm workers, by 1980 the proportion had decreased to 45 percent. In this group farm laborers showed the most dramatic decline, from more than 20 percent (in 1950) to only 10 percent of the rural farm labor force by 1980. It is equally important to note that the rural farm and rural nonfarm labor forces have increasingly come to be composed of persons employed in operator, precision production, and service occupations while urban populations have increasingly become involved in managerial and professional as well as service occupations. It is evident, then, that rural farm populations are increasingly employed in nonagricultural industries as well as nonagricultural occupations.

Table 7.16 presents data on the educational characteristics of rural farm populations. These data suggest that the loss of farm populations and of persons employed in agriculture (as clearly shown in the tables presented above) may have assisted rural farm populations in achieving

Table 7.14. Labor force by occupation and urban, rural, rural farm, and rural nonfarm residence for the United States, 1950

	Labor force					
Occupation group	Number	% of total	Urban %	Rural %	Rural farm %	Rural nonfarm %
Managerial occupations	5,076,848	8.8	10.0	6.1	2.0	9.4
Professional/specialty occupations	4,988,963	8.7	10.1	5.4	2.5	7.7
Technical and support occupations	11,708,022	20.3	21.5	17.8	8.9	24.4
Sales occupations	4,044,251	7.0	8.3	4.2	1.6	6.1
Administrative occupations	7,071,283	12.3	15.4	5.4	2.4	7.7
Service occupations	4,511,677	7.8	9.3	4.5	1.5	6.8
Private household occupations	1,488,388	2.6	2.8	2.0	1.2	2.7
Farm operators and managers	4,322,809	7.5	0.3	23.2	49.8	2.4
Farm workers and laborers	2,514,843	4.4	0.6	12.6	21.3	5.9
Operators, fabricators, and laborers	3,765,394	6.5	6.4	7.1	3.8	9.8
Precision production craft and repair	8,162,499	14.1	15.3	11.7	5.0	17.1
Total	57,654,977	100.0	39,657,765	17,997,212	7,930,868	10,066,344

Source: U.S. Census of Population and Housing (U.S. Department of Commerce, Bureau of the Census 1950).

Table 7.15. Labor force by occupation and urban, rural, rural farm, and rural nonfarm residence for the United States, 1980

	Labor force					
Occupation group	Number	% of total	Urban %	Rural %	Rural farm %	Rural nonfarm %
Managerial occupations	10,133,551	11.0	11.9	8.1	4.8	8.5
Professional/specialty occupations	12,018,097	13.0	14.1	9.7	6.8	10.1
Technical and support occupations	2,981,951	3.2	3.5	4.8	1.3	5.4
Sales occupations	9,760,157	10.6	11.3	8.3	5.0	8.9
Administrative occupations	16,851,398	18.3	19.9	13.1	9.1	13.2
Service occupations	12,040,073	13.1	13.5	11.4	6.7	11.9
Private household occupations	589,352	0.6	0.6	0.6	0.4	0.6
Farm operators and managers	1,298,670	1.4	0.2	5.0	35.9	1.5
Farm workers and laborers	1,334,123	1.5	0.9	3.2	10.1	2.5
Operators, fabricators, and laborers	12,495,844	13.6	11.5	19.6	11.1	20.3
Precision production craft and repair	12,594,175	13.7	12.6	16.2	8.8	17.1
Total	92,097,391	100.0	69,351,204	22,746,187	2,395,268	20,350,919

Source: U.S. Census of Population and Housing (U.S. Department of Commerce, Bureau of the Census 1980).

Table 7.16. Median school years completed for persons 25 years old and older for the United States by urban, rural, rural farm, and rural nonfarm residence, 1950–1980

| | Median school years completed | | | |
Year	Urban	Rural	Rural farm	Rural nonfarm
1950	10.2	8.6	8.8	8.4
1960	11.1	9.2	8.8	9.5
1970	12.2	11.0	10.7	11.2
1980	12.5	12.3	12.3	12.3

Source: *U.S. Census of Population and Housing* (U.S. Department of Commerce, Bureau of the Census 1950–1980).

greater equity with nonfarm populations for those who have remained behind in rural farm populations. Whereas the rural farm population lagged behind the urban population by 1.4 years in terms of median years of education in 1950, by 1980 the difference had been reduced to 0.2 years. Recent decades have thus seen significant progress in the educational status of the rural farm population.

The data in Tables 7.12–7.16 provide additional evidence concerning the adaptation of the rural farm population to the changing farm ecosystem. An examination of the data in these tables indicates that rural farm populations have adapted to reduced needs for agricultural labor both by dramatically reducing the size of their work forces and the proportion of their work forces engaged in agriculture and by expanding into nonagricultural forms of employment. Clearly, the rural farm population has made progress in closing the educational disparities that have traditionally existed between farm and urban populations. Thus the adaptation of the rural farm population has been both substantial in magnitude and successful in altering the socioeconomic conditions of this population.

REGIONAL AND STATE VARIATION IN THE DEMOGRAPHIC AND SOCIOECONOMIC CHARACTERISTICS OF RURAL FARM POPULATIONS IN THE UNITED STATES

As noted in Chapter 4, the agricultural environment in the United States is diverse with extreme variation in climate, soil type and quality, and numerous other factors. As a result, one can expect that nearly all aspects of the rural ecosystem will show variation from one region of the nation to another. In this section we examine some of the variation in rural farm populations compared to other population components for different regions and states. Because the diversity is so extensive, even a regional and state analysis cannot adequately describe it. However, a more detailed analysis is not possible here, and we believe the analysis is sufficient to display the variability in the U.S. farm population. In the section that follows, emphasis is placed on regional differences with variation in the total rural farm and rural nonfarm populations being shown for each of the states.

Demographic Characteristics of Rural Farm Populations in Different Regions of the United States

Table 7.17 provides data showing change in the size of the farm population by region from 1930 to 1985. As noted above, the U.S. farm population declined by over 25 million persons between 1930 and 1985, a reduction of over 82 percent. Regional variations in decline were extensive, however. The northeastern United States lost 1.9 million persons

Table 7.17. Regional distribution of the U.S. farm population, 1930–1985 (numbers in thousands)

| Year | U.S. farm population | | | |
	Northeast	North central	South	West
	Current farm definition			
1985	313	2,602	1,718	723
1984	322	2,516	2,052	864
1983	358	2,548	2,035	846
1982	419	2,512	1,964	732
1981	355	2,688	2,029	778
1980[a]	443	2,730	2,162	716
	Previous farm definition			
1983	467	2,955	2,576	1,030
1982	527	2,907	2,517	930
1981	488	3,050	2,563	913
1980[a]	487	3,252	2,629	873
1970	699	4,305	3,754	954
1960	1,119	5,836	7,160	1,520
1950	1,791	7,433	11,896	1,929
1940	2,411	9,349	16,400	2,387
1930	2,287	9,583	16,364	2,295
Percentage change 1930–1985	−86.3	−72.8	−89.5	−68.5

Source: Table 1 in U.S. Department of Commerce, Bureau of the Census (1985).
[a]The 1980 estimates are based on the population controls from the 1970 census and thus are not directly comparable to the estimates for 1981 and later years.

representing an 86.3 percent decline and 7.9 percent of the total decline for the United States. The north central region declined by 6.9 million persons, a regional decline of more than 72 percent representing more than 27 percent of the total national decline of 25 million. The South lost 14.6 million rural farm residents from 1930 to 1985, which represented more than 89.5 percent of its 1930 farm population and more than 58 percent of the total number of persons lost from farm populations in the United States from 1930 to 1985. The West lost 1.5 million persons during this period, representing a 68 percent decline on its 1930 rural farm population base and 6.2 percent of the national decline in the rural farm population from 1930 to 1985. Although the South had the largest farm population of any region in the United States in 1930, with more than 53 percent of the total rural farm population in the United States, by 1985 it had only 32 percent of the rural farm population and its rural farm population was one-third smaller than that in the north central region. By 1985 the north central region had a farm population of 2.6 million, the South's farm population was 1.7 million, the West's, 723,000, and the Northeast's, 313,000. The size of the rural farm populations in the different regions in 1985 thus appears to largely reflect the differential carrying capacities of the regions.

An examination of the data in Tables 7.18 and 7.19 further reveals that such changes resulted in all regions in the nation having less than 5 percent of their populations living on farms by 1980. By comparison, all regions had at least 25 percent of their population living on farms in 1930. Overall, then, an examination of the data on rural farm population change suggests that the southern region has shown the most dramatic adaptations to changes in farm structure over the past fifty years, but all regions have displayed patterns that show that extensive adaptations have occurred, resulting in the loss of millions of farm residents.

The age and sex composition of the rural farm population for each of the regions in 1980 is shown in Tables 7.20–7.22. An analysis of these data show that although the rate of decline in the size of rural populations has varied from one region to another (see Table 7.17), the age and sex characteristics of the rural farm populations in these regions are quite similar. Thus, in 1980 all of the regions, except the Northeast, had a higher proportion of aged persons in rural areas than in urban areas, and all areas with the exception of the South had a higher proportion of youth in their rural and rural farm populations than in their urban populations (Tables 7.20 and 7.21). These exceptions (in the percentage

Table 7.18. Total population of the United States by region and percentage in urban, rural, rural farm, and rural nonfarm residence, 1950–1980

Year	U.S. total	Northeast total	Urban %	Rural %	Rural farm %	Rural nonfarm %	North central total	Urban %	Rural %	Rural farm %	Rural nonfarm %
1950	150,697,361	39,477,986	79.5	20.5	4.5	16.0	44,460,762	64.1	35.9	16.7	19.2
1960	179,325,675	44,681,702	80.2	19.8	2.0	17.8	51,623,773	68.7	31.3	10.4	20.9
1970	203,212,877	49,044,420	80.4	19.6	2.0	17.6	56,566,372	71.5	28.5	8.1	20.4
1980	226,545,805	49,135,283	79.2	20.8	0.7	20.1	58,865,670	70.5	29.5	4.9	24.6

Year	South total	Urban %	Rural %	Rural farm %	Rural nonfarm %	West total	Urban %	Rural %	Rural farm %	Rural nonfarm %
1950	47,197,088	48.6	51.4	25.2	26.2	19,561,525	69.8	30.2	10.0	20.2
1960	54,963,474	58.5	41.5	10.8	30.7	28,056,726	77.7	22.3	4.4	17.9
1970	62,793,311	64.6	35.4	6.4	29.0	34,808,774	82.9	17.1	2.9	14.2
1980	75,372,362	66.9	33.1	2.4	30.7	43,172,490	83.9	16.1	1.4	14.7

Source: *U.S. Census of Population and Housing* (U.S. Department of Commerce, Bureau of the Census 1950–1980).

Table 7.19. Percentage change in U.S. population by region and urban, rural, rural farm, and rural nonfarm residence for 1950–1960, 1960–1970, 1970–1980, and 1950–1980

Population Change Percentage

Time period	U.S. total	Northeast total	Urban	Rural	Rural farm	Rural nonfarm	North central total	Urban	Rural	Rural farm	Rural nonfarm
1950–1960	18.9	13.1	14.2	9.0	−49.0	25.5	16.1	24.5	1.0	−27.4	25.8
1960–1970	13.3	9.7	10.0	8.5	8.4	8.5	9.5	14.0	−0.2	−14.7	7.0
1970–1980	11.4	0.1	−1.3	6.5	−63.9	14.7	4.0	2.5	7.7	−37.4	25.8
1950–1980	50.3	24.4	24.0	26.1	−80.0	56.3	32.3	45.7	8.6	−61.2	69.4

Population Change Percentage

Time period	South total	Urban	Rural	Rural farm	Rural nonfarm	West total	Urban	Rural	Rural farm	Rural nonfarm
1950–1960	16.4	40.1	−5.9	−50.1	36.6	43.4	59.6	5.9	−35.5	26.0
1960–1970	14.2	26.0	−2.4	−32.6	8.1	24.0	32.4	−5.1	−18.9	−1.7
1970–1980	20.0	24.3	12.2	−55.4	2.7	24.0	25.4	17.0	−39.9	28.6
1950–1980	59.6	119.6	2.9	−85.0	87.7	120.7	165.3	17.0	−68.6	59.4

Source: U.S. Census of Population and Housing (U.S. Department of Commerce, Bureau of the Census 1950–1980).

174

Table 7.20. Age distribution of the population in the United States by region and urban, rural, rural farm, and rural nonfarm residence, 1980

Northeast

Age	Number	% of total	Urban %	Rural %	Rural farm %	Rural nonfarm %
<20	14,897,093	30.3	29.6	33.4	35.0	33.3
20–34	12,056,763	24.6	24.8	23.4	18.9	23.5
35–49	8,076,896	16.5	16.1	17.7	17.9	17.6
50–64	8,042,300	16.2	16.8	14.9	18.5	14.9
65+	6,062,231	12.4	12.7	10.6	9.7	10.7
Total	49,135,283	100.0	38,908,074	10,227,209	357,295	9,869,914

North central

Age	Number	% of total	Urban %	Rural %	Rural farm %	Rural nonfarm %
<20	19,215,037	32.6	31.8	34.8	33.9	35.0
20–34	15,007,627	25.5	26.7	22.3	17.4	23.3
35–49	9,300,150	15.7	15.4	16.9	17.6	16.8
50–64	8,657,005	14.7	14.8	14.6	19.5	13.5
65+	6,685,851	11.5	11.3	11.4	11.6	11.4
Total	58,865,670	100.0	41,518,921	17,346,749	2,878,280	14,468,469

South

Age	Number	% of total	Urban %	Rural %	Rural farm %	Rural nonfarm %
<20	24,567,325	32.6	31.7	34.5	27.8	34.9
20–34	19,368,346	25.6	26.9	23.2	15.8	23.8
35–49	12,178,587	16.2	15.8	16.9	18.1	16.8
50–64	10,788,634	14.3	14.2	14.3	22.4	13.8
65+	8,469,470	11.3	11.4	11.1	15.9	10.7
Total	75,372,362	100.0	50,413,049	24,959,313	1,776,962	23,182,351

West

Age	Number	% of total	Urban %	Rural %	Rural farm %	Rural nonfarm %
<20	13,736,849	31.9	31.2	34.8	33.5	35.0
20–34	12,042,452	27.9	28.6	24.0	18.2	24.5
35–49	7,106,847	16.4	16.3	17.3	18.6	17.1
50–64	6,005,508	13.9	13.9	14.4	19.5	14.0
65+	4,280,834	9.9	10.0	9.5	10.2	9.4
Total	43,172,490	100.0	36,214,594	6,957,896	605,366	6,352,530

Source: U.S. Census of Population and Housing (U.S. Department of Commerce, Bureau of the Census 1980).

Table 7.21. Youth and old age dependency ratios for the U.S. population by region and urban, rural, rural farm, and rural nonfarm residence, 1980

	Youth dependency ratio				Old age dependency ratio			
Region	Urban	Rural	Rural farm	Rural nonfarm	Urban	Rural	Rural farm	Rural nonfarm
Northeast	51.2	59.6	63.5	59.4	22.2	18.9	17.7	19.0
North central	55.8	64.7	62.1	65.2	19.9	21.2	21.3	21.2
South	55.6	63.2	49.6	64.3	19.8	20.3	28.1	27.6
West	53.2	62.6	59.2	62.9	17.0	17.2	18.1	26.2

Source: U.S. Census of Population and Housing (U.S. Department of Commerce, Bureau of the Census 1980).

of elderly in the Northeast and the percentage of persons under twenty in the South) were the result of the concentration of the elderly in large cities in the Northeast and the concentration of minority youth in large cities in the South. If such effects are removed (the results of this analysis are not shown here), the age patterns of the rural farm, rural nonfarm, and urban population groups are similar. In like manner, the sex composition of the populations in the four regions is also quite similar with the majority of residents in rural farm populations in all regions (see Table 7.22) being male, while females predominate in the urban populations of each region.

The racial/ethnic composition of the population of the four regions remains somewhat more diverse (Table 7.23), with the percentage of blacks (14.5 percent) remaining higher in rural nonfarm areas in the South than in any of the other regions. At the same time, however, the number of nonwhites in the farm population is now so small even in the South that the rural farm population can be said to be largely a racially homogeneous population.

Information on the patterns of fertility in rural farm and other populations in different regions of the nation is shown in Table 7.24.

Table 7.22. Percentage of population by sex, region, and urban, rural, rural farm, and rural nonfarm residence in the United States, 1980

	Urban		Rural		Rural farm		Rural nonfarm	
Region	Male %	Female %	Male %	Female %	Male %	Female %	Male %	Female %
Northeast	47.3	52.7	49.7	50.3	52.4	47.6	49.6	50.4
North central	47.9	52.1	50.2	49.8	52.3	47.7	49.8	50.2
South	48.0	52.0	50.4	49.6	51.1	48.9	49.5	50.5
West	49.2	50.8	51.3	48.7	52.3	47.7	51.2	48.8

Source: U.S. Census of Population and Housing (U.S. Department of Commerce, Bureau of the Census 1980).

Table 7.23. U.S. population by race, region, and urban, rural, rural farm, and rural nonfarm residence, 1980

Area	Urban Population	White %	Black %	Other %	Rural Population	White %	Black %	Other %	Rural farm White %	Black %	Other %	Rural nonfarm White %	Black %	Other %
Northeast	38,905,545	83.0	12.2	4.8	10,229,738	98.0	1.1	0.9	99.4	0.3	0.3	98.0	1.4	0.6
North central	41,519,746	84.7	12.6	2.7	17,345,924	98.2	0.7	1.1	99.6	0.1	0.3	98.2	0.8	1.0
South	50,414,258	75.4	20.7	3.9	24,958,104	83.8	14.5	1.7	93.3	6.0	0.7	83.8	15.2	1.0
West	36,211,443	79.6	6.1	14.3	7,016,351	86.6	0.8	12.6	96.0	0.3	3.7	91.2	0.9	7.9
Total	167,050,992	80.4	13.5	6.1	59,494,813	90.8	6.5	2.7	97.2	2.0	0.8	91.2	7.1	1.7

Source: U.S. Census of Population and Housing (U.S. Department of Commerce, Bureau of the Census 1980).

Table 7.24. Children ever born per 1,000 women by age, region, and urban, rural, rural farm, and rural nonfarm residence, 1980

Children ever born per 1,000 women by age of women

Region	Urban Total (all ages)	15–24	25–34	35–44	Rural Total (all ages)	15–24	25–34	35–44	Rural farm Total (all ages)	15–24	25–34	35–44	Rural nonfarm Total (all ages)	15–24	25–34	35–44
Northeast	1,144	222	1,273	2,443	1,394	260	1,539	2,729	1,565	192	1,916	3,239	1,389	263	1,530	2,678
North central	1,243	301	1,443	2,657	1,565	345	1,807	2,955	1,649	226	2,002	3,210	1,551	367	1,781	2,905
South	1,276	348	1,454	2,596	1,542	431	1,782	2,827	1,493	257	1,767	2,693	1,545	441	1,783	2,837
West	1,232	311	1,367	2,535	1,572	382	1,737	2,901	1,642	267	1,888	2,989	1,566	392	1,727	2,892

Source: U.S. Census of Population and Housing (U.S. Department of Commerce Bureau of the Census 1980).

178   These data provide additional evidence of the similarity among rural farm populations in different regions of the United States. Rural farm populations clearly have a larger number of children ever born than urban populations in all regions, and, in general, rural farm fertility is higher than rural nonfarm fertility (except in the South where the large concentration of minorities with high fertility levels in rural nonfarm areas results in higher rural nonfarm than rural farm fertility). In fact, the ratio of the total number of children ever born in rural nonfarm areas is over 30 percent higher than the number in urban areas in every region except the South where a higher rate of urban and a lower rate of rural farm fertility result in the ratio of children ever born in the rural farm population being only 17 percent higher than that for the urban population.

Overall, the data in Tables 7.17–7.24 suggest that the rural farm populations in the different regions of the United States have experienced somewhat different levels of decline in their farm population bases but that the demographic characteristics of such populations are now quite similar among the regions. Given the diversity of environmental and other conditions among these regions, the similarity in the demographic characteristics of these populations suggests, as noted in earlier chapters, that other ecosystem dimensions such as agricultural technology and organizational changes may have had even greater influences than differences in environments in shaping the characteristics of the farm population of the United States.

Socioeconomic Characteristics of Rural Farm Populations in Different Regions of the United States

The socioeconomic characteristics of farm populations in different regions of the United States are shown in Tables 7.25–7.28. An examination of the data in Table 7.25 indicates that in each of the four regions less than one-half of the labor force in rural farm populations is engaged in agriculture and, in the South the proportion drops to less than one-third. In addition, in all regions except the West, rural manufacturing and services are the next most important sectors of employment for rural farm residents. In the South, manufacturing employs nearly half as many persons as agriculture. These data clearly show that the sustenance bases of rural farm populations are increasingly diverse and increasingly show substantial involvement in nonagricultural activities.

Northeast

Industry	Labor force	% of total	Urban %	Rural %	Rural farm %	Rural nonfarm %
Agriculture	247,647	0.9	0.4	3.3	44.7	1.8
Forestry and fisheries	17,885	0.1	0.0	0.2	0.2	0.2
Mining	73,016	0.3	0.1	0.9	0.5	0.9
Construction	928,519	3.5	3.2	5.1	3.2	5.2
Manufacturing	5,407,236	20.7	19.9	24.1	11.3	24.6
Transportation	1,568,295	6.0	6.2	5.5	3.0	5.6
Wholesale trade	904,194	3.5	3.6	2.9	2.1	2.9
Retail trade	3,241,006	12.4	12.5	11.9	6.3	12.1
Finance, insurance, real estate	1,468,801	5.6	6.1	3.6	1.7	3.7
Services	6,465,894	24.8	25.4	22.3	14.1	22.6
Professional and related services	4,714,842	18.1	18.4	16.6	10.8	16.8
Public administration	1,070,813	4.1	4.2	3.6	2.1	3.6
Total	26,108,148	100.0	20,921,179	5,186,969	189,357	4,997,612

North central

Industry	Labor force	% of total	Urban %	Rural %	Rural farm %	Rural nonfarm %
Agriculture	1,000,758	3.3	0.5	10.6	45.4	3.5
Forestry and fisheries	12,865	0.0	0.0	0.1	0.0	0.1
Mining	146,109	0.5	0.3	1.0	0.5	1.1
Construction	1,239,313	4.0	3.5	5.5	3.5	6.0
Manufacturing	6,609,245	21.5	21.4	21.8	11.5	24.0
Transportation	1,771,016	5.8	5.9	5.5	3.1	6.0
Wholesale trade	1,107,996	3.6	3.7	3.5	2.7	3.6
Retail trade	4,182,972	13.6	14.1	12.2	6.5	13.3
Finance, insurance, real estate	1,400,364	4.6	5.1	3.2	2.1	3.4
Services	7,003,146	22.8	24.1	19.3	12.8	20.6
Professional and related services	5,205,736	16.9	17.8	14.5	10.2	15.4
Public administration	1,043,293	3.4	3.6	2.8	1.7	3.0
Total	30,722,813	100.0	22,444,894	8,277,919	1,406,775	6,871,144

South

Industry	Labor force	% of total	Urban %	Rural %	Rural farm %	Rural nonfarm %
Agriculture	907,137	2.4	1.0	5.8	31.3	3.6
Forestry and fisheries	58,395	0.1	0.1	0.3	0.3	0.3
Mining	592,983	1.6	1.2	2.5	1.2	2.6
Construction	2,345,810	6.2	5.6	7.6	5.1	7.8
Manufacturing	6,526,362	17.3	14.7	23.3	14.7	24.1
Transportation	2,342,456	6.2	6.3	5.9	4.2	6.1
Wholesale trade	1,378,220	3.7	3.8	3.3	2.8	3.3
Retail trade	5,071,254	13.4	14.2	11.7	7.7	12.0
Finance, insurance, real estate	1,742,176	4.6	5.3	3.0	2.5	3.1
Services	8,763,057	23.2	25.0	19.0	15.0	19.3
Professional and related services	6,092,374	16.1	17.2	13.5	11.8	13.7
Public administration	1,950,529	5.2	5.6	4.1	3.4	4.1
Total	37,770,753	100.0	26,472,995	11,297,758	874,607	10,423,151

West

Industry	Labor force	% of total	Urban %	Rural %	Rural farm %	Rural nonfarm %
Agriculture	604,671	2.7	1.4	10.0	45.5	6.3
Forestry and fisheries	64,231	0.3	0.2	1.0	0.4	1.0
Mining	216,070	0.9	0.7	2.3	0.7	2.5
Construction	1,225,956	5.4	5.0	7.7	3.9	8.1
Manufacturing	3,371,911	14.8	15.3	11.4	6.2	11.9
Transportation	1,405,688	6.2	6.2	6.1	3.9	6.3
Wholesale trade	826,822	3.6	3.7	2.9	2.5	3.0
Retail trade	3,221,462	14.1	14.3	12.8	6.9	13.4
Finance, insurance, real estate	1,286,718	5.6	5.9	3.8	2.4	4.0
Services	5,744,233	25.1	25.7	21.9	13.9	22.7
Professional and related services	3,798,867	16.6	16.9	15.0	10.7	15.4
Public administration	1,082,831	4.7	4.7	5.1	3.0	5.4
Total	22,849,460	100.0	19,658,770	3,190,690	301,395	2,889,295

Source: U.S. Census of Population and Housing (U.S. Department of Commerce Bureau of the Census 1980).

An evaluation of the data in Table 7.26 further verifies the pervasiveness of the patterns of nonfarm employment noted in the description of Table 7.25 and the similarity of patterns among regions of the nation. In each of the regions, less than 40 percent of the rural farm labor force in 1980 indicated that their major occupation was farm manager or farm laborer. When compared to the larger percentage of the labor force that indicated they were involved in agriculture (Table 7.25), this suggests that for many rural farm residents (see Chapter 3) agriculture is a part-time activity rather than a major means of earning a living. The data further suggest that for many rural farm residents, employment in professional and related activities and employment as operatives were also important means of obtaining sustenance from the environment. Again it is evident that although rural farm residents in the South have a somewhat lower rate of involvement in agriculture than residents in the rural farm populations of other regions, the general patterns of employment by occupation are similar in rural farm populations in all regions of the nation. In fact, it is also important to point out that if employment in farm managerial and farm laborer occupations is removed from the occupational distributions of the rural farm population, the occupational patterns for rural farm populations are very similar to those in urban and rural nonfarm areas in all regions.

Tables 7.27 and 7.28 examine educational and income characteristics in different regions of the United States by residence category. The data in these tables indicate that the rural farm population in the South lags behind that in other regions of the nation. Thus, median years of education completed by rural farm residents in the South was nearly one-half year less than in other regions, and the median family income was $1,500 less. Income differences between the South and other regions exist for all population components. For education, the data suggest that although residents in the urban South are similar to residents in urban areas in other regions, rural residents in the South have substantially lower levels of education than their counterparts in other regions.

Overall, then, the data on socioeconomic characteristics show similar sustenance patterns for rural farm populations across the United States. However, educational and income levels are substantially lower in the South. Although the South has historically shown the most substantial reduction in the size of its rural farm population of any region, it appears that even a loss of over 14 million persons from its farm popula-

Northeast

Occupation	Labor force	% of total	Urban %	Rural %	Rural farm %	Rural nonfarm %
Professional, technical, and kindred	9,702,398	30.7	31.6	26.8	16.7	27.2
Farm and farm managers	95,457	0.3	0.0	1.4	28.8	0.4
Managers, officers, proprietors, executives	5,224,287	16.5	16.7	15.6	10.1	15.8
Clerical and kindred workers	4,074,995	12.9	13.6	9.9	6.0	10.0
Sales workers	2,030,673	6.4	6.5	5.9	3.5	6.0
Craftsmen, foremen, and kindred workers	2,530,320	8.0	7.4	10.7	5.7	10.9
Operatives and kindred workers	3,836,636	12.1	11.3	15.5	9.9	15.7
Private household workers	109,972	0.3	0.3	0.4	0.5	0.4
Service workers	2,650,478	8.4	8.5	7.9	4.8	8.0
Farm laborers and farm foremen	155,120	0.5	0.3	1.3	10.9	1.0
Laborers except farm and mine	1,220,768	3.9	3.8	4.6	3.1	4.6
Total	31,631,104	100.0	25,533,274	6,097,830	206,641	5,891,189

North central

Occupation	Urban %	Rural %	Rural farm %	Rural nonfarm %	Labor force	% of total
Professional, technical, and kindred	30.3	22.9	15.7	24.4	10,432,467	28.3
Farm and farm managers	0.0	6.4	32.6	1.4	640,576	1.7
Managers, officers, proprietors, executives	15.8	12.0	7.6	12.9	5,426,412	14.7
Clerical and kindred workers	12.5	9.2	6.7	9.6	4,259,097	11.6
Sales workers	7.0	5.7	3.4	6.2	2,467,210	6.7
Craftsmen, foremen, and kindred workers	7.9	11.0	6.4	11.9	3,212,426	8.7
Operatives and kindred workers	12.7	16.5	10.5	17.6	5,045,418	13.7
Private household workers	0.3	0.3	0.3	0.3	112,073	0.3
Service workers	9.0	8.5	5.5	9.1	3,281,063	8.9
Farm laborers and farm foremen	0.3	2.5	8.0	1.3	323,419	0.9
Laborers except farm and mine	4.2	5.0	3.3	5.3	1,640,809	4.5
Total	27,240,537	9,600,433	1,539,544	8,060,889	36,840,975	100.0

South

Occupation	Labor force	% of total	Urban %	Rural %	Rural farm %	Rural nonfarm %
Professional, technical, and kindred	12,986,356	28.3	30.5	22.8	19.6	23.0
Farm and farm managers	393,893	0.9	0.2	2.6	21.0	1.1
Managers, officers, proprietors, executives	6,814,143	14.8	16.3	11.3	10.5	11.3
Clerical and kindred workers	5,177,030	11.3	12.1	9.3	7.9	9.4
Sales workers	3,209,180	7.0	7.5	5.8	4.6	5.9
Craftsmen, foremen, and kindred workers	4,399,634	9.6	8.4	12.4	8.1	12.8
Operatives and kindred workers	6,221,209	13.5	11.1	19.5	13.1	20.0
Private household workers	265,624	0.6	0.6	0.5	0.3	0.6
Service workers	3,692,914	8.0	8.2	7.5	5.2	7.7
Farm laborers and farm foremen	454,838	1.0	0.6	2.0	5.7	1.7
Laborers except farm and mine	2,322,906	5.0	4.5	6.3	4.0	6.5
Total	45,937,727	100.0	32,561,206	13,376,521	991,477	12,385,044

West

Occupation	Urban %	Rural %	Rural farm %	Rural nonfarm %	Labor force	% of total
Professional, technical, and kindred	31.1	24.9	18.2	25.8	8,490,382	30.5
Farm and farm managers	0.1	3.6	26.7	1.3	168,744	0.6
Managers, officers, proprietors, executives	17.1	14.5	10.4	15.0	4,686,806	16.9
Clerical and kindred workers	12.4	9.0	7.0	9.2	3,340,276	12.0
Sales workers	7.5	6.4	4.2	6.7	1,835,094	6.6
Craftsmen, foremen, and kindred workers	8.4	11.7	5.7	11.6	2,481,795	8.9
Operatives and kindred workers	9.6	11.3	7.6	11.8	2,756,080	9.9
Private household workers	0.4	0.3	0.3	0.3	101,683	0.4
Service workers	8.6	9.0	4.9	9.5	2,415,618	8.8
Farm laborers and farm foremen	1.0	4.3	11.9	3.6	400,746	1.4
Laborers except farm and mine	3.9	5.0	3.1	5.2	1,121,053	4.0
Total	24,236,407	3,749,870	336,290	3,413,580	27,798,277	100.0

Source: U.S. Census of Population and Housing (U.S. Department of Commerce Bureau of the Census 1980).

Table 7.27. Median years of school completed for persons 25 years old and older by regions and urban, rural, rural farm, and rural nonfarm residence, 1980

Region	Median years of school completed			
	Urban	Rural[a]	Rural farm	Rural nonfarm
Northeast	12.5	12.5	12.4	12.6
North central	12.5	12.4	12.4	12.4
South	12.5	12.0	12.0	12.0
West	12.8	12.6	12.6	12.6
Total	12.5	12.3	12.3	12.3

Source: U.S. Census of Population and Housing (U.S. Department of Commerce Bureau of the Census 1980).
[a]Rural is calculated as the average of rural farm and rural nonfarm.

Table 7.28. Median family income by region and urban, rural, rural farm, and rural nonfarm residence, 1960–1980

Year	Northeast				North central				South				West			
	Urban	Rural	Rural farm	Rural nonfarm	Urban	Rural	Rural farm	Rural nonfarm	Urban	Rural	Rural farm	Rural nonfarm	Urban	Rural	Rural farm	Rural nonfarm
1960	6,354	5,033[a]	4,389	5,676	6,422	4,386[a]	3,590	5,181	5,246	3,057[a]	2,433	3,681	6,654	5,022[a]	4,653	5,390
1970	10,632	9,495[a]	9,148	9,841	10,710	8,445[a]	7,914	8,976	8,920	6,413[a]	5,962	6,864	10,563	8,506[a]	8,252	8,760
1980	20,817	20,124	18,149	[b]	21,759	19,294	18,072	[b]	18,985	16,066	16,538	[b]	21,362	19,068	20,157	[b]

Source: U.S. Census of Population and Housing (U.S. Department of Commerce Bureau of the Census 1960, 1970, 1980).
[a]Average of rural farm and rural nonfarm.
[b]Not available.

tion base has not allowed the South to establish income and educational **183** parity for its rural farm residents.

The data in Tables 7.17–7.28 provide an indication of the potential diversity in rural farm population patterns in the four census regions of the United States. In general, these data verify the patterns of extensive change in rural populations shown in the previous section of the chapter. Clearly, in all regions of the nation rural farm populations have adapted to the changing structure of agriculture by reducing the number of persons in such populations and broadening their sustenance bases to include nonagricultural activities. Although a comparison of the data in these tables shows the rural farm population in the southern region to be substantially different from the rural farm populations in other regions, the similarity in farm populations in different regions of the nation remains the most obvious result of the regional comparisons. Farm populations, no matter where they are located, tend to have experienced decline, to be composed of older persons, to be increasingly homogeneous in racial/ethnic composition, to be predominantly male, to be increasingly involved in nonagricultural forms of sustenance activities, and to have somewhat lower levels of education and income than their urban counterparts. The similarity of such patterns among regions suggests that pervasive national patterns of adaptation in agriculture have been required in all regions of the nation in the past half century.

Despite the similarity of the patterns among the regions, the distinct patterns for the South should not be discounted. It is clear that the South has been required to make the most substantial changes in its population base, that these changes have removed its rural farm population farther from dependence on agriculture than in other regions but that adaptation has not brought about parity between the South and other regions of the nation or even among population groups within the South in terms of socioeconomic factors. Rural farm populations in the South have shown particularly dramatic patterns of population decline while retaining a disadvantageous position relative to other regions. It appears that southern rural farm populations are likely to have at least some unique characteristics for some time to come.

Rural Farm and Nonfarm Populations by State

Although extensive comparisons by state are beyond the scope of the present effort, Table 7.29 provides information on the size and

Table 7.29. Rural farm and rural nonfarm population and population change, 1950–1980, by state

State	1950	Change 1950–1960	1960	Change 1960–1970	1970	Change 1970–1980	1980	Change 1950–1980
				Rural farm population				
Alabama	960,493	−557,638	402,855	−180,659	222,196	−134,439	87,757	−872,736
Alaska[a]	—	—	2,171	2,186	4,357	−3,535	822	−1,349
Arizona	76,914	−27,493	49,421	−3,463	45,958	−32,188	13,770	−63,144
Arkansas	801,827	−470,182	331,645	−106,000	225,645	−117,997	107,648	−694,179
California	568,231	−233,915	334,266	−86,030	248,236	−71,776	176,460	−391,771
Colorado	198,181	−70,620	127,561	−23,796	103,765	−44,613	59,152	−139,029
Connecticut	62,656	−38,142	24,514	24,762	49,276	−41,893	7,383	−55,273
Delaware	34,225	−12,404	21,821	−2,068	19,753	−9,507	10,246	−23,979
Florida	232,806	−127,387	105,419	44,196	149,615	−90,936	58,679	−174,127
Georgia	962,435	−555,157	407,278	−153,739	253,539	−132,450	121,089	−841,346
Hawaii[a]	—	—	10,936	−2,899	8,037	−3,514	4,523	−6,413
Idaho	164,960	−32,178	132,782	−28,980	103,802	−34,673	69,129	−95,831
Illinois	763,196	−200,351	562,845	−61,171	501,674	−187,696	313,978	−449,218
Indiana	667,154	−181,680	485,474	−21,241	464,233	−188,079	276,154	−391,000
Iowa	782,650	−120,411	662,239	−127,516	534,723	−143,653	391,070	−391,580
Kansas	443,739	−123,231	320,508	−67,979	252,529	−79,628	172,901	−270,838
Kentucky	974,170	−426,347	547,823	−96,533	451,290	−206,701	244,589	−729,581
Louisiana	567,455	−334,317	233,138	−62,636	170,502	−111,557	58,945	−508,510
Maine	121,828	−73,676	48,152	−5,478	42,674	−28,711	13,963	−107,865
Maryland	183,476	−73,319	110,157	−6,451	103,706	−58,772	44,934	−138,542
Massachusetts	79,976	−44,030	35,946	27,377	63,323	−53,484	9,839	−70,137
Michigan	694,742	−253,805	440,937	−46,148	394,789	−217,198	177,591	−517,151
Minnesota	739,799	−152,251	587,548	−99,263	488,285	−172,885	315,400	−424,399
Mississippi	1,097,207	−554,368	542,839	−281,347	261,492	−176,734	84,758	−1,012,449
Missouri	863,496	−322,698	540,798	−132,954	407,844	−125,770	282,074	−581,422
Montana	135,939	−30,341	105,598	−17,138	88,460	−30,064	58,396	−77,543
Nebraska	391,435	−82,676	308,759	−61,436	247,323	−69,210	178,113	−231,322
Nevada	13,461	3,355	10,106	104	10,210	−4,671	5,539	−7,922
New Hampshire	47,170	−28,536	18,634	4,755	23,389	−16,749	6,640	−40,530
New Jersey	105,300	−53,943	51,357	29,335	80,692	−61,708	18,984	−86,316
New Mexico	131,823	−73,559	58,264	−6,206	52,058	−31,971	20,087	−111,736
New York	577,654	−252,908	324,746	−24,427	300,319	−177,210	123,109	−454,545
North Carolina	1,376,560	−568,181	808,379	−278,063	530,316	−341,879	188,437	−1,188,123
North Dakota	254,487	−50,089	204,398	−48,518	155,880	−51,999	103,881	−150,606

Table 7.29. (Continued)

State	1950	Change 1950–1960	1960	Change 1960–1970	1970	Change 1970–1980	1980	Change 1950–1980
				Rural farm population				
Ohio	853,088	−333,575	519,513	−16,081	503,432	−231,890	271,542	−581,546
Oklahoma	553,066	−294,117	258,949	−60,766	198,183	−68,309	129,874	−432,192
Oregon	228,235	−89,932	138,303	−5,194	133,109	−55,064	78,045	−150,190
Pennsylvania	705,207	−348,934	356,273	30,498	386,771	−228,588	158,183	−547,024
Rhode Island	10,338	−6,382	3,956	3,814	7,770	−6,555	1,115	−9,223
South Carolina	700,611	−349,457	351,154	−173,945	177,209	−123,614	53,595	−647,016
South Dakota	253,545	−47,857	205,688	39,281	166,407	−53,553	112,854	−140,691
Tennessee	1,016,204	−429,460	586,744	−194,241	392,503	−216,830	175,673	−840,531
Texas	1,292,267	−597,785	694,482	−222,440	472,042	−203,149	268,893	−1,023,374
Utah	80,620	−37,209	43,411	−10,709	32,702	−14,330	18,372	−62,248
Vermont	81,132	−32,287	48,845	−13,032	35,813	−17,734	18,079	−63,053
Virginia	731,961	−334,785	397,176	−129,893	267,283	−154,168	113,115	−618,846
Washington	273,771	−110,529	163,242	−21,689	141,553	−59,889	81,664	−192,107
West Virginia	410,922	−289,984	120,938	−24,826	96,112	−67,382	28,730	−382,192
Wisconsin	725,234	−171,370	553,864	−71,205	482,659	−199,937	282,722	−442,512
Wyoming	56,704	−13,658	43,046	−7,950	35,096	−15,689	19,407	−37,297
				Rural nonfarm population				
Alabama	760,313	308,403	1,068,716	140,680	1,209,396	259,702	1,469,098	708,785
Alaska[a]	—	—	138,229	11,267	149,496	−7,188	142,308	4,079
Arizona	256,673	25,451	282,124	34,737	316,861	108,710	425,571	168,898
Arkansas	477,093	212,231	689,324	45,870	735,194	265,244	1,000,438	523,345
California	1,478,572	331,210	1,809,782	−238,019	1,571,763	311,099	1,882,862	404,290
Colorado	295,590	38,006	333,596	33,816	367,412	133,705	501,117	205,527
Connecticut	385,982	139,171	525,153	113,702	638,855	12,105	650,960	264,978
Delaware	84,738	46,945	131,683	1,507	133,190	30,696	163,886	79,148
Florida	724,609	460,149	1,184,758	−12,001	1,172,757	300,975	1,473,732	749,123
Georgia	922,696	432,906	1,355,602	213,850	1,569,452	364,297	1,933,749	1,011,053
Hawaii[a]	—	—	137,875	−15,101	122,774	2,671	125,445	−12,430
Idaho	171,128	46,184	217,312	4,353	221,665	143,341	365,006	193,878
Illinois	1,189,709	188,273	1,377,982	7,892	1,385,874	208,098	1,593,972	404,263
Indiana	909,874	356,812	1,266,686	91,740	1,358,426	330,573	1,688,999	779,125

185

Table 7.29. (Continued)

Rural nonfarm population

State	1950	Change 1950–1960	1960	Change 1960–1970	1970	Change 1970–1980	1980	Change 1950–1980
Iowa	587,485	44,329	631,814	41,014	672,828	141,997	814,825	227,340
Kansas	468,340	61,023	529,363	−19,548	509,815	104,816	614,631	146,291
Kentucky	886,566	250,552	1,137,118	−55,147	1,081,971	472,861	1,554,832	668,266
Louisiana	644,365	318,913	963,278	98,604	1,061,882	197,672	1,259,554	615,189
Maine	319,946	104,053	423,999	20,883	444,882	132,034	576,916	256,970
Maryland	543,623	193,077	736,700	77,095	813,795	−28,447	785,348	241,725
Massachusetts	651,299	158,803	810,102	5,449	815,551	102,309	917,860	266,561
Michigan	1,173,940	469,185	1,643,125	281,992	1,925,117	608,100	2,533,217	1,359,277
Minnesota	617,770	87,543	705,313	84,813	790,126	244,804	1,034,930	417,160
Mississippi	474,545	339,952	814,497	153,611	968,108	275,535	1,243,643	769,098
Missouri	658,442	244,016	902,458	89,383	991,841	293,302	1,285,143	626,701
Montana	197,051	33,661	230,712	2,893	233,605	78,430	312,035	114,984
Nebraska	312,170	24,348	336,518	14,406	322,112	81,726	403,838	91,668
Nevada	54,997	19,471	74,468	8,839	83,307	28,585	111,892	56,895
New Hampshire	179,266	55,255	234,521	63,080	297,601	136,247	433,848	254,582
New Jersey	543,822	97,864	641,686	72,522	714,208	73,961	788,169	244,347
New Mexico	207,475	60,110	267,585	−14,348	253,237	89,521	342,758	135,283
New York	1,570,092	555,541	2,125,633	206,584	2,332,217	244,222	2,576,439	1,006,347
North Carolina	1,317,268	628,587	1,945,855	320,367	2,266,222	603,927	2,870,149	1,552,881
North Dakota	200,332	5,008	205,340	−17,101	188,239	42,387	230,626	30,294
Ohio	1,515,265	548,457	2,063,722	61,519	2,125,241	482,817	2,608,058	1,092,793
Oklahoma	540,804	63,559	604,363	15,665	620,028	240,196	860,224	319,420
Oregon	473,788	56,474	530,262	25,503	555,765	211,011	766,776	292,988
Pennsylvania	2,389,769	471,648	2,861,417	118,339	2,979,756	504,125	3,483,881	1,094,112
Rhode Island	114,346	−1,711	112,635	3,160	115,795	5,520	121,315	6,969
South Carolina	638,495	415,559	1,054,054	127,360	1,181,414	197,504	1,378,918	740,423
South Dakota	182,485	25,161	207,646	−5,176	202,470	54,760	257,230	74,745
Tennessee	822,912	292,605	1,115,517	108,960	1,224,477	416,635	1,641,112	818,200
Texas	1,580,867	117,779	1,698,646	96,210	1,794,856	833,865	2,628,721	1,047,854
Utah	158,387	21,671	180,058	−6,801	173,257	36,520	209,777	51,390
Vermont	159,003	32,112	191,115	74,530	265,645	54,881	320,526	161,523
Virginia	1,026,604	325,736	1,352,340	97,717	1,450,057	253,416	1,703,473	676,869
Washington	602,026	144,697	746,723	44,396	791,119	219,915	1,011,034	409,008
West Virginia	900,143	128,239	1,028,382	−59,782	968,600	246,874	1,215,474	315,331
Wisconsin	721,453	154,281	875,734	149,887	1,025,621	377,379	1,403,000	681,547
Wyoming	89,207	10,262	99,469	−3,026	96,443	59,506	155,949	66,742

Source: U.S. Census of Population and Housing (U.S. Department of Commerce, Bureau of the Census 1950–1980).
ªData for Alaska and Hawaii are not shown for 1950 because these areas did not become states until after 1950.

change in the rural farm and rural nonfarm populations from 1950 to **187**
1980 for each of the fifty states. An examination of the data in this table
indicates how pervasive patterns of decline in the farm population have
been. In all states patterns of decline are evident for the period from
1950 to 1980. Only three states, Iowa, Illinois, and Minnesota, had rural
farm populations exceeding 300,000 in 1980, and only six other states,
Indiana, Kentucky, Missouri, Ohio, Texas, and Wisconsin, had farm
populations that exceeded 200,000. Such data clearly show the dominance of agriculture in the north central or Midwest states but also show
the extensive decline in farm population, particularly in the South. Thus,
from 1950 to 1980 three states, Mississippi, North Carolina, and Texas,
lost more than 1 million rural farm residents. Clearly, then, although
patterns of decline are evident in all states, the extent of adaptation
required has varied substantially among states.

At the same time, the data on the rural nonfarm population suggests that such populations have shown growth despite the declines in the
rural farm population. All states except Hawaii have shown growth in
their rural nonfarm populations between 1950 and 1980 and seven states
(Georgia, Michigan, New York, North Carolina, Ohio, Pennsylvania,
and Texas) have gained more than 1 million new rural nonfarm residents
from 1950 to 1980. Such growth in the nonfarm population in rural
areas, when compared to the decline in the farm population, clearly
shows that the carrying capacity of rural environments has grown as a
result of the diversification of its sustenance base beyond agricultural
production.

Overall, an examination of the data presented above showing regional and state variation in the demographic and socioeconomic characteristics of the rural farm population suggests that differential patterns
of adaptation among regions over several decades have produced increasingly similar rural farm populations in different areas in the United
States. Such a finding suggests that environmental differences among
regions of the United States have required different levels of adaptation
but that similarities in other factors (e.g., technology and social organizational factors) have resulted in similar population characteristics
among rural farm populations. Thus, although different regions have
shown different rates of adaptation, the results have produced population bases that display extensive similarities. This clearly points to the
pervasive national (and perhaps international) basis for many of the
forces to which agricultural populations have adapted and that have
shaped the structure of agriculture in the United States.

188 SUMMARY AND IMPLICATIONS

The population structure of rural America affects, and is affected by, the structure of agriculture. In this chapter we have traced some of the conceptual linkages between population factors and the structure of agriculture in the United States and presented data that allow the characteristics of rural populations and the variation and changes in such characteristics to be described. The analysis has emphasized the rural farm population since it is this population that must directly adapt to changes in the structure of agriculture. In the discussion of both its conceptual and empirical findings, this chapter has obviously examined only a few of the many dimensions that could have been examined.

The interrelationships between the structure of agriculture and populations are numerous and complex. The declining size of the rural farm population has reflected the application of technology to agricultural production processes and the changing organizational patterns in agricultural structure that have led to farm consolidation. These changes have produced a surplus of farm labor that has required extensive out-migration from rural areas even during periods when growth occurred in other segments of the rural population. In like manner, the distribution of the population has reflected differences in the ecological carrying capacity of the land and in original patterns of settlement. The composition of the population also reflects original patterns of settlement and the differential abilities of different segments of the population to adapt to patterns of change in agricultural structure. Thus, the nonwhite rural farm population has declined rapidly, in part because it was disproportionately concentrated on small rented land holdings during a period in which larger-sized farms and landownership enhanced the probability of remaining in agricultural production.

Similarly, the demographic processes of fertility, mortality, and migration can be seen as reflecting agricultural patterns. Fertility among rural farm populations may reflect historical patterns of extensive labor demands in labor-intensive forms of agricultural production; mortality patterns reflect, in part, differences in population structures in the rural areas, access to health care systems in rural areas, and the relative safety of agricultural production processes; and migration may reflect the reduced need for labor brought about by the increased use of technology and the consolidation of farms into increasingly larger units.

It is equally evident that the structure of agriculture is affected by the characteristics of the rural farm population. The size, distribution, **189** and composition of that population determines the magnitude and types of public and private services that can be supported in an area, and basic demographic processes alter the characteristics of the population so that its potential for agricultural and nonagricultural forms of sustenance diversity is altered.

Understanding the linkages between the ecological components of population and the structure of agriculture is thus essential for understanding change. The characteristics of rural populations, particularly the farm population, and the changes in these populations that have occurred in recent decades were analyzed extensively in this chapter.

The analysis of rural farm populations presented here indicated that they have had to make extensive adaptations due to changes in agriculture. These adaptations have resulted in the loss of over 80 percent of the rural farm population in the last fifty years, in the loss of nearly all nonwhites from the farm population, in a farm population that is increasingly composed of the very young and the very old and of more males than females.

Despite such dramatic changes, it has not been possible for rural farm populations to find adequate sustenance in economic activities tied to agriculture. Rural farm residents increasingly have been required to pursue nonagricultural forms of employment so that in 1980 less than one-half of the rural farm labor force was employed in agriculture. Work in manufacturing and service-industries, particularly as operatives and laborers, has become important secondary employment for the rural farm population.

The adaptations required of the rural farm population have been so pervasive that rural farm populations are increasingly similar in different regions of the nation. Overall adaptations have apparently been at least partially successful in that the socioeconomic characteristics of rural farm populations are increasingly similar to those for rural nonfarm and urban populations. Only in the South have these adaptations failed to provide near parity between rural farm and other populations.

Overall, then, we find that the population component of the ecological complex reflects the structure of agriculture. Interrelationships between agricultural structure and population patterns are not only conceptually important but, as the analysis in this chapter has indicated, can provide empirical evidence of dramatic changes in agriculturally dependent rural areas.

190   Our findings are thus both conceptually revealing and descriptively useful. In addition, however, the relationships described and analyzed here have important implications in two areas: the further development of ecological theories of agriculture and understanding the likely future of U.S. agriculture. These implications are briefly described below.

The changes that have occurred in the rural farm population, the pervasiveness of change patterns among regions of the United States, and the increasing similarity in characteristics of rural farm populations in different regions suggest (1) that the organizational and technological factors requiring adaptation in agriculture have been extremely dominant and (2) that the processes of adaptation they have required have been pervasive. The fact that many of the differentials in characteristics among farm populations in different regions have decreased over time suggests that the forces requiring adaptation have been so powerful as to produce similar isomorphic responses in different regions of the United States. Unique environmental factors have affected such factors as the nature of the commodities grown, farm size, and the size of farm populations, but similar adaptive mechanisms such as farm consolidation and the extensive decline in tenant and other nonownership categories of producers have occurred in nearly all environmental settings.

This finding tells us that ecological theories of agriculture must employ a concept of multiple ecosystems of influence and that the national ecosystem and the organizational dimensions emanating from national farm policies must be included in ecological analyses. It is apparent that a complex mix of local and national processes have shaped the present structure of agriculture in the United States and that analyses of multiple systems of influence are needed to understand present, as well as the likely future, structure of agriculture.

Although the results in this chapter suggest that farm populations are becoming increasingly homogeneous, it is clear that subpopulation differences continue and that an ecological analysis of agricultural structure must carefully account for differential adaptive abilities of subcomponents of the population base within a given set of regional and national ecosystems. For example, when examined in retrospect the decline in the number of nonwhites in the farm population appears to reflect a disproportionate concentration of nonwhite producers who have been unsuccessful in adapting organizational forms and types of technology that have been associated with survival in agriculture over the past decades. The loss of producers in the middle categories of farm size (see Chapter 3) reflects similar technological and organizational forces. Such patterns suggest the need for ecological analysts to use the population component as a causative factor in the ecological complex rather than simply as a convenient means of referring to the unit of analysis. Multiple ecological theories of adaptation may be necessary for different subcomponents of the population. Just as different types of environments often require unique forms of adaptation that merit separate analysis so different population components are likely to have different adaptive abilities that merit careful and individualized forms of analysis.

The results presented in this chapter also have implications for understanding the future of agriculture in the United States. It is evident, for example, that past patterns of adaptation have produced an increasingly homogeneous farm population base. Such a homogeneous base has allowed a system of agriculture to develop in which responses to past trends have been quite efficient. However, if analyses of physical ecosystems are at all applicable to social and ecological ecosystems, then it must also be acknowledged that a homogeneous population base is more limited in its adaptive ability than a more diverse population and thus likely to be uniformly negatively or positively affected by environmental, organizational, or technological changes in its ecosystem. Although the data presented here and in Chapter 3 show agricultural producers to be increasingly involved in nonagricultural economic activities that have decreased their dependence on agriculture, the present structure of the farm population base may be one that will lead to increasingly uniform patterns of response and similar patterns of positive or negative effects. Thus, one might argue that the farm crisis of the 1980s was pervasive, at least in part, because the population being affected and the organizational structure of agriculture were so similar among producers. It may thus be that "crises" in agriculture are likely to be more severe in the future due to the decreased range of adaptive characteristics in the farm population.

In sum, then, the structure of the rural farm population is one that has been molded by patterns of extensive adaptation to the changing structure of agricultural production. Populations affect and are affected by that structure. Whether viewed historically or in terms of potential future changes, it is apparent that the population component of the ecological complex is one that both reflects and limits the ecosystem in numerous and complex ways. Its size, distribution, and composition have thus been critical forces in shaping the past and are likely to be equally important in determining the future structure of agriculture in the United States.

The Relationship between
Agriculture and Rural Communities

With the westward expansion of American agriculture, numerous rural communities emerged to provide for the needs of the growing farm population. The number and sizes of these communities were largely dependent on the quality and quantity of available resources important to agriculture, the type of agricultural enterprises that emerged, and the level of technological development to utilize available resources (Larson 1981). Through the years changes that occurred in agriculture had a direct bearing on life in these communities. In fact, much of the rationale for the current interest in the sociology of agriculture is a result of this hypothesized close relationship between agriculture and the community.

Changes in the structure of agriculture have been seen as basic to the survival of the rural community and to its quality of life. As farm operators leave farming, the base of support for rural businesses declines, the base of service clientele essential to justify rural public services is eroded, and the community loses key participants in community organizations and community leadership. In addition, the form of agriculture practiced seems to affect community stratification, the perceptions of residents toward their community and its resource base, and the likelihood that community residents will be integrated with the larger society outside the local area. Agricultural structure and rural communities' characteristics are thus seen as intimately linked.

Despite the obvious importance of identifying the effects of changes **193**

194   in the structure of agriculture for agriculturally dependent rural communities, empirical analysis of the relationships between agriculture and rural community change have been infrequent and attempts to develop theoretical explanations for these changes have seldom been formulated (see Leistritz and Ekstrom [1986] for a recent listing of the literature on this topic). The human ecological framework, however, suggests some of the forms and areas of change likely to accompany a change in the structure of agriculture. We begin then by examining some of the relationships expected on the basis of ecological theory, then examine the existing related literature, and finally suggest areas where additional research is required.

Viewed ecologically, the effects of agricultural structure changes on rural communities must be seen in the context of the effects of an organizational change occurring within a wider ecosystem involving population, technological, environmental, and other organizational dimensions. Thus, the effects of organizational change must be seen as conditional on the state of each of the other elements operating within an ecosystem. Some of the ecological relationships likely to determine how changes in the structure of agriculture affect rural communities are delineated below. The relationships examined are only some of those of relevance, but one hopes they are both exemplary of the complexity of this issue and of the utility of the ecological framework for providing insight concerning them.

Changes in the structure of agriculture represent changes in the means by which sustenance is extracted from the environment. As such they can be expected to occur in response to changes in the environment occurring primarily through the alteration of the environment by the application of different forms of technology. Such sustenance organizations are the major activities through which human populations respond to the constraints placed on their ecosystems by the environment. For communities the extent to which structural changes in sustenance activities affects them will depend on the extent to which such activities are the key functional activities within the ecosystem.

Human ecological theory thus suggests that the extent to which changes in agriculture affect communities will be a function of the range of sustenance activities and the dominance of such activities in the ecosystem. This dominance is, in turn, largely a function of differences in the environmental resource base of an area. As a result, human ecological theory would suggest that examinations of the effects of the structure of agriculture on rural communities must begin with an examination of the range of sustenance activities operating in the environment and the relative role of agriculture among such activities. So seen, the effects of agriculture on rural communities would be expected to be quite different in different environments. Areas such as the Great Plains where few alternative sustenance activities exist should be affected differently by changes in the structure of agriculture than many areas in the West, Northeast, or South where manufacturing and other alternative sustenance activities are more common.

In like manner the effects may be expected to vary with the type of technology that is being applied to the organizational base of the sustenance activity of agriculture. Commensalistic forms of technology, for example, tend to increase efficiency and to allow a given unit of work to be completed with less inputs, particularly labor. When such forms of technology are applied to an environment, the effects are likely to be the reduction of the need for labor and thus the reduction of the overall population base of the area. This in turn will lead to a decrease in the customer base for local businesses and to a decline in the clientele base for local services.

When symbiotic forms of technology are involved, the effects are more complex, but changes resulting in a stabilization of the population base and/or an increase in the base may be expected to occur. In reality, of course, both commensalistic and symbiotic forms of technology occur simultaneously in any given area. As a result, in many areas the manifestation of a mix of the two forms of technology simply has been a slower rate of population decline. For example, in many areas with irrigated agriculture population decline has occurred, but it has been less apparent than in other areas (Albrecht and Murdock 1986b).

The effects will also vary with the nature of the population base in the area. Areas with abundant labor supplies may be expected to delay implementing laborsaving forms of technology because abundance generally reduces the cost of labor. As long as the use of labor is more cost effective than the use of technology, labor rather than technology will probably continue to be used. However, because the costs of most forms of technology tend to decline per unit of production over time, in most cases a point is reached in which the use of the technology is more efficient than the use of labor. Although it is obvious that the labor supply existing in an area at the time a new form of technology is introduced is a product of past adaptive activities, it is nevertheless apparent that because of existing labor supplies and because of the variation in the costs of labor, different areas will make different organizational responses to changing environmental and technological factors.

It is also clear that the nature of the structural changes likely to occur in agriculture and their subsequent effects on rural communities will vary with the nature of other characteristics of the organizational base in an area including, as indicated above, the range of sustenance activities prevailing in an area. Although this range is largely a function of the environment, areas also vary in their organizational structures due to historical organizational factors. Thus, some areas may be county seats or the sites of state capitals. In like manner these communities may have been able due to past patterns of dominance to influence the routes and form of construction of major types of transportation resulting in additional organizational opportunities for sustenance diversity.

In addition, the forms and level of differentiation and dominance in an area may affect the form in which an organizational change is implemented. In most ecosystems a system of dominance is perpetuated by the existing elements unless the maintenance of such dominance is rendered impossible by the nature of the change. For example, if the existing base of differentiation is one that is largely bipolar involving a relatively small number of dominants and a large number of subdominants then it is likely that the ecosystem will attempt to array the new organizational changes in a similar manner. On the other hand, if the existing system of differentiation is one in which there is largely a uniform distribution of dominance, then it is likely that organizational change will be implemented with a view toward retaining that uniform distribution. What this ecological premise suggests is that the organizational history of an area cannot be ignored in attempting to interpret how it has reacted to new requirements for organizational change. History cannot be ignored in attempting to understand the differences in stratification systems among, for example, rural areas in the Midwest and those in southern California, Texas, or the South.

In sum, an ecological perspective on the interrelationships between changes in the structure of agriculture and changes in the rural community suggests that in order to adequately understand the effects of changes, a number of interrelated factors affecting the ecosystems of the areas of interest must be examined. Included among these factors are differences (1) in the environmental base, (2) in the diversity of the sus-

tenance activities, (3) in the form and type of technological change re-   **197**
quiring the organizational adaptation, (4) in the present characteristics
of the population (particularly the labor force dimensions of that population), and (5) in the organizational history of the area. The determination of the effects of changes in the structure of agriculture on rural areas
clearly requires complex and multifaceted comparative and longitudinal
analysis.

In comparison with the types of analyses essential to the ecological
perspective, analyses completed to date have been relatively simplistic. It
is this existing literature that is our next topic of concern. After re-
viewing Goldschmidt's study, which is the exemplar in this area, we then
examine the three major foci of studies of the effects of changes in the
structure of agriculture on rural communities. These include the effects
on population, on community services, and on community stratification
systems.

THE GOLDSCHMIDT HYPOTHESIS

Much of the current interest in the sociology of agriculture in general, and interest in the relationship between agriculture and the community in particular, can be traced to the now classic study by Walter
Goldschmidt (Goldschmidt 1946, 1978b). In 1944 Goldschmidt completed a thorough comparison of two California communities: Arvin in
Kern County and Dinuba in Tulare County. The two communities were
selected for the study because they were very similar in many respects.
The two communities were about the same size, and economically both
were about equally dependent on agriculture. Approximately the same
dollar volume of agricultural products were brought to market in the
two communities. There were, however, major differences in the scale of
agriculture surrounding the two communities. The average farm size in
the Arvin area (497 acres) was nine times larger than the average farm in
the Dinuba area (57 acres). While gross farm sales were about equal in
the two communities, they were divided among about five times as many
farmers in Dinuba.

Goldschmidt's intention was to isolate the effects of farm size to
determine the influence this factor had on various aspects of the community. He admits, however, that other factors in addition to farm size may

198 be at least partially responsible for the differences found. Acknowledging this limitation, his analysis of the social and economic conditions in the two communities revealed that (Nuckton et al. 1982):

1. Dinuba (with small farms) supported twice as many local businesses as Arvin
2. the volume of retail trade was 61 percent greater in Dinuba than in Arvin
3. expenditures for household and building supplies were over three times greater in Dinuba than Arvin
4. Dinuba supported 20 percent more people per dollar volume of agricultural sales and these people had a better average standard of living than residents of Arvin
5. in the large farm community nearly two-thirds of all people gainfully employed were agricultural wage laborers. In comparison, less than one-third of those employed in the small farm community were agricultural wage laborers. In contrast, the proportion of businesspeople and white collar workers was much greater in Dinuba
6. public services such as paved streets, sidewalks, and garbage disposal were much superior in Dinuba compared to Arvin
7. there were more schools, parks, churches, civic improvement organizations, and similar entities in Dinuba than in Arvin
8. decision making was more democratic in Dinuba, while in Arvin decisions tended to be made by county officials

Based on these findings Goldschmidt concluded that the quality of life in a rural community surrounded by small farms was superior to the quality of life in a community surrounded by large farms. He also stated that he expected that the results obtained in his study would be applicable to any other place where similar economic conditions existed. This expectation that smaller-sized farms would result in an improved quality of life in neighboring communities has become known as the Goldschmidt hypothesis.

An extension of the Goldschmidt hypothesis is that an increase in the scale of agriculture in an area will result in a decreased quality of life in affected communities. Since its original publication, various aspects of the Goldschmidt hypothesis have been tested numerous times (e.g., Eberts 1979; Flora et al. 1977; Gilles et al. 1984; Green 1985; Harris and Gilbert 1982; Heffernan 1972; Heffernan and Lasley 1978; La Rose 1973;

LeVeen 1979; Small Farm Viability Project 1977; Sonka 1979). While **199** this literature is conceptually rich with important and interesting hypotheses, it currently lacks sound scientific underpinnings. A study of two communities in California does not permit wide generalization, and researchers since Goldschmidt have generally failed to build on the base he established (Nuckton et al. 1982).

One fundamental problem that researchers have confronted is the difficulty in measuring quality of life. Due to the lack of an appropriate measure they have typically used a variety of factors as indicators of quality of life. Among the indicators have been population trends, the quality and quantity of community services available, and the class structure in the community. In the sections that follow, the literature will be reviewed relative to the aspect of the community that is hypothesized to be impacted by the scale of farming in an area.

A further problem with the literature is that much of the research has dealt only with the effects of farm size. Obviously, numerous other dimensions of agriculture have important consequences for rural communities. A review of the existing literature suggests several potential relationships between agriculture and the quality of life in rural communities that merit attention. In the sections that follow, we examine a few of these relationships.

AGRICULTURE AND COMMUNITY POPULATION TRENDS

The relationship between agricultural structure and community population trends is well documented in the literature (Beale 1978; 1980), and discussed in detail in Chapter 7. As noted in Chapters 3 and 7, structural changes in agriculture, which have included a declining number of farms, a reduced farm population, and much larger farm units have resulted in extensive declines in the populations of agriculturally based rural communities. This reflects the ecological principle that population size achieves a balance with available opportunities. Technological developments in agriculture replaced labor and consequently resulted in reduced employment opportunities. Thus, between 1940 and 1970 the population in many rural communities declined by more than 50 percent as numerous rural residents moved to the city in search of economic opportunities (Beale 1978, 1980; Larson 1981). Even during the more recent population turnaround of the 1970s, counties heavily dependent on agricultural employment remained about as likely to experience a declining population as they were in the past. The primary difference was that there were fewer areas heavily dependent on agricultural employment than in the past (Albrecht 1986).

Research from the Great Plains has provided further evidence of the strong relationship between farm structure and community population trends. Albrecht and Murdock (1985b, 1986a, 1986b) found that counties experiencing large-scale irrigation development between 1940 and 1980 were also likely to experience population growth. In contrast, those counties without irrigation development were more likely to experience declining populations, a trend typical in agriculturally based rural counties of that era. The reason for these differences in population trends is the mediating effect of farm structure. Extensive irrigation development results in greater agricultural production per acre and a system of agriculture that is more labor intensive and that has thus been more resistant to farm consolidation. As a result, more persons have remained in agriculture, and this more productive agricultural base has resulted in allied and secondary growth in surrounding communities. Consequently, high rates of irrigation development have resulted in population increases in some areas and population stability in others.

One problem with the literature on agricultural structure and population trends is that it has failed to determine the extent to which population declines in agriculturally based rural areas are a result of farm structure changes as opposed to other factors. Brown (1979), for example, notes that demographic change in small towns is a result of two major factors: (1) changes in transportation and communication and (2) changes in the structure of agriculture. He notes that prior to about 1920 rural communities were relatively isolated, autonomous, and self-sufficient trade centers, and residents of these communities were dependent on their local community for the majority of their goods and services. Later developments in transportation and communication permitted rural residents to extend their life beyond the boundaries of their local community so that they were no longer required to shop at local stores. Instead, many travel to remote but larger cities to obtain some of their goods and services. Some small trade centers have become like the neighborhood store in large cities. People use them to pick up small items to avoid traveling long distances, but they make their major purchases elsewhere. Thus, these transportation and communication advancements would have resulted in extensive changes in rural population patterns **201** without corresponding changes in the structure of agriculture.

Additional research is needed to improve our understanding of the relationship between agricultural structure and changes therein and population trends in rural communities. There is little question that future developments that result in fewer and larger farms will also exert downward pressure on the population of nearby rural communities. However, the extent of this relationship in different contexts and the importance of other variables remains unknown.

AGRICULTURAL STRUCTURE AND COMMUNITY SERVICES

A number of researchers have documented that the changes occurring in agriculture have implications for the quality and quantity of community services available in rural areas (e.g., Adams 1969; Rogers 1982). Goldschmidt contended that a greater choice of services available to residents meant a higher quality of life. In his own research, Goldschmidt (1946, 1978b) found that the community service base in Dinuba (surrounded by small farms) was substantially superior to the community service base in Arvin (surrounded by large farms).

The reason for this expected relationship between farm structure and community services is that these community services are subject to economies of scale. Consequently, since large-scale farming by definition means fewer farms and fewer farm people, the trend toward larger farms results in a smaller population to support these businesses. In addition to the effects of absolute numbers, researchers have also hypothesized that family farmers would have higher levels of participation in community organizations than the managers and laborers from large-scale agriculture (Heffernan 1982a; Rodefeld 1974). Thus, large-scale farming is hypothesized to result in both fewer farm families and a type of farm family that will be less involved in community organizations.

Most of the research completed on this topic has found some support for the Goldschmidt hypothesis. During the 1970s, 130 rural communities in the San Joaquin Valley of California were studied and ranked on an index of seventeen community services. The researchers found a positive relationship between family farm agriculture and available community services (Small Farm Viability Project 1977). This research, however, used proxy measures of farm size based on aerial photography, and thus the conclusions must be questioned. A 1970 restudy of Arvin and Dinuba (La Rose 1973) found that differences in the level of services provided by the two communities were as great or greater than in the 1940s. However, the communities had changed so much from the 1940s that they would not have been selected for a comparative study in 1970.

Several studies have also explored the relationship between farm structure and the level of involvement and participation in community activities or organizations (Heffernan 1982a). After studying poultry growers in Louisiana, Heffernan (1972) concluded that there was little difference between growers (those working in a corporate-type structure) and family farmers with regard to community involvement. Within corporate structures, however, he found that owners and managers were more involved in community and political activities than hired workers. Researchers in Wisconsin found that individuals on family farms were more involved in local voluntary organizations and political or social activities than were the workers on other types of farms (Rodefeld 1974; Martinson et al. 1976). Similarly, Heffernan and Lasley (1978) found a relationship between the type of farm structure and involvement in the social activities of the local community among Missouri grape producers. In a study of Maryland dairy farmers Poole (1981) found that farm scale was inversely related to social participation in formal community organizations. Thus, most, but not all, of the studies on community involvement have provided some support for the Goldschmidt hypothesis.

Other researchers have found that declining populations in rural communities resulting from structural changes in agriculture as well as other factors have an important effect on community services. A long line of community research has shown a direct relationship between the quality and quantity of services provided in rural communities and the size of the community (Harden 1960; Jesser 1963). It appears obvious that larger communities should be able to provide a broader range of services and that the quality of the services provided should also be better. This contention is generally supported by both subjective and objective research. A body of subjective literature has shown that satisfaction with services is greater among the residents of larger communities (Johnson and Knop 1970; Goudy 1977; Rojek et al. 1975). Similarly, the more objective research has shown smaller communities to be at a disadvantage with factors such as the number of doctors per capita, teachers per student, and so on (Leistritz and Murdock 1981; Rogers 1982).

The situation is made even more severe by the nature of population declines. The typical pattern of change with population decline is that the youth leave, the average age rises, birth rates fall, and incomes decline. This selective movement of people increases the burden on remaining residents through extra costs and lower levels of service (Rogers 1982). Adams (1969) found that when a community declines the first services to leave are the professionals such as doctors, dentists, and lawyers. The second to go are the large dry goods dealers such as car and appliance salespersons, and the third to go are the duplicate businesses. In each case, the declining community finds itself unable to compete with larger neighboring communities.

In sum, much of the previous research has found that a trend toward larger farms results in the quality and quantity of services in rural communities being reduced. Studies have also found that family farmers often participate more in community activities and organizations than the managers and workers on large-scale or corporate-type farms. Additional research, especially longitudinal research, is needed to determine the impact of different types of structural changes in agriculture and to determine which types of community services are most affected by these changes.

AGRICULTURE AND THE COMMUNITY CLASS STRUCTURE

An important assumption of Goldschmidt's research was that the effects of farm size on the community were mediated through social class. That is, large-scale agriculture results in a large number of people employed in low-scale, often seasonal, wage labor. Some argue that if agricultural holdings and production are concentrated in the hands of a few, then income, educational opportunities, the level of living, and other advantages will also be tilted in favor of these few. For example, T. Lynn Smith (1972, 8) notes that

> closely associated with a high degree of concentration . . . are such phenomena as the following: (1) a sharp division of the rural popu-

lation into a small, highly developed group of the elite at the apex of the socioeconomic scale and a huge mass of persons who are only slightly above the creature or brute level of existence at the base; (2) practically no shifting up or down in the scale, or from one class to another; (3) a strong cast element in that the status of human beings is determined largely by that of their parents; (4) widespread poverty and low average levels of living among those engaged in agricultural pursuits; (5) a rural or agricultural population in which the average level of intelligence is low and in which the differences between the extremes are very great, i.e., a condition in which only a small fraction of the human potential is realized.

A number of studies in recent years have attempted to test this aspect of the Goldschmidt hypothesis and explore the consequences of farm structure in general and large-scale farming in particular on the social class structure of rural areas. Using 1959 Census of Agriculture data, Smith (1969) attempted to divide the farm population of the United States into five social class categories including upper class, upper-middle class, middle-middle class, lower-middle class, and lower class. He found that the proportion of the farm population that fell into the different social class categories varied extensively from one part of the country to another and was largely dependent on the farm structure and the type of agricultural enterprises that persisted in these different areas. For example, less than 15 percent of the farm population was in the lower class in the midwestern states of Iowa, Wisconsin, Minnesota, North Dakota, South Dakota, Nebraska, and Kansas. Agriculture in these states is dominated by family farms that provide most of the capital, management, and labor on the farms. Consequently, there is little need for a hired farm labor force. In fact, a vast majority of the farm population in these states fell into the upper-middle and middle-middle classes with a relatively small lower class and upper class.

In contrast, more than one-half of the farm population was in the lower class in the states of Arizona, Hawaii, California, Florida, Rhode Island, Mississippi, and New Mexico. In each of these states agriculture was dominated by large-scale operations, and as a consequence there was a large labor force of hired workers. The states with a large lower class also tend to have a relatively large upper class. Table 8.1 presents the data from Smith's analysis. This table shows that nearly one-third of the farm population nationwide was in the lower class, 2 percent was in the upper class, and the remaining two-thirds were in the middle-class categories.

Goldschmidt (1978a) correlated the percentage of the farm population in the lower class as reported by Smith (1969) with the extent of large-scale farming as defined by the proportion of agricultural sales from farms with sales of $100,000 or more. He found a strong correlation between the two ($r = .76$) showing that areas characterized by large-scale farming are more likely to have a large proportion of their farm population in the lower class.

More recently Harris and Gilbert (1982) attempted to expand the Goldschmidt research by examining in more detail the relationship between farm scale and rural income. Utilizing measures similar to those used by Goldschmidt as well as some additional measures, they found some support for Goldschmidt's contentions. However, they also found some relationships that were contrary to their expectations. Specifically, they found that the size of the lower class was positively related to the prevalence of large farms. They also found a negative relationship between farm structure and both farmers' income and farm workers' income. They found a positive relationship between farm income and rural income, and they found that large farms and rural income are negatively related. All of these findings support their hypotheses and Goldschmidt's contentions. Contrary to their hypotheses, however, they found that the prevalence of large farms had a positive effect on both farmers' income and farm workers' income. They concluded that the uncritical acceptance of Goldschmidt's thesis would be unwarranted.

LeVeen (1979) conducted a study to discern the consequences of enforcing the Reclamation Act of 1902. This act has a provision that farms receiving water from a federally funded reclamation project cannot be greater than 160 acres in size. The focus of his study was Fresno County, California, where the Reclamation Act has been ignored as it has in nearly all other areas in the nation. LeVeen found that people living in areas dominated by smaller farms had larger incomes, and the proportion of the population living in the lower class was reduced. However, he noted that moving to a system of smaller farms in California would do little to help the most disadvantaged people who are living in poverty. The nature of California agriculture is that it uses a low-income, seasonal labor force, and such a labor force is needed whether the farms are large or small.

Pfeffer (1983) described the emergence of three systems of agriculture and noted how each was related to the resulting class structure in that area. In each case the system of agriculture that emerged was in

Table 8.1. Proportions of the farm personnel in the United States classified upper, upper-middle, middle-middle, lower-middle, and lower class, by state, 1959

Geographic division and state	Farm personnel				
	Upper class %	Upper-middle class %	Middle-middle class %	Lower-middle class %	Lower class %
United States	2.1	14.5	26.6	25.7	31.1
New England					
Maine	2.9	18.5	16.1	27.9	34.6
New Hampshire	1.5	15.0	17.8	29.6	36.1
Vermont	1.0	22.8	28.8	18.6	28.8
Massachusetts	2.0	16.5	16.1	19.1	46.3
Rhode Island	2.6	18.8	14.9	13.3	50.4
Connecticut	3.1	18.0	12.5	17.9	48.5
Middle Atlantic					
New York	1.2	20.7	25.3	20.1	32.7
New Jersey	3.0	24.3	16.3	13.9	42.5
Pennsylvania	0.8	17.0	25.8	30.1	26.3
East north central					
Ohio	0.7	14.5	32.8	31.6	20.4
Indiana	0.9	19.7	33.3	28.6	17.5
Illinois	2.3	31.4	30.9	16.7	18.7
Michigan	0.5	12.5	30.8	32.0	24.2
Wisconsin	0.4	19.2	49.1	16.6	14.7
West north central					
Minnesota	0.8	22.2	45.1	17.1	14.8
Iowa	2.7	36.1	36.7	10.9	13.6
Missouri	0.8	13.0	34.3	32.3	19.6
North Dakota	0.8	22.7	50.6	11.4	14.5
South Dakota	1.2	23.0	50.2	13.3	12.3
Nebraska	2.3	32.1	42.1	10.4	13.1
Kansas	2.1	25.7	40.4	18.0	13.8
South Atlantic					
Delaware	3.9	25.8	21.1	18.3	30.9
Maryland	1.7	17.0	21.5		

Table 8.1. (Continued)

Geographic division and state	Upper class %	Upper-middle class %	Middle-middle class %	Lower-middle class %	Lower class %
Virginia	0.7	6.5	18.6	38.0	36.2
West Virginia	0.3	3.7	11.1	58.5	26.4
North Carolina	0.3	6.3	28.0	27.8	37.6
South Carolina	0.5	4.8	16.6	31.3	46.8
Georgia	0.9	9.1	19.2	28.4	42.4
Florida	2.6	7.4	11.9	22.5	55.6
West south central					
Kentucky	0.2	5.6	25.6	38.8	29.8
Tennessee	0.2	3.8	20.3	39.5	36.2
Alabama	0.6	5.0	14.7	41.8	37.9
Mississippi	0.7	3.3	11.5	34.2	50.3
Arkansas	1.5	7.7	14.2	27.5	49.1
Louisiana	0.9	5.5	12.2	37.7	43.7
Oklahoma	0.9	12.8	28.4	32.0	25.9
Texas	2.5	12.7	19.0	24.5	41.3
Mountain					
Montana	2.6	28.6	29.5	14.5	24.8
Idaho	2.6	25.8	29.5	18.3	23.8
Wyoming	3.5	26.0	25.7	12.9	31.9
Colorado	3.9	25.4	25.2	16.3	29.2
New Mexico	2.7	11.5	13.3	22.3	50.2
Arizona	5.0	8.8	6.1	8.7	71.4
Utah	2.0	16.8	28.4	27.9	24.9
Nevada	5.8	16.1	15.8	16.9	45.4
Pacific					
Washington	3.1	18.5	18.6	31.8	28.0
Oregon	2.8	15.2	20.1	32.4	29.5
California	5.2	12.9	11.9	14.3	55.7
Alaska	2.8	17.9	13.3	37.2	28.8
Hawaii	0.9	4.4	9.8	19.4	65.5

Farm personnel

Source: Smith (1969, 506–7); published with the permission of the Rural Sociological Society.

response to differing labor needs in agriculture. He described how a system of small family farms emerged in the Midwest and resulted in a largely middle-class farm population. In contrast, in both California and the South a small upper class owns the land and makes the decisions, while a relatively large lower class provides the labor on these farms. In California these workers typically came from a disadvantaged class of people and were often hired on a seasonal basis, while in the South the labor force initially consisted of slaves. Later most of these slaves became sharecroppers.

CONCLUSIONS

Obviously a great deal of additional research is needed on the relationship between agriculture and the community. Following the classic study of Goldschmidt, most analyses have focused on the size of the farm units surrounding a community as the major determinant affecting the community. In addition, most of the analyses have been limited to examinations of the effects on population retention, services, and stratification in the community.

From the ecological theory standpoint, however, such studies have failed to examine some of the most critical conditions determining the effects of the structure of agriculture on communities. Thus, few studies have been made of communities in truly different environmental settings, few have examined the role of the organizational history of the area on its response to organizational change, and few have evaluated the differences in response to different types of technology. In addition, few analyses have compared community responses in areas that are different on such key dimensions as the diversity of their sustenance bases, the types and forms of agricultural commodities produced (which also has sustenance implications for organization), or the availability and costs of labor.

From an ecological perspective the major failure of past efforts is that they have tended to see organizational factors as causes rather than consequences of change. If viewed ecologically, however, such changes must be seen as major consequences of changes that are a result of a complex set of interactions between population, environment, technology, and other organizational dimensions. It is critical to recognize that the effects of change in the structure of agriculture on rural communities occurs as a result of a total complex of ecosystem change that involves **209** complex actions and reactions among diverse elements.

Given a more complex and integrative approach to the study of agricultural and community interdependencies, a number of specific research issues can be identified. Among these are

1. A majority of the previous research on the relationship between agriculture and the community has focused on the effects of farm size. No doubt numerous other agricultural factors are important. For example, the literature to date has generally assumed that farm structure and farm scale were synonymous, with large-scale agriculture being equal to corporate agriculture (Green 1985). Often, however, this is not the case. Furthermore, the tenure structure of the farms, the extent of off-farm employment, and numerous other agricultural factors may be related to the quality of life in rural communities but have not yet been examined (Heffernan 1982a). Similarly, researchers have failed to account for potential implications of the type of commodity being produced. For example, does it make a difference if a community is surrounded by wheat producers or lettuce producers (if other factors are equal)? Further, does the corporate production of hogs have similar consequences on the community as the corporate production of oranges?

From an ecological perspective these various agricultural dimensions would be expected to have important implications for the community. The type of agricultural structure that emerges in an area is a product of the combination of environmental resources available, the technological practices that can be used to deal with these resources, and organizational and other factors. No doubt the population and organizational adaptations to these variations will be different.

2. Researchers have yet to examine the characteristics of the community that are likely to influence the extent to which the community is impacted by changes in agriculture. For example, in some rural areas agriculture employs only a small proportion of the total work force, and changes that occur in agriculture may not be consequential for these communities. In contrast, changes in agriculture may be more profound in communities that are more economically dominated by agriculture. Thus, one could hypothesize that the effects of agricultural change will be greater in communities that are more economically dependent on agriculture.

3. Researchers have failed to examine the effects of economic cycles

in agriculture on the viability of rural communities. In Chapter 2 it was noted that from an ecological perspective humans tend to expand their lives to the fullest extent possible. Thus, in a time when farm incomes are relatively high this should lead to economic prosperity in rural communities. Likewise during hard economic times in agriculture (such as the recent farm crisis), agriculturally based rural communities are likely to face economic decline. In a similar manner, rural communities in a productive agricultural region should be more viable than rural communities in an area where resources important to agricultural production are limited.

4. To date we have only a limited understanding of which aspects of the community are affected by changes in agriculture. Further, researchers in the sociology of agriculture have seldom used the literature on and the measures of variables such as community viability, community satisfaction, and social class membership.

5. Researchers are becoming increasingly aware that not only do changes in agriculture affect rural communities, but that changes in rural communities also affect agriculture (Beaulieu and Molnar 1985; Buttel 1983). In many instances the survival of small and limited-resource farms is directly dependent on the availability of part-time employment in nearby communities. Also, land and water resources critical to agriculture are being used increasingly for nonfarm uses. The diversion of such resources away from agriculture will no doubt have important consequences for the farm population.

The analysis of the effects of agricultural structure and of changes in this structure on rural communities is thus clearly important, but broader and more inclusive research efforts than most of those completed to date are essential. Although we are under no illusion that organizing, funding, and completing such efforts will be easy, we believe that our understanding in this area will not increase appreciably until broader and more inclusive research efforts are completed.

Agriculture in the United States
in the 1990s

griculture in the United States faces a future of revolutionary
changes in technology and in its organizational base. This future will be influenced by numerous factors reflecting not only
changes in agricultural technology but also changing patterns
of international trade, national agricultural and trade policy, world population growth and other factors. In this chapter human ecological
theory and the findings reported in the previous chapters are used to
logically integrate key trends and to indicate how these trends are likely
to form the future of agriculture in the United States in the coming
years. In so doing an attempt is made both to provide the reader with
insight concerning the possible future of agriculture in the United States
and to further indicate the utility of a human ecological perspective for
understanding the structure of agriculture. The changes discussed are
ones suggested from the use of a human ecological perspective and in
many cases are incremental changes rather than abrupt departures from
existing trends. In addition, we do not claim that the changes examined
are either exhaustive of the changes that will occur or the most significant changes of those that may occur in the future. In sum, the discussion in this chapter is both speculative and limited in a number of regards.

211

212   Ecologically Based Patterns of Change in the Future of U.S. Agriculture

One means of examining the future of U.S. agriculture is to examine changes that may occur in the basic ecological dimensions of agriculture. In particular, returning to the concepts outlined in Chapter 2, the potential changes can be analyzed in relation to basic dimensions such as environment, technology, population, and organization and in terms of processual factors such as adaptation, symbiotic and commensalistic interdependence, functionality, differentiation, key function, dominance, and isomorphism. By describing likely changes in these factors, insight concerning changes in the coming decade can be obtained.

Before discussing change in each of the factors noted above, an overview of possible change in the total ecosystem of agriculture is provided. In so doing, it is necessary to briefly introduce conditions that will be discussed in detail for each factor. The intent, however, is not to describe the major changes within each factor but to display some of the many interactions that are crucial to understanding the total ecological context, or ecosystem.

Future Ecosystem of U.S. Agriculture

Changes in agricultural ecosystems in the past appear to have largely been driven by technological developments and interrelated adaptations in the ecological organization of agriculture (Berardi and Geisler 1984). Such changes can be recognized ecologically as representing populations' attempts to improve their ability to adapt by using means (technology) that both expand the environmental base and improve their ability to exploit that base. These patterns reflect the basic premises of human ecology that populations will attempt to expand to the limits of the environment (see Chapter 2). The future of the agricultural ecosystem may continue to be determined, in large part, by technological and organizational change. Among the key technological and organizational changes expected are those resulting from the recent economic crisis in agriculture, those related to biotechnology and the information revolution, and the organizational changes related to these technological changes.

Although the causes for the 1980 farm crisis in U.S. agriculture were complex (involving U.S. monetary and trade policy, the changing value of the U.S. dollar, and numerous other factors), the crisis can be **213** seen ecologically as resulting, at least in part, from the declining dominance of U.S. agriculture in the world food supply system. As such dominance declined and other countries came to be major food and fiber exporters, the ability of U.S. agriculture to control world markets declined. As a factor's dominance in an ecosystem declines, it will experience increased competition and may play a decreasing role in determining the characteristics of the ecosystem. It could respond by seeking to more completely dominate its immediate environment, by seeking to expand the number of niches it addresses in that environment, and by attempting to further exploit its dominance within those niches in the larger ecosystem where its control is most effective. For U.S. agriculture the base of competitors in world markets is likely to continue to expand. Its expected ecological response is thus one that should lead it to exploit its traditional strengths in agricultural technology development, to search for means to fill new niches in the domestic food market, and to specialize in specific commodities in international markets.

Among the major strengths of U.S. agriculture has been its development and use of advanced forms of technology. In fact, it can be persuasively argued that it is the diffusion of United States' agricultural technology that has allowed other nations to become effective competitors with the United States (Paarlberg 1980; Ashby 1982; Goss 1979). As the biotechnological and information revolutions impact agriculture, the effect should be a lessening of the environmental constraints to the types of commodities produced in different locations. This will occur as plants and animals that are resistant to temperature and rainfall extremes are developed and better means of marketing goods are developed. Both the range of crops and livestock that can be raised in a given environment and the efficiency of production of such commodities should increase. The United States may attempt to rapidly expand its technology base and to export that technology and will attempt to provide a larger proportion of its own food products by expanding its base of products. It should attempt to exert greater domination of its own immediate environment and to specialize in a few products that it can dominate in world markets. Similar patterns should develop within regions in the United States as attempts to prevent loss in local markets and attempts by producers in certain regions to enhance their competitive advantages relative to producers in other regions intensify.

In like manner, both the new financial and market realities facing producers and the new technologies will affect the organizational base of agriculture. This base is likely to expand as populations of producers not only adopt new technology but also search for new niches in which to seek more profitable (more adaptable) markets. This should lead to a diversification of the types of commodities produced by farmers in different environments. This diversification should lead to an increased range of farm production units as new products come to provide the sustenance base for these production units. It may in fact lead to a further acceleration of the bipolar organizational structure in agriculture as small producers attempt to expand into new product areas and to produce multiple products while larger producers attempt to compete in a few very specialized commodity areas. Although new technologies and marketing requirements are likely to be so costly that only a few producers will be able to afford them for production of very specialized commodities that are competitive in worldwide markets, the new biotechnologies should also allow small producers to remain profitable in certain types of commodities.

As a result of such diversification, the farm population should become increasingly bipolar and diverse. In those areas of the nation where farming can be combined with other work activities, the number of part-time production units will increase and an increasingly diverse range of persons who have not previously been involved in agriculture will come to seek involvement in small-scale agriculture (Schroeder et al. 1983). On the other hand, in areas with few alternatives to agriculture a continued domination by populations with traditional farm population characteristics can be expected.

In sum, then, the expansion of agriculture into an increasingly worldwide ecosystem of competition and biotechnological and other technological developments offers to substantially increase the range of commodities that can be produced within a given set of environmental limitations. It may also lead to an increasingly bipolar organizational structure in agriculture as large-scale production units compete in a few very specialized commodity areas while small-scale producers compete in an increasingly diverse range of commodity areas. This will result in a diversification in both the structure of agriculture and the farm population and will likely further emphasize the dual structure of agriculture promoting greater bipolarization of the size of units into an increasing number of very small production units that account for a limited proportion of overall commodity production and a decreasing number of very

large units that account for a large proportion of total agricultural pro-   **215**
duction.

Although the bipolar structural pattern described above appears to point to little more than the continuation of past trends, the fact that the characteristics of the total population of producers may become increasingly diverse promises to have significant implications for agriculture and particularly for agricultural policy. As the characteristics of persons involved in agriculture diversify, agricultural policy may be less dominated by commodity programs, and as Paarlberg (1980) has noted, an increasing range of nonagricultural groups will be involved in the formulation of agricultural and food policy. In like manner, as the population of producers broadens, state and local service providers such as extension services and experiment stations are likely to experience increased demands from small producers who, although managing farms that are limited in production, are nevertheless attuned to the need for continually updated information and technology. If such demands lead to dramatic changes in the service and research base for agriculture, the long-term implications for agriculture could be extensive. As the ecological processes interactively evolve, then, the changes expected in the next decade could provide the basis for a substantially altered ecosystem in the next century.

If the patterns of ecosystem change hypothesized above are correct, the major ecological factors and processes should come to display distinct characteristics. The examination of these characteristics and their possible forms and patterns of change in the next decade are discussed below.

Environment

As noted in Chapter 4, the diverse environment of the United States has produced crop specialization and regionally distinct forms of agriculture. The biotechnical and other technological development projected for agriculture in the coming years can be expected, in the long run, to free agriculture from some of the environmental constraints that have affected it in the past. Such technology (United States Department of Agriculture 1986b) is expected to produce plants that will mature in shorter growing seasons with more resistance to temperature variations and animals with extensive disease resistance and other desirable growth and structural characteristics. In addition, as noted above and in Chap-

216 ter 5, these methods may increase the level of production per unit and even alter the patterns of change in farm size.

It must be recognized, however, that many of the new technologies will require many years of basic research before they can be safely and efficiently applied to agricultural production. Thus, although long-term effects are expected to occur, many of these effects will not be apparent in the next decade. In addition, at least for the next few years, environmental variations will largely persist, and to some extent, no matter how developed the technology base, the natural advantages existing for the production of certain commodities within certain areas will continue to impact levels of productivity.

Ecological theory suggests that the impact of biotechnology will vary widely among different environmental bases. The impact of biotechnology may provide the greatest range of alternative products in the richest environments that provide the most alternative resources from which products can be developed. Clearly, products will be developed specifically for environments that have historically been less productive, but the viable options are less in such environments than in more diverse environments. We expect that biotechnology will not reverse the competitive advantages that exist due to environmental differences in the United States, except for a limited number of agricultural commodities. In fact, such technologies may exaggerate existing environmental differences and the competitive advantages created by these differences (for example, such appears to be the case for the bovine growth hormone [Smith and Bauman 1986]). In addition, some maintain that it is unclear how many of these technologies may impact the environment and that concerns exist (Curry 1986) about how bioengineered products may impact the biological ecosystem.

In sum, then, although environmental limitations on production will be different with new technologies and reduced in significance for some products, particularly in the long run, environmental differences will continue to be of importance in determining both the form and productivity of agriculture in different regions of the nation in the coming decade.

Technology

The technological base of agriculture may be impacted by at least two major developments. These two developments are biotechnology

(United States Department of Agriculture 1986b) and information   **217**
management technology (Dillman 1985). As noted in Chapter 5, the
impact of these forms of technology may vary with the form of interdependence developed between them and the existing agricultural base. In
this regard information technology is largely commensalistic and its major effect will probably be to increase the efficiency of the farm operation
by allowing the operator to access information more rapidly and to
perform activities such as marketing and production management with
more developed information bases. As a result, computer and other
forms of information technology in the coming years should continue to
increase the efficiency of existing producers but with increasingly dimin-
ishing returns as new technology is incorporated by competitors and
information bases are widely and rapidly disseminated.

The expected forms and effects of biotechnology have also been
described in Chapter 5, but it is essential to note here that this technology is likely to be adopted at increasingly rapid rates as populations of
producers recognize the competitive advantages associated with the use
of such technology. Because the rate of adoption of new technology will
probably be increasingly rapid, it appears that the effect of biotechnology may be that of raising the total level of technology use rather
than increasing the level of use among only certain groups. Although
some (Buttel et al. 1983) would argue that the costs of biotechnology will
allow larger producers to obtain a competitive advantage over smaller
farms by more quickly adopting such technologies, we anticipate that
because the changes brought about by such technology will be so substantial they will be adapted at more rapid and uniform rates than anticipated. Because the importance of the use of technology will be widely
recognized, the new political forces in agriculture may support a subsidized dissemination of this technology. As a result, biotechnology will
dramatically affect agricultural production in the coming decades, and
its adoption rate will probably be sufficiently rapid so that it will largely
increase the overall level of technology use rather than provide marked
shifts in the competitive advantages for only certain groups.

In addition, because biotechnology is a symbiotic form of technology it should substantially alter the resource bases of many rural environments causing them to both develop new products and to be able to
produce commodities that were previously deemed to be inappropriate
for certain environments. It is such effects that will lead to the diversification of agriculture described in the introduction of this section. As

noted in Chapter 5, however, the equity effects of biotechnology will likely vary with the policies developed for their dissemination.

Population

As of 1985, the farm population of the United States consisted of only 5.4 million people or only 2.2 percent of the total U.S. population. In addition, only about 50 percent of that population was engaged primarily in agricultural production. Even when nonmetropolitan populations were growing in the United States during the late 1960s and 1970s (Beale 1975; Engels 1986), the rural farm population continued to decline. Past trends would thus lead one to anticipate continued decline. From an ecological perspective, however, it is the interaction of environmental, technological, and organizational factors that determine the size of the farm population, and, as noted above, the patterns for these factors point to increasingly diversified environmental, technological, and organizational bases. Since many of these changes should lead to a growth in the total number of farms (particularly small farms) (Harper et al. 1980), the farm population should begin to stabilize in the coming decade as opportunities for involvement in agriculture by nontraditional populations expand.

Because of the bipolar structure in farm organization and the fact that nontraditional groups may begin to enter small-scale agriculture, an increasingly bipolar distribution in the rates of growth and the characteristics of the farm population can also be expected. In areas such as the Great Plains, farm populations can be expected to decline further as adaptations to technology occur. In these areas, a majority of producers have few opportunities to combine farm and nonfarm employment because of the lack of nonfarm employment. In addition, such areas are ones likely to have the organizational forms of agriculture that will be involved in the national and international competition for commodity markets. As such, the use of efficient techniques that reduce the costs for labor may continue to be emphasized, resulting in reduced farm populations. Finally, because of the lack of nonfarm employment opportunities, the scale of agriculture, and its national and international competitive base, the entry of new persons into agriculture in these areas will be limited. Those remaining in the farm population are likely to be the sons and daughters of existing producers and thus the population may have characteristics that are homogeneous with the existing farm population **219** bases in these areas.

In other rural farm areas of the nation, particularly those areas in close proximity to nonfarm employment opportunities, the farm population may increase as people move to farms to seek the perceived benefits of farm life (surveys continue to show strong preferences for obtaining the life-style believed to be associated with rural farm life [Molnar and Duffy 1986; Schroeder et al. 1985]). For such areas, a farm population composed of increasingly diverse socioeconomic groups can be expected. In fact, because this new farm population may be highly dependent on the nonfarm sustenance base, its size and its characteristics are likely to vary more with the nonfarm environment and economy than with the conditions in the farm environment and its economy.

In regard to population, then, a stabilization of the total farm population can be expected, but the nature of change in the farm population will be highly variable from one geographical and farming area to another. The trends toward more diverse population bases on farms should serve to at least partially reverse the trend toward increasing homogeneity in the farm population that has dominated rural farm population patterns in the past.

Organization

Many of the expected patterns in the organizational base of agriculture have already been described. Trends producing a bipolar composition of farms by size as well as an expansion in the number of countries competing for world commodity markets will probably continue. At the same time, however, ecological processes occurring as a result of the adaptation of new technology should also lead to patterns that have occurred infrequently in the past. The anticipated increase in the number of producers originating from nonfarm groups is, for example, a new pattern that could lead to a new set of interactional and organizational processes, to new forms of competition for resources and services, and to an evolving sociopolitical base that is likely to produce dramatic changes in the structure of agriculture in the future.

Because many of the new producers will possess considerable nonfarm resources including relatively high levels of education and extensive knowledge of bureaucratic and governmental processes, they should ex-

220   ert an increasing influence on the formulation of farm policy. Their successful adaptation to agriculture may depend on resources and technologies quite different from those that have led to the expansion of commercial-scale agriculture, and such organizational change may lead to an increased demand by these new producers for new agricultural services and research bases and to new small-scale producer-oriented farm policies. Although such a pattern may only begin to emerge in the coming decade, the anticipated diversification of the technology base, its effect in diversifying the forms of agriculture being developed around given environmental bases, and the very different population characteristics expected for the new producer groups make projections of dramatic changes in the dominance and power structure of agriculture increasingly feasible.

Such changes should, in turn, affect the key nonfarm organizational groups involved in agriculture. Given an evolving power structure, governmental programs may increasingly reflect policies that are scale neutral if not oriented specifically toward small producers. Although they will probably continue to be important players in the determination of agricultural policy, historically powerful commodity groups should be expected to be joined by an increasing number of new commodity groups whose memberships will probably be composed of small-scale producers. This should result in a reduction in the dominance and power of the traditional commodity groups. Agribusiness firms may become increasingly responsive to new markets for small producers and may find it more difficult to exert historic patterns of control, concentration and vertical integration. In sum, the new environment for agriculture may produce unprecedented changes in its organizational structure.

Adaptation

Of the ecological processes, adaptation is clearly among the most critical in shaping the future structure of U.S. agriculture. In fact, many of the anticipated trends in the future of U.S. agriculture are based on specific assumptions about the major types of adaptation that will occur as a result of the application of new technologies and the continuing expansion of competitors in international commodity markets. We have hypothesized two major forms of adaptation. One form is projected to involve large-scale producers increasingly specializing and utilizing new technological developments to compete more effectively. The second type will involve part-time producers and new producers pursuing the production of new products and a diversified range of products. Of these types of adaptation, the expectation that new forms of technology will lead to the entry of new persons into agriculture marks a sharp departure from past trends. However, from an ecological perspective the creation of new niches in the ecosystem, which can be expected to result from the use of the new technologies, should lead to the development of new competitors attempting to fill these niches. Three competitive groups participating in two major types of adaptation can be anticipated. For large producers the types of adaptation will be largely a continuation of historic patterns. For small part-time producers presently engaged in agriculture, adaptation may require both the continuation of historic patterns and attempts to respond to new technologies that are feasible for small-scale operations. For the new producer groups adaptation will involve not only the acquisition of standard producer patterns of behavior but also the introduction of new behaviors derived from their principal activities in other nonagricultural sustenance bases. As noted above, these new producers will eventually markedly affect the organizational structure of U.S. agriculture.

Differentiation

The agricultural ecosystem is likely to become increasingly diverse. The bipolar structure of agriculture, with a small number of large farms, a large number of small farms, and a declining number of medium-sized farms can be expected to be accelerated in the coming decade due to the processes noted above. Rather than a pattern involving occasional conflicts between large and small producer groups, a three-tier system of differentiation could develop, with the tiers consisting of large producers: traditional, small-scale, part-time producers; and new small-scale producers. Behaviorally, large producers should display preferences similar to those they have displayed in the past, seeking programs and policies that support large-scale commercial production. Traditional small-scale producers may continue to be relatively ineffective in promoting policies beneficial to their interests unless they work in conjunction with the new producer groups. The new producers may be more active than traditional small-scale producers both in pursuing information of utility to their production activities and in asserting the need for policies that assist small-scale producers. As a result of such differences, in the coming years conflicts may increase between large and small producers (especially between large producers and new small-scale producers).

Interdependence

The patterns previously described suggest the potential for an emergence of new types of commensalistic and symbiotic relationships. The new producers and traditional small-scale producers may develop commensalistic relationships relative to one another and relative to nonfarm constituencies because of the nonfarm base and origins of many new producers. In like manner, such commensalistic relationships may occur across space, so that constituencies of new producers may emerge. Symbiotic relationships also seem likely to develop among producer groups across the world as producers in nations come to serve specific needs in the worldwide markets for food and fiber products. In particular, as noted previously, the United States may come to serve in the role of a major agricultural technology exporter and as a supplier of raw commodities that will be processed in other nations. Large producers will probably continue their commensalistic relationships among themselves through commodity group memberships. Finally, the symbiotic relationships often believed to exist between large producers and agricultural research and extension agencies may become increasingly supplemented by the development of symbiotic relationships between these agencies and small producers. As the number and political influence of small producers grow, they should be able to increasingly attract the attention of the administrators of research and extension organizations.

Dominance and Key Function

Agriculture employs a decreasing number of persons, and the number of areas for which agriculture is the major sustenance base has continued to decline for several decades. As a result of processes described previously, the number of counties in the United States for which agriculture is a key function will continue to decline. Although the increase in the number of new producers will add to the farm population in some areas, it is unlikely that the size of these production units will be such as to offset the declining proportions of economic activity being derived from agriculture in such areas. In like manner, due to increased international competition agriculture may play a decreasing role as a source of

U.S. export activity. If this proves to be the case, the implications for **223** U.S. agriculture could be significant.

As a result of these trends the dominance of U.S. agriculture may decrease in several regards. Thus, agriculture may have a decreasing influence as the major industry in many rural areas within the United States. In like manner, the dominance of U.S. agriculture in world markets has declined and is likely to continue to decline. In the area of policy development, the declining power of agriculture also suggests that the number of groups (e.g., consumers, environmentalists, new producers, etc.) involved in the formulation of food and agricultural policy will, as Paarlberg (1980) has noted, extend to an increasing number of persons who have interests beyond those of large-scale production agriculture and who will exert an increasing influence as the power base of traditional groups declines. In sum, then, a continued decline in the dominance of U.S. agriculture in national and international affairs and the influence of traditional large-scale producers in the determination of domestic agricultural policy can be expected.

Isomorphism

Finally, with the continued rapid development of agricultural technology, the rapid dissemination of that technology, and the continued increase in the internationalization of agricultural markets, an increase in isomorphism, the similarity among the forms of agriculture in different regions in the United States and in different parts of the world, can be anticipated. As noted in the discussion of the environment, these similarities will only begin to become apparent in the coming decade and major environmental differences will continue to exist no matter what forms of technology are developed, but a trend toward increasing homogeneity in agriculture seems likely.

SUMMARY AND CONCLUSIONS

In this chapter some tentative projections of characteristics and trends likely to characterize U.S. agriculture in the coming decade have been described using key ecological dimensions and processes expected to operate in any ecosystem. The discussion suggests that increasing rates of use of new and revolutionary forms of technology such as biotechnology and information management technology, coupled with

224   the organizational changes being brought about by the financial crisis in agriculture in the 1980s and the expanding ecosystem of international agricultural competition will produce numerous changes in key dimensions of U.S. agriculture. Among the changes anticipated are an increase in the range of products that can be produced in different environments, which will increase the number of agricultural niches in numerous areas and increase the number of persons entering agriculture as an economic activity to be managed in conjunction with other nonfarm activities.

In addition, the group of new producers expected to enter agriculture will diversify the population and political power base of agriculture. Although large-scale commercial agricultural interests will continue to be dominant in those areas of the country where few alternatives to agricultural production exist, substantial growth in the number of small-scale local and regionally oriented producers should occur in other parts of the nation. United States' agriculture is expected to decrease in dominance both within the economic structure of the nation and in the international community. Finally, we expect that agricultural policy and research and extension activities will increasingly be impacted by new producers and by nonfarm interest groups. In sum, the structure of U.S. agriculture should become increasingly diverse and be impacted by an increasing number of factors in the coming decade.

Although the future as outlined is congruent with the predictions of others in some regards (e.g., in projecting a wider number of decision makers in agriculture [see Paarlberg 1980]), it is quite different in its projection of a diversifying base of agricultural activities, the introduction of new producer groups, and its projection of an increasingly diversified farm population base. It is clearly a highly speculative perspective on the future of U.S. agriculture, and even if only some of the major trends anticipated materialize, dramatic changes would occur in the coming decades. Such changes will alter the basic structure of the agricultural ecosystem.

Monitoring such changes should prove to be a challenging task for agricultural and social scientists in the coming decades. We suggest that researchers who are involved in that monitoring choose to use an ecological perspective to guide their efforts. By so doing, their analyses should both retain the broad-based interactive perspective essential to understanding the complexity of the forces affecting the structure of agriculture in the United States and provide the bases for further conceptual and empirical development of the human ecological perspective in the sociology of agriculture.

References

Adams, Bert N. 1969. The small trade center: Processes and perceptions of growth or decline. In *The Community: A Comparative Perspective,* ed. R. M. French. Itasca, Ill.: F. E. Peacock.

Adams, Michael E. 1986. Altering insect brain chemistry. In *Research for Tomorrow,* United States Department of Agriculture, 152–57. 1986 Yearbook of Agriculture. Washington, D.C.: United States Department of Agriculture.

Albrecht, Don E. 1986. Agriculture dependence and the population turnaround: Evidence from the Great Plains. *Journal of the Community Development Society* 17(1): 1–15.

Albrecht, Don E., and Howard Ladewig. 1982. Corporate agriculture and the family farm. *Rural Sociologist* 2(6): 376–83.

_____. 1985. The adoption of irrigation technology: The effects of personal, structural, and environmental variables. *Southern Rural Sociology* 3: 26–41.

Albrecht, Don E., and John K. Thomas. 1986. Farm tenure: A retest of conventional knowledge. *Rural Sociology* 51(1): 18–30.

Albrecht, Don E., and Steve H. Murdock. 1984. Toward a human ecological perspective on part-time farming. *Rural Sociology* 49(3): 389–411.

_____. 1985a. In defense of ecological analyses of agricultural phenomena: A reply to Swanson and Busch. *Rural Sociology* 50(3): 437–56.

_____. 1985b. *The Consequences of Irrigation Development in the Great Plains.* Department of Rural Sociology Technical Report 85-1. College Station: Texas Agricultural Experiment Station.

_____. 1986a. Natural resource availability and social change. *Sociological Inquiry* 56(3): 381–400.

_____. 1986b. Understanding farm structure and demographic change: An ecological analysis of the impacts of irrigation. *Sociological Perspectives* 29(4): 484–505.

Albrecht, Don E., Steve H. Murdock, Rita R. Hamm, and Kathy L. Schiflett. 1987a. *The Farm Crisis in Texas: Changes in the Financial Condition of Texas Farmers and Ranchers, 1985–86.* Department of Rural Sociology Technical Report 87-3. College Station: Texas Agricultural Experiment Station.

_____. 1987b. *Farm Crisis: Impact on Producers and Rural Communities in*

225

226   *Texas.* Department of Rural Sociology Technical Report 87-5. College Station: Texas Agricultural Experiment Station.

Alihan, M. A. 1938. *Social Ecology.* New York: Columbia University Press.

American Institute of Banking. 1969. *Agricultural Finance.* The American Bankers Association.

Appelbaum, Richard C. 1970. *Theories of Social Change.* Chicago: Markham.

Argenzio, Robert A. 1986. Membrane research: New approach to treatment of gastrointestinal illnesses. In *Research for Tomorrow,* ed. United States Department of Agriculture, 77–79. 1986 Yearbook of Agriculture. Washington, D.C.: United States Department of Agriculture.

Armbruster, W., D. Henderson, and R. Knutson, eds. 1983. *Federal Marketing Programs in Agriculture.* Danville, Ill.: The Interstate Printers and Publishers, Inc.

Ashby, Jacqueline A. 1982. Technology and ecology: Implications for innovation research in peasant agriculture. *Rural Sociology* 47(2): 234–50.

Babb, E. M. 1979. Some causes of structural change in U.S. agriculture. In *Structure Issues of American Agriculture,* ed. Economics, Statistics, and Cooperatives Service, 51–60. Agricultural Economic Report 438. Washington, D.C.: U.S. Department of Agriculture.

Banks, Vera J., and Karen M. Mills. 1983. Farm population of the United States: 1982. *Current Population Reports.* P-27, No. 56. Washington, D.C.: U.S. Department of Commerce, Bureau of the Census.

Barnes, P., and L. Casalino. 1972. *Who Owns the Land? A Primer on Land Reform in the U.S.A.* Berkeley, Calif.: Center for Rural Studies.

Barry, Peter J. 1984. *Impacts of Financial Stress and Regulatory Forces on Financial Markets for Agriculture.* Washington, D.C.: National Planning Association.

Beachy, Roger N. 1986. Producing disease-resistant plants. In *Research for Tomorrow,* ed. United States Department of Agriculture, 121–23. 1986 Yearbook of Agriculture. Washington, D.C.: United States Department of Agriculture.

Beale, Calvin L. 1975. The revival of population growth in nonmetropolitan America. Economic Research Service, ERS-605. Washington, D.C.: U.S. Department of Agriculture.

_____. 1978. People on the land. In *Rural U.S.A.: Persistence and Change,* ed. Thomas R. Ford. Ames: Iowa State University Press.

_____. 1979. Demographic aspects of agricultural structure. In *Structure Issues of American Agriculture,* ed. Economics, Statistics, and Cooperatives Service, 80–85. ESCS Agricultural Economic Report 438. Washington, D.C.: U.S. Department of Agriculture.

_____. 1980. The changing nature of rural employment. In *New Directions in Urban-Rural Migration.* ed. D. L. Brown and J. W. Wardwell. New York: Academic Press.

Beaulieu, Lionel J., and Joseph J. Molnar. 1985. Community change and the farm sector: Impacts of rural development on agriculture. *Rural Sociologist* 5(1): 15–22.

Bender, Lloyd D., Bernal L. Green, Thomas F. Hady, John A. Kuen, Marlys K. Nelson, Leon B. Perkinson, and Peggy J. Ross. 1985. *The Diverse Social and Economic Structure of Nonmetropolitan America.* Economic Research

Service, Rural Development Research Report Number 40. Washington, **227**
D.C.: United States Department of Agriculture.

Bennett, Hugh H. 1940. The land we defend. Speech given before the 78th
annual meeting of the National Education Association, Milwaukee, Wis.

Bennett, J. W. 1976. *The Ecological Transition.* New York: Pergamon.

Berardi, Gigi M. 1981. Socio-economic consequences of agricultural mechanization in the United States: Needed redirections for mechanization research.
Rural Sociology 46(3): 483–504.

Berardi, Gigi M., and Charles C. Geisler. 1984. *The Social Consequences and
Challenges of New Agricultural Technologies.* Boulder, Colo.: Westview
Press.

Berry, Brian J. L., and Frank E. Horton. 1970. *Geographic Perspectives on
Urban Systems.* Englewood Cliffs, N.J.: Prentice-Hall.

Berry, Brian J. L., and John D. Kasarda. 1977. *Contemporary Urban Ecology.*
New York: Macmillan.

Bertrand, Alvin L. 1958. *Rural Sociology.* New York: McGraw-Hill.

_____. 1978. Rural social organizational implications of technology and in-
dustry. In *Rural U.S.A.: Persistence and Change,* ed. T. R. Ford. Ames:
Iowa State University Press.

Bertrand, Alvin L., J. L. Charlton, Harold A. Pedersen, R. L. Skrabanek, and
James D. Tarver. 1956. *Factors Associated with Agricultural Mechanization
in the Southwest Region.* Agricultural Experiment Station Bulletin 567.
Fayetteville: University of Arkansas.

Bittinger, Morton W., and Elizabeth B. Green. 1980. *You Never Miss the
Water . . . (The Ogallala Story).* Littleton, Colo.: Water Resources.

Blum, Udo. 1986. Plants defend themselves chemically. In *Research for Tomorrow,* ed. United States Department of Agriculture, 139–42. 1986 Yearbook
of Agriculture. Washington, D.C.: United States Department of Agriculture.

Blumer, Herbert. 1969. *Symbolic Interactionism: Perspective and Method.*
Englewood Cliffs, N.J.: Prentice-Hall.

Boland, Walter. 1966. American institutions of higher education: A study of size
and complexity. Ph.D. diss., University of Michigan.

Bottomore, T. B., trans. and ed. 1964. *Karl Marx: Early Writings.* New York:
McGraw-Hill.

Breimyer, Harold F. 1977. The changing American farm. *Annals of the American Academy of Political and Social Science* 429: 12–22.

Brewster, John M. 1950. The machine process in agriculture and industry.
Journal of Farm Economics 32(1): 69–81.

Brooks, Nora L., Thomas A. Stucker, and Jennifer A. Bailey. 1986. Income and
well-being of farmers and the farm financial crisis. *Rural Sociology* 51(4):
391–405.

Brown, David L. 1979. Farm structure and the rural community. In *Structure
Issues of American Agriculture,* ed. Economics, Statistics, and Coopera-
tives Service, 283–87. Agricultural Economic Report 438. Washington,
D.C.: U.S. Department of Agriculture.

Brown, David L., and Calvin L. Beale. 1981. Diversity in post-1970 population
trends. In *Nonmetropolitan America in Transition.* ed. A. H. Hawley and
S. M. Mazie, 27–71. Chapel Hill: University of North Carolina Press.

228

Brown, Lester R. 1981. *Building a Sustainable Society.* New York: W. W. Norton.

Browne, William P. 1982. Farm organizations and agribusiness. In *Food Policy and Farm Programs.* Proceedings of the Academy of Political Science, Volume 34. New York: Academy of Political Science.

Brunner, Edmund deS., and J. H. Kolb. 1933. *Rural Social Trends.* New York: McGraw-Hill.

Bultena, Gordon L., and Eric O. Hoiberg. 1983. Factors affecting farmers' adoption of conservation tillage. *Journal of Soil and Water Conservation* 38(3): 281–83.

Bultena, Gordon, Paul Lasley, and Jack Geller. 1986. The farm crisis: Patterns and impacts of financial distress among Iowa farm families. *Rural Sociology* 51(4): 436–48.

Burgess, Ernest W., and R. D. McKenzie, eds. 1925. *The City.* Chicago: University of Chicago Press.

Busch, Lawrence, and William B. Lacy. 1983. *Science, Agriculture, and the Politics of Research.* Boulder, Colorado: Westview Press.

Buttel, Frederick H. 1982. Rural resource use and the environment. In *Rural Society in the U.S.: Issues for the 1980s.* ed. D. A. Dillman and D. J. Hobbs, 359–72. Boulder, Colo.: Westview Press.

————. 1983. Farm structure and rural development. In *Farms in Transition,* ed. D. Brewster, W. Rasmussen, and G. Youngberg, 103–24. Ames: Iowa State University Press.

————. 1985. Biotechnology and genetic information: Implications for rural people and the institutions that serve them. *Rural Sociologist* 5(2): 68–78.

Buttel, Frederick H., Gilbert W. Gillespie, Jr., Oscar W. Larson, III, and Craig K. Harris. 1981. The social bases of agrarian environmentalism: A comparative analysis of New York and Michigan farm operators. *Rural Sociology* 46(3): 391–410.

Buttel, Frederick H., and Howard Newby. 1980. *The Rural Sociology of Advanced Societies: Critical Perspectives.* Montclair, N.J.: Allanhead, Osmun.

Buttel, Frederick H., Jack Kloppenburg, Jr., Martin Kenney, and J. Tadlock Cowan. 1983. Genetic engineering and the restructuring of agricultural research. *Rural Sociologist* 3: 132–44.

Buttel, Frederick H., and Oscar W. Larson, III. 1982. Political implications of multiple jobholding in U.S. agriculture: An exploratory analysis. *Rural Sociology* 47(2): 272–94.

Carlin, Thomas A., and Linda M. Ghelfi. 1979. Off-farm employment and the farm sector. In *Structure Issues of American Agriculture,* ed. Economics, Statistics, and Cooperatives Service, 270–73. Agricultural Economics Report 438. Washington, D.C.: U.S. Department of Agriculture.

Carroll, Glen R., and Yangchung Paul Huo. 1986. Organizational task and institutional environments in ecological perspective: Findings from the local newspaper industry. *American Journal of Sociology* 91(4): 838–73.

Casey, James, Ronald D. Lacewell, and Lonnie L. Jones. 1975. *Impact of Limited Fuel Supplies on Agricultural Output and Net Returns: Southern High Plains of Texas.* MP-1175. College Station: Texas Agricultural Experiment Station.

Caswell, Julie A. 1984. Direct and network control of firms in the agribusiness sector. Ph.D. diss., University of Wisconsin, Madison.

Cavazzani, Ada. 1979. *Part-Time Farming in Advanced Industrial Societies:*

Role and Characteristics in the United States. Rural Sociology Bulletin No. **229**
106. Ithaca, N.Y.: Cornell University.
Christenson, James A., and Lorraine E. Garkovich. 1985. Fifty years of rural sociology: Status, trends, and impressions. *Rural Sociology* 50(4): 503–22.
Ciriacy-Wantrup, S. V. 1952. *Resource Conservation: Economics and Policies.* Berkeley: University of California Press.
Clarke, Neville P. 1986. Implications of the biotechnology revolution for agriculture. In *Research for Tomorrow,* ed. United States Department of Agriculture, 37–41. 1986 Yearbook of Agriculture. Washington, D.C.: United States Department of Agriculture.
Clifford, William B., Michael K. Miller, and C. Shannon Stokes. 1986. Rural urban differences in mortality in the United States, 1970 to 1980. In *New Dimensions in Rural Policy: Building Upon Our Heritage,* ed. D. Jahr, J. W. Johnson, and R. C. Wimberly. Washington, D.C.: U.S. Government Printing Office.
Cochrane, Willard W. 1979. *The Development of American Agriculture: A Historical Analysis.* Minneapolis: University of Minnesota Press.
Cohen, L. E., and M. Felson. 1979. Social change and crime rate trends: A routine activity approach. *American Sociological Review* 44: 588–608.
Connor, John M., Richard T. Rogers, Bruce W. Marion, and Willard F. Mueller. 1985. *The Food Manufacturing Industries: Structure, Strategies, Performance, and Policies.* Lexington, Mass.: Lexington Books.
Cooley, Charles H. 1964. *Human Nature and the Social Order.* New York: Schocken.
Copp, James H., et al. 1983. *Agricultural Mechanization: Physical and Societal Effects, and Implications for Policy Development.* Report No. 96. Ames, Iowa: Council for Agricultural Science and Technology.
Coser, Lewis. 1956. *The Functions of Social Conflict.* New York: Free Press.
Coughenour, C. Milton. 1984. Social ecology and agriculture. *Rural Sociology* 49(1): 1–22.
Coughenour, C. Milton, and Louis Swanson. 1983. Work statuses and occupations of men and women in farm families and the structure of farms. *Rural Sociology* 48(1): 23–43.
Curry, Judith R. 1986. Biotechnology policy—public perception, participation, and the law. In *Research for Tomorrow,* ed. United States Department of Agriculture, 24–37. 1986 Yearbook of Agriculture. Washington, D.C.: United States Department of Agriculture.
Dahrendorf, Ralf. 1958. Out of Utopia: Toward a reorientation of sociological analysis. *American Journal of Sociology* 64 (September): 115–27.
Dale, Tom, and Vernon Gill Carter. 1955. *Topsoil and Civilization.* Norman: University of Oklahoma Press.
Davie, Maurice. 1938. The pattern of urban growth. In *Studies in the Science of Society,* ed. George P. Murdock. New Haven: Yale University Press.
Dickins, Dorothy. 1937. White owner and tenant cotton farm families. *Rural Sociology* 2(4): 409–14.
Dillingham, Harry C., David F. Sly. 1966. The mechanical cotton-picker, Negro migration, and the integration movement. *Human Organization* 25(4): 344–51.
Dillman, Don A. 1985. The social impacts of information technologies in rural North America. *Rural Sociology* 50(1): 1–26.
Dilworth, Machi F. 1986. Plant growth regulators. In *Research for Tomorrow,*

230   ed. United States Department of Agriculture, 117–20. 1986 Yearbook of Agriculture. Washington, D.C.: United States Department of Agriculture.

Doeksen, Gerald A. 1987. The agricultural crisis as it affects rural communities. *Journal of the Community Development Society* 18(1): 78–88.

Donaldson, F. G., and J. P. McInerney. 1973. Changing machinery technology and agricultural adjustment. *American Journal of Agricultural Economics* 55(December): 829–39.

Dorner, Peter. 1983. Technology and U.S. agriculture. In *Technology and Social Change in Rural Areas: A Festschrift for Eugene A. Wilkening,* ed. G. F. Summers, 73–86. Boulder, Colo.: Westview Press.

Duncan, Otis D. 1959. Human ecology and population studies. In *The Study of Human Population,* ed. P. M. Hauser and O. D. Duncan, 678–716. Chicago: University of Chicago Press.

_____. 1961. From social system to ecosystem. *Sociological Inquiry* 31 (Spring): 140–49.

_____. 1964. Social organization and the ecosystem. In *Handbook of Modern Sociology,* ed. Robert Faris, 36–82. Chicago: Rand McNally and Co.

Duncan, Otis D., and A. J. Reiss. 1956. *Social Characteristics of Urban and Rural Communities.* New York: Wiley.

Duncan, Otis D., and Leo Schnore. 1959. Cultural, behavioral, and ecological perspectives in the study of social organizations. *American Journal of Sociology* 65: 132–46.

Duncan, O. D., W. R. Scott, S. Lieberson, B. Duncan, and H. H. Winsborough. 1960. *Metropolis and Region.* Baltimore: Johns Hopkins University Press.

Dunham, H. Warren. 1937. The ecology of the functional psychoses in Chicago. *American Sociological Review* 2(August): 467–79.

Dunlap, Riley E., and Kenneth E. Martin. 1983. Bringing environment into the study of agriculture: Observations and suggestions regarding the sociology of agriculture. *Rural Sociology* 48(2): 201–18.

Durost, Donald D., and Warren R. Bailey. 1970. What's happened to farming. In *Contours of Change: The Yearbook of Agriculture 1970,* 2–10. Washington, D.C.: U.S. Department of Agriculture.

Eberstein, I. W., and W. P. Frisbie. 1982. Metropolitan function and interdependence in the U.S. urban system. *Social Forces* 60(3): 676–700.

Eberts, Paul. 1979. The changing structure of agriculture and its effects on community life in northeastern U.S. counties. Paper presented at the annual meetings of the Rural Sociological Society, Burlington, Vt.

Engels, Richard A. 1986. The metropolitan/nonmetropolitan population at mid-decade. Paper presented at the annual meetings of the Population Association of America, San Francisco.

Falk, William W., and Jess Gilbert. 1985. Bringing rural sociology back in. *Rural Sociology* 50(4): 561–77.

Federal Depositors Insurance Corporation. 1982–1988. Annual Report. Washington, D.C.: Federal Depositors Insurance Corporation.

Firey, Walter. 1945. Sentiment and symbolism as ecological variables. *American Sociological Review* 10(2): 140–48.

Fite, Gilbert C. 1981. *American Farmers: The New Minority.* Bloomington: Indiana University Press.

Fliegel, Frederick C., and J. C. van Es. 1983. The diffusion-adoption process in agriculture: Changes in technology and changing paradigms. In *Technology and Social Change in Rural Areas,* ed. G. F. Summers, 13–28. Boulder, Colo.: Westview Press.

Flora, Jan L., Ivan Brown, and Judith Lee Conby. 1977. Impact of type of **231** agriculture on class structure, social well-being, and inequalities. Paper presented at the annual meetings of the Rural Sociological Society, Madison, Wis.

Frederick, Kenneth D., and James C. Hanson. 1982. *Water for Western Agriculture.* Washington, D.C.: Resources for the Future.

Friedland, William H. 1973. *Social Sleepwalkers: Scientific and Technological Research in California Agriculture.* Research Monograph No. 13. Davis: Department of Applied Behavioral Sciences, University of California.

Friedland, William H., and A. Barton. 1975. *Destalking the Wily Tomato: A Case Study in Social Consequences in California Agricultural Research.* Research Monograph No. 15. Davis: University of California.

Friedland, William H., Amy E. Barton, and Robert J. Thomas. 1981. *Manufacturing Green Gold: Capitol, Labor, and Technology in the Lettuce Industry.* New York: Cambridge University Press.

Frisbie, W. Parker, and Dudley L. Poston, Jr. 1975. Components of sustenance organization and nonmetropolitan population change: A human ecological investigation. *American Sociological Review* 40(December): 773–84.

_____. 1976. The structure of sustenance organization and population change in nonmetropolitan America. *Rural Sociology* 41(3): 354–70.

Gardner, B. Delworth, and Rulon D. Pope. 1978. How is scale and structure determined in agriculture? *American Journal of Agricultural Economics* 60: 295–302.

Gee, Wilson. 1942. *The Social Economics of Agriculture.* New York: Macmillan.

Gibbs, Jack P., and Walter T. Martin. 1959. Toward a theoretical system of human ecology. *Pacific Sociological Review* 2: 29–36.

_____. 1962. Urbanization, technology, and the division of labor: International patterns. *American Sociological Review* 27: 667–77.

Gilles, Jere L., Don Hirschi, Rex Campbell, and William Heffernan. 1984. Agricultural change and quality of life in three major land resource regions: A correlation analysis. Paper presented at the annual meetings of the Rural Sociological Society, College Station, Texas.

Gillette, John Morris. 1913. *Constructive Rural Sociology.* New York: Sturgis and Walton.

_____. 1936. *Rural Sociology.* New York: Macmillan.

Goldschmidt, Walter. 1946. *Small Business and the Community: A Study in Central Valley of California on Effects of Scale of Farm Operation.* Report to the Special Committee to Study Problems of American Small Business, United States Senate, December 23.

_____. 1978a. Large-scale farming and the rural social structure. *Rural Sociology* 43(3): 362–66.

_____. 1978b. *As You Sow: Three Studies in the Social Consequences of Agribusiness.* Montclair, N.J.: Allanhead, Osmun.

Goss, Kevin F. 1979. Consequences of diffusion of innovations. *Rural Sociology* 44 (4): 754–72.

Goss, Kevin F., Richard Rodefeld, and Frederick Buttel. 1980. The political economy of class structure in U.S. agriculture. In *The Rural Sociology of Advanced Societies: Critical Perspectives,* ed. F. Buttel and H. Newby, 83–132. Montclair, N.J.: Allanhead, Osmun.

Goudy, Willis J. 1977. Evaluations of local attributes and community satisfaction in small towns. *Rural Sociology* 42(3): 371–82.

Gould, C. N. 1907. *The Geological and Water Resources of the Western Portion of the Panhandle of Texas.* Water Supply Paper 191. Washington, D.C.: U.S. Geological Survey.

Green, Donald E. 1973. *Land of the Underground Rain.* Austin: University of Texas Press.

Green, Gary P. 1984. Credit and agriculture: Some consequences of the centralization of the banking system. *Rural Sociology* 49(4): 568–79.

————. 1985. Large-scale farming and the quality of life in rural communities: Further specification of the Goldschmidt hypothesis. *Rural Sociology* 50(2): 262–74.

Green, Gary P., and William D. Heffernan. 1984. Economic dualism in American agriculture. *Southern Rural Sociology* 2: 1–10.

Guither, Harold D. 1980. *The Food Lobbyists.* Lexington, Mass.: Lexington Books.

Hadwiger, Don F., and William P. Browne, eds. 1978. *The New Politics of Food.* Lexington, Mass.: Lexington Books.

Hamilton, Horace C. 1939. The social effect of recent trends in the mechanization of agriculture. *Rural Sociology* 4(March): 3–19.

Hamm, L. G. 1979. Farm inputs industries and farm structure. In *Structure Issues of American Agriculture,* ed. Economics, Statistics, and Cooperatives Service. Agricultural Economics Report 438. Washington, D.C.: U.S. Department of Agriculture.

Hannan, Michael T., and John Freeman. 1977. The population ecology of organizations. *American Journal of Sociology* 82: 929–64.

Harden, Warren R. 1960. Social and economic effects of community size. *Rural Sociology* 25: 204–11.

Hardesty, Donald L. 1977. *Ecological Anthropology.* New York: Wiley.

————. 1980. The ecological perspective in anthropology. *American Behavioral Scientist* 24: 107–24.

Hargrove, David S. 1986. Mental health response to the farm foreclosure crisis. *The Rural Sociologist* 6(2): 88–95.

Harlander, Susan K., and Richard G. Garner. 1986. The future of biotechnology in food processing. In *Research for Tomorrow,* ed. United States Department of Agriculture, 52–55. 1986 Yearbook of Agriculture. Washington, D.C.: United States Department of Agriculture.

Harper, Emily B., Frederick C. Fliegel, and J. C. van Es. 1980. Growing numbers of small farms in the North Central states. *Rural Sociology* 45(4): 608–20.

Harris, Craig K., and Jess Gilbert. 1982. Large-scale farming, rural income, and Goldschmidt's agrarian thesis. *Rural Sociology* 47(3): 449–58.

Harris, Marshall. 1941. Landless farm people in the United States. *Rural Sociology* 6(2): 107–16.

Hauser, P. M., and L. F. Schnore, eds. 1965. *The Study of Urbanization.* New York: Wiley.

Hauser, P. M., and O. D. Duncan, eds. 1959. *The Study of Human Population.* Chicago: University of Chicago Press.

Hawley, Amos H. 1944. Ecology and human ecology. *Social Forces* 22: 398–405.

————. 1950. *Human Ecology: A Theory of Community Structure.* New York: Ronald Press.

————. 1968. Human ecology. In *International Encyclopedia of the Social*

Sciences, Volume 4, ed. D. L. Sills, 328–37. New York: Crowell, Collier and **233** Macmillan.

———. 1971. *Urban Society: An Ecological Approach.* New York: Ronald Press.

———. 1986. *Human Ecology: A Theoretical Essay.* Chicago: University of Chicago Press.

Heaton, Tim B. 1980. Metropolitan influence on United States farmland use and capital intensivity. *Rural Sociology* 45(3): 501–8.

Heaton, T. B., W. B. Clifford, and G. V. Fuguitt. 1981. Temporal shifts in the determinants of young and elderly migration in nonmetropolitan areas. *Social Forces* 60(1): 41–60.

Heffernan, William D. 1972. Sociological dimensions of agricultural structure in the United States. *Sociologia Ruralis* 12(3/4): 481–99.

———. 1982a. Structure of agriculture and quality of life in rural communities. In *Rural Society in the U.S.: Issues for the 1980s,* ed. D. A. Dillman and D. J. Hobbs, 337–46. Boulder, Colo.: Westview Press.

———. 1982b. Reducing uncertainty: Changes in the U.S. poultry industry. Paper presented at the annual meetings of the Rural Sociological Society, San Francisco.

Heffernan, William D., and Gary P. Green. 1986. Farm size and soil loss: Prospects for a sustainable agriculture. *Rural Sociology* 51(1): 31–42.

Heffernan, William D., Gary P. Green, R. Paul Lasley, and Michael F. Nolan. 1981. Part-time farming and the rural community. *Rural Sociology* 46(2): 245–62.

Heffernan, William D., and Judith B. Heffernan. 1986. Impact of the farm crisis on rural families and communities. *The Rural Sociologist* 6(3): 160–70.

Heffernan, William D., and Paul Lasley. 1978. Agricultural structure and interaction in the local community: A case study. *Rural Sociology* 43(3): 348–61.

Hickey, Jo Ann S., and Anthony Andrew Hickey. 1987. Black farmers in Virginia, 1930-1978: An analysis of the social organization of agriculture. *Rural Sociology* 52(1): 75–88.

Hightower, Jim. 1971. Corporate power in rural America. Paper presented at the New Democratic Coalition Hearing, Washington, D.C., October 12.

———. 1973. *Hard Tomatoes, Hard Times.* Cambridge, Mass.: Schenckman.

———. 1975. *Eat Your Heart Out.* New York: Vintage.

Hoffsommer, Harold. 1937. The disadvantaged farm family in Alabama. *Rural Sociology* 2(4): 382–92.

Hoiberg, Eric O., and Gordon L. Bultena. 1981. Farm operator attitudes toward governmental involvement in agriculture. *Rural Sociology* 46(3): 381–90.

Hottel, Bruce, and David H. Harrington. 1979. Tenure and equity influences on the incomes of farmers. In *Structure Issues of American Agriculture,* ed. Economics, Statistics and Cooperatives Service, 97–107. Agricultural Economic Report 438. Washington, D.C.: U.S. Department of Agriculture.

Howe, Carolyn. 1986. Farmers' movements and the changing structure of agriculture. In *Studies in the Transformation of U.S. Agriculture,* ed. A. E. Havens, G. Hooks, P. H. Mooney, and M. J. Pfeffer, 104–49. Boulder, Colo.: Westview Press.

Hughes, William F., and A. C. Magee. 1960. *Some Economic Effects of Adjust-*

234

ing to a Changing Water Supply. Bulletin 966. College Station: Texas Agricultural Experiment Station.

Hughes, William F., and Joe R. Motheral. 1950. *Irrigated Agriculture in Texas.* Miscellaneous Publication 59. College Station: Texas Agricultural Experiment Station.

Hurt, R. Douglas. 1981. *The Dust Bowl: An Agricultural and Social History.* Chicago: Nelson-Hall.

Hwang, Sean-Shong. 1983. *Suburbanization as a Sociocultural and Ecological Process: A Theoretical Synthesis and Empirical Investigation.* Ph.D. diss., Texas A&M University.

Hwang, Sean-Shong, and Steve H. Murdock. 1983. Segregation in nonmetropolitan and metropolitan Texas in 1980. *Rural Sociology* 48(4): 607–23.

Jesser, Clinton. 1963. Community satisfaction patterns of professionals in rural areas. *Rural Sociology* 32: 56–69.

Johnson, C. S., E. R. Embree, and W. W. Alexander. 1935. *The Collapse of Cotton Tenancy.* Chapel Hill: University of North Carolina Press.

Johnson, D. Gale, Kenso Hemmi, and Pierre Lardinois. 1985b. *Agricultural Policy and Trade: Adjusting Domestic Programs in an International Framework.* New York: New York University Press.

Johnson, Jim, Kenneth Baum, and Richard Prescott. 1985a. *Financial Characteristics of U.S. Farms, 1985.* Agricultural Information Bulletin No. 495. Washington, D.C.: U.S. Department of Agriculture, Economic Research Service.

Johnson, Lawrence A. 1986. Gender preselection in farm animals. In *Research for Tomorrow,* ed. United States Department of Agriculture, 73–77. 1986 Yearbook of Agriculture. Washington, D.C.: United States Department of Agriculture.

Johnson, Ronald L., and Edward Knop. 1970. Rural-urban differentials in community satisfaction. *Rural Sociology* 35(4): 544–48.

Jorgenson, Neal. 1986. Bovine growth hormone research at the University of Wisconsin-Madison. Written statement presented at a hearing of the subcommittee on livestock, dairy, and poultry, Committee on Agriculture, U.S. House of Representatives, Washington, D.C., June 11.

Kahl, Joseph. 1959. Some social concomitants of industrialization and urbanization. *Human Organization* 18: 35–71.

Kalbacher, Judith Z., and Diana DeAre. 1986. Farm population of the United States 1985. *Current Population Reports.* P-27, No. 59. Washington, D.C.: U.S. Department of Commerce, Bureau of the Census.

Kalter, Robert J., Robert Milligan, William Lesser, William Magrath, Loren Tauer, and Dale Bauman. 1985. *Biotechnology and the Dairy Industry: Production Costs, Commercial Potential, and the Economic Impact of the Bovine Growth Hormone.* Department of Agricultural Economics, A.E. Research 85-20. Ithaca, N.Y.: Cornell University.

Kasarda, John D., and Charles E. Bidwell. 1984. A human ecological theory of organizational structuring. In *Sociological Human Ecology,* ed. M. Micklin and H. M. Choldin, 183–236. Boulder, Colo.: Westview Press.

Kearney, Philip C. 1986. Soil microbes could help clean the environment. In *Research for Tomorrow,* ed. United States Department of Agriculture, 60–61. 1986 Yearbook of Agriculture. Washington, D.C.: United States Department of Agriculture.

Kinloch, Graham C. 1977. *Sociological Theory: Its Development and Major* **235**
Paradigms. New York: McGraw-Hill.
Kloppenburg, Jack, Jr. 1984. The social impacts of biogenetic technology in
agriculture: Past and future. Chap. 19 in *The Social Consequences and
Challenges of New Agricultural Technologies,* ed. G. M. Berardi and C. C.
Geisler. Boulder, Colo.: Westview Press.
Kloppenburg, Jack, Jr. 1988. *First the Seed: The Political Economy of Plant
Biotechnology, 1492–2000.* Cambridge: Cambridge University Press.
Kloppenburg, Jack R., Jr., and Charles C. Geisler. 1985. The agricultural ladder:
Agrarian ideology and the changing structure of U.S. agriculture. *Journal
of Rural Studies* 1(1): 59–72.
Knapp, Joseph G. 1973. *The Advance of American Cooperative Enterprise:
1920–1945.* Danville, Ill.: The Interstate Printers and Publishers, Inc.
Knutson, R. D., E. G. Smith, J. W. Richardson, J. B. Penson, Jr., D. W.
Hughes, M. S. Paggi, R. D. Yonkers, and D. T. Chen. 1987. *Policy Alterna-
tives for Modifying the 1985 Farm Bill.* Agricultural and Food Policy Cen-
ter B-1561. College Station: Texas Agricultural Experiment Station.
Knutson, R. D., J. B. Penn, and W. T. Boehm. 1983. *Agricultural and Food
Policy.* Englewood Cliffs, N.J.: Prentice-Hall.
Knutson, R. D., J. W. Richardson, D. A. Klinefelter, M. S. Paggi, and E. G.
Smith. 1986. *Policy Tools for U.S. Agriculture.* Agricultural and Food Pol-
icy Center B-1548. College Station: Texas Agricultural Experiment Station.
Kolb, J. H., and Edmund de S. Brunner. 1935. *A Study of Rural Society: Its
Organization and Changes.* Boston: Houghton Mifflin.
Korsching, Peter F., Curtis W. Stofferahn, Peter J. Nowak, and Donald
Wagener. 1983. Adoption characteristics and adoption patterns of minimum
tillage: Implications for soil conservation programs. *Journal of Soil and
Water Conservation* 38(5): 428–30.
Kraenzel, Carl Frederick. 1955. *The Great Plains in Transition.* Norman: Univer-
sity of Oklahoma Press.
Lacewell, Ronald D., and Glenn S. Collins. 1986. Energy inputs on western
groundwater irrigated areas. In *Energy and Water Management in Western
Irrigated Agriculture,* ed. N. K. Whittlesey, 155–76. Boulder, Colo.: West-
view Press.
La Rose, Bruce. 1973. Arvin and Dinuba revisited: A new look at community
structure and the effects of scale of operation. In *Role of Giant Corpora-
tions,* ed. Select Committee on Small Business, U.S. Senate, 4076–83.
Hearings before the subcommittee on Monopoly of the Select Committee
on Small Business, U.S. Senate. Washington, D.C.: U.S. Government
Printing Office.
Larson, Olaf F. 1981. Agriculture and the community. In *Nonmetropolitan
America in Transition,* ed. A. H. Hawley and S. M. Mazie, 147–93. Chapel
Hill: University of North Carolina Press.
Lawson, Merlin P., and Maurice E. Baker. 1981. *The Great Plains: Perspectives
and Prospects.* Lincoln: University of Nebraska Press.
Leholm, Arlen G., F. Larry Leistritz, Brenda Ekstrom, and Harvey G.
Vreugdenhil. 1985. *Potential Secondary Effects of Farm Financial Stress in
North Dakota.* Department of Agricultural Economics Report No. 199.
Fargo: North Dakota State University.
Leistritz, F. L., and Brenda L. Ekstrom. 1986. *Interdependencies of Agriculture*

and *Rural Communities: An Annotated Bibliography.* New York: Garland.

Leistritz, F. L., D. E. Albrecht, A. G. Leholm, and S. H. Murdock. 1986. Impact of agricultural development on socioeconomic change in rural areas. In *Interdependencies of Agriculture and Rural Communities in the 21st Century: The North Central Region,* ed. P. F. Korsching and J. Gildner, 109–38. Ames, Iowa: The North Central Regional Center for Rural Development.

Leistritz, F. L., H. G. Vreugdenhil, B. L. Ekstrom, and A. G. Leholm. 1985. *Off-Farm Income and Employment of North Dakota Farm Families.* Agricultural Economics Misc. Report No. 88. Fargo: North Dakota Agricultural Experiment Station.

Leistritz, F. L., and Steve H. Murdock. 1981. *The Socioeconomic Impact of Resource Development: Methods for Assessment.* Boulder, Colo.: Westview Press.

LeVeen, E. Phillip. 1979. Enforcing the Reclamation Act and rural development in California. *Rural Sociology* 44(4): 667–90.

Levin, Yale, and Alfred Lindesmith. 1937. English ecology and criminology of the past century. *Journal of Criminal Law and Criminology* 27(March): 801–16.

Lockeretz, William. 1981. The dust bowl: Its relevance to contemporary environmental problems. In *The Great Plains: Perspectives and Prospects,* ed. M. P. Lawson and M. E. Baker, 11–31. Lincoln: University of Nebraska Press.

Lowdermilk, Walter C. 1953. *Conquest of the Land Through 7,000 Years.* USDA-SCS Information Bulletin 99. Washington, D.C.: U.S. Department of Agriculture.

Lund, Daryl B. 1986. Using biotechnology in food processing today. In *Research for Tomorrow,* ed. United States Department of Agriculture, 48–51. 1986 Yearbook of Agriculture. Washington, D.C.: United States Department of Agriculture.

McConnell, Grant. 1969. *The Decline of Agrarian Democracy.* New York: Atheneum.

McIntosh, Wm. Alex, and Mary Zey-Ferrell. 1986. *Factors Involved in Texas Loan Officers' Decisions to Recommend Agricultural Technology to Farmers.* Department of Rural Sociology Technical Report 86-1. College Station: Texas Agricultural Experiment Station.

Madden, J. P. 1967. *Economies of Size in Farming.* Agricultural Economic Report No. 107. Washington, D.C.: U.S. Department of Agriculture.

Mandle, Jay R. 1983. Sharecropping and the plantation economy in the United States South. In *Sharecropping and Sharecroppers,* ed. T. J. Byre, 120–29. Bristol, Great Britain: Frank Cass.

Mann, Susan A. 1984. Sharecropping in the cotton south: A case of uneven development in agriculture. *Rural Sociology* 49(3): 412–29.

Maret, Elizabeth, and James H. Copp. 1982. Some recent findings on the economic contributions of farm women. *Rural Sociologist* 2: 112–15.

Marion, Bruce W., ed. 1978. *Agricultural Cooperatives and the Public Interest.* Research Publication 256. Madison, Wis.: North Central Regional Research Committee.

_____. 1986. *The Organization and Performance of the U.S. Food System.* Lexington, Mass.: Lexington Books.

Martin, Iris F. 1986. Nitrogen fixation in non-leguminous plants. In *Research for* **237** *Tomorrow,* ed. United States Department of Agriculture, 112–16. 1986 Yearbook of Agriculture. Washington, D.C.: United States Department of Agriculture.

Martin, Marshall A., and Joseph Havlicek, Jr. 1977. Some welfare implications of the adoption of mechanical cotton harvesters in the United States. *American Journal of Agricultural Economics* 59: 739–44.

Martinson, O. B., E. A. Wilkening, and R. D. Rodefeld. 1976. Validity and reliability of indicators of alienation and integration applied to a selected rural sample. Unpublished manuscript. Madison, Department of Rural Sociology, University of Wisconsin.

Matras, Judah. 1973. *Populations and Societies.* Englewood Cliffs, N.J.: Prentice-Hall.

Mead, George Herbert. 1934. *Mind, Self, and Society.* Ed. Charles W. Morris. Chicago: University of Chicago Press.

Merton, Robert K. 1968. *Social Theory and Social Structure.* New York: Free Press.

Michelson, W. 1976. *Man and His Urban Environment: A Sociological Approach.* Rev. ed. Reading, Mass.: Addison-Wesley.

Micklin, Michael. 1973. *Population, Environment, and Social Organization.* Hinsdale, Ill.: Dryden Press.

Micklin, Michael, and Harvey M. Choldin, eds. 1984. *Sociological Human Ecology: Contemporary Issues and Applications.* Boulder, Colo.: Westview Press.

Molnar, Joseph J., and Patricia A. Duffy. 1986. Urban and suburban residents' perceptions of farmers and agriculture. Paper presented at the National Conference on Sustaining Agriculture Near Cities, Boston.

Molnar, Joseph J., and Henry Kinnucan. 1989. *Biotechnology and the New Agricultural Revolution.* Boulder, Colo.: Westview Press.

Molnar, Joseph J., and Peter F. Korsching. 1983. Consequences of concentrated ownership and control in the agricultural sector for rural communities. *Rural Sociologist* 3(5): 298–302.

Murdock, Steve H. 1975. Ecological expansion in southern Appalachia: A theoretical and empirical assessment. Ph.D. Diss., University of Kentucky.

———. 1979. The potential role of the ecological framework in impact analysis. *Rural Sociology* 44(3): 543–65.

Murdock, Steve H., and Don E. Albrecht. 1985. The consequences of technological developments in American agriculture: A human ecological perspective. Paper presented at the annual meetings of the Pacific Sociological Association, Albuquerque, New Mexico.

Murdock, Steve H., Don E. Albrecht, Rita R. Hamm, F. Larry Leistritz, and Arlen G. Leholm. 1986. The farm crisis in the Great Plains: Implications for theory and policy development. *Rural Sociology* 51(4): 406–35.

Murdock, Steve H., and F. Larry Leistritz. 1979. *Energy Development in the Western United States: Impact on Rural Areas.* New York: Praeger.

———. 1988. *Farm Financial Crisis: Socioeconomic Dimensions and Implications for Producers and Rural Areas.* Boulder, Colo.: Westview Press.

Murdock, Steve H., F. Larry Leistritz, Arlen G. Leholm, Rita R. Hamm, and Don E. Albrecht. 1987. Impacts of the farm crisis on a rural community. *Journal of the Community Development Society* 18(1): 30–49.

238   Murdock, Steve H., Rita R. Hamm, Don E. Albrecht, John K. Thomas, and Janelle Johnson. 1985. *The Farm Crisis in Texas: An Examination of the Characteristics of Farmers and Ranchers Under Financial Stress in Texas.* Department of Rural Sociology Technical Report 85-2. College Station: The Texas Agricultural Experiment Station.

Murdock, Steve H., and Willis A. Sutton, Jr. 1974. The new ecology and community theory: Similarities, differences, and convergencies. *Rural Sociology* 39(3): 319–33.

Napier, Ted L., Cameron S. Thraem, Akia Gore, and W. Richard Goe. 1984. Factors affecting adoption of conventional and conservation tillage practices in Ohio. *Journal of Soil and Water Conservation* 39(3): 205–8.

National Resources Committee. 1937. *Farm Tenancy: Report of the President's Committee.* Washington, D.C.: U.S. Government Printing Office.

National Water Commission. 1973. *New Directions in U.S. Water Policy: Summary, Conclusions, and Recommendations.* Final Report of National Water Commission, Superintendent of Documents. Washington, D.C.: U.S. Government Printing Office.

Navarro, V. 1976. The political and economic determinants of health and health care in rural America. *Inquiry* 13: 111–21.

Neal, Ernest E., and Lewis W. Jones. 1950. The place of the Negro farmer in the changing economy of the cotton south. *Rural Sociology* 15(1): 30–41.

Nelson, Aaron G., and William G. Murray. 1967. *Agricultural Finance.* 5th ed. Ames: Iowa State University Press.

Nowak, Peter J. 1983. Adoption and diffusion of soil and water conservation practices. *The Rural Sociologist* 3(2): 83–91.

Nowak, Peter J., and Peter F. Korsching. 1982. Social and institutional factors affecting the adoption and maintenance of agricultural BMPs. In *Agricultural Management and Water Quality,* ed. F. Schaller and G. Bailey. Ames: Iowa State University Press.

Nuckton, Carol Frank, Refugio I. Rochin, and Douglas Gwynn. 1982. Farm size and community welfare: An interdisciplinary approach. *Rural Sociology* 47(1): 32–46.

Odum, H. P. 1971. *Fundamentals of Ecology.* 3rd ed. Philadelphia: W. B. Saunders.

Odum, Howard T., and Elizabeth C. Odum. 1976. *Energy Basis for Man and Nature.* New York: McGraw-Hill.

Office of Technology Assessment. 1986. *Technology, Public Policy, and the Changing Structure of American Agriculture.* Washington, D.C.: Office of Technology Assessment.

Paarlberg, Don. 1980. *Farm and Food Policy: Issues of the 1980s.* Lincoln: University of Nebraska Press.

Pampel, Fred, Jr., and J. C. van Es. 1977. Environmental quality and issues of adoption research. *Rural Sociology* 42(1): 57–71.

Papavizas, George C., and Joyce E. Loper. 1986. Biotechnology and soilborne plant diseases. In *Research for Tomorrow,* ed. United States Department of Agriculture, 62–65. 1986 Yearbook of Agriculture. Washington, D.C.: United States Department of Agriculture.

Park, Robert E. 1936. Human ecology. *American Journal of Sociology* 42 (July): 1–15.

Parsons, Talcott. 1937. *The Structure of Social Action.* New York: McGraw-Hill.

Penn, J. B. 1979. The structure of agriculture: An overview of the issue. In **239** *Structure Issues of American Agriculture,* ed. Economics, Statistics, and Cooperatives Service. Agricultural Economics Report 438. Washington, D.C.: U.S. Department of Agriculture.

Penson, John B., Jr., Rulon D. Pope, and Michael L. Cook. 1986. *Introduction to Agricultural Economics.* Englewood Cliffs, N.J.: Prentice-Hall.

Perkinson, Leon B., and Dale M. Hoover. 1984. University involvement in social impact analysis of changing agricultural technologies: Tobacco harvest mechanization in the Southeast. In *The Social Consequences and Challenges of New Agricultural Technologies,* ed. G. M. Berardi and C. C. Geisler. Boulder, Colo.: Westview Press.

Peterson, Trudy Huskamp, ed. 1980. *Farmers, Bureaucrats, and Middlemen: Historical Perspectives on American Agriculture.* Washington, D.C.: Howard University Press.

Pfeffer, Max J. 1983. Social origins of three systems of farm production in the United States. *Rural Sociology* 48(4): 540–62.

Pimentel, D., E. C. Terhune, R. Dyson-Hudson, S. Rochereau, R. Samis, E. Smith, D. Denman, D. Reifschneider, and M. Shepard. 1976. Land degradation: Effects on food and energy resources. *Science* 194: 149–55.

Poincelot, Raymond P. 1986. *Toward a More Sustainable Agriculture.* Westport, Conn.: AVI Publishing.

Poindexter, John R., and William B. Clifford. 1983. Components of sustenance organization and nonmetropolitan population change: The 1970s. *Rural Sociology* 48: 421–35.

Poole, Dennis L. 1981. Farm scale, family life, and community participation. *Rural Sociology* 46(1): 112–27.

Poston, Dudley L., Jr., W. Parker Frisbie, and Michael Micklin. 1984. Sociological human ecology: Theoretical and conceptual perspectives. In *Sociological Human Ecology: Contemporary Issues and Applications,* ed. M. Micklin and H. M. Choldin, 91–123. Boulder, Colo.: Westview Press.

Preston, Samual H. 1976. *Mortality in National Populations.* New York: Academic Press.

Quaintance, H. W. 1904. *The Influence of Farm Machinery on Production and Labor.* Publication of the American Economic Association. New York: Macmillan.

Quinn, James A. 1939. The nature of human ecology: Reexamination and redefinition. *Social Forces* 18(December): 161–68.

Raup, Philip M. 1978. Cooperatives, Capper-Volstead and the organization and control of agriculture. In *Agricultural Cooperatives and the Public Interest,* ed. B. W. Marion, 11–17. Research Publication 256. Madison, Wis.: North Central Regional Research Committee.

Reckless, Walter C. 1926. The distribution of commercialized vice in the city: A sociological analysis. *Publications of the American Sociological Society* 20: 164–76.

Reimund, Donn. 1979. Form of business organization. In *Structure Issues of American Agriculture,* ed. Economics, Statistics, and Cooperatives Service. Agricultural Economics Report 438, Washington, D.C.: U.S. Department of Agriculture.

Richter, Kerry. 1985. Nonmetropolitan growth in the late 1970s: The end of the Turnaround? *Demography* 22: 245–63.

Robinson, B. H. 1983. The agricultural policy environment in 1983: Where we

240

are and how we got here. In *Farm and Food Policy: Critical Issues for Southern Agriculture,* ed. M. D. Hammig and H. M. Harris, Jr., 17–42. Clemson, S.C.: Clemson University.

Rodefeld, R. D. 1974. The changing organizational and occupational structure of farming and the implications for farm work force individuals, families, and communities. Ph.D. Diss., University of Wisconsin.

Rodefeld, R. D., J. Flora, D. Voth, I. Fujimoto, and J. Converse. 1978. *Change in Rural America: Causes, Consequences, and Alternatives.* St. Louis, Mo.: Mosby.

Roemer, M. I. 1976. *Rural Health Care.* St. Louis: Mosby.

Rogers, David L. 1982. Community services. In *Rural Society in the U.S.: Issues for the 1980s,* ed. D. A. Dillman and D. J. Hobbs, 146–55. Boulder, Colo.: Westview Press.

Rogers, Everett. 1983. *Diffusion of Innovations.* New York: Free Press.

Rohrer, Wayne C. 1970. Agrarianism and the social organization of U.S. agriculture: The concomitance of stability and change. *Rural Sociology* 35(1): 5–14.

Rojek, Dean G., Frank Clemente, and Gene F. Summers. 1975. Community satisfaction: A study of contentment with local services. *Rural Sociology* 40(2): 177–92.

Roy, Ewell Paul. 1970. *Collective Bargaining in Agriculture.* Danville, Ill.: The Interstate Printers and Publishers, Inc.

Sampson, R. Neil. 1981. *Farmland or Wasteland: A Time to Choose.* Emmaus, Penn.: Rodale Press.

Samualson, Paul A. 1964. *Economics: An Introductory Analysis.* New York: McGraw-Hill.

Schertz, Lyle P., ed. 1979. *Another Revolution in U.S. Farming?* Economics, Statistics, and Cooperatives Service, Agricultural Economic Report 441. Washington, D.C.: U.S. Department of Agriculture.

Schlebecker, John T. 1975. *Whereby We Thrive: A History of American Farming, 1607–1972.* Ames: Iowa State University Press.

Schmelzer, John R., and Gerald R. Campbell. 1978. An overview of the number, size, diversification, and market share of agricultural marketing cooperatives in various commodity subsectors. In *Agricultural Cooperatives and the Public Interest,* ed. B.W. Marion, 71–104. Research Publication 256. Madison, Wis.: North Central Regional Research Committee.

Schmieder, Edgar. 1941. Will history repeat in rural America? *Rural Sociology* 6(4): 291–99.

Schmitz, Andrew, and David Seckler. 1970. Mechanized agriculture and social welfare: The case of the tomato harvester. *American Journal of Agricultural Economics* 54(4): 569–77.

Schnore, Leo F. 1958. Social morphology and human ecology. *American Journal of Sociology* 63(May): 620–34.

_____. 1961. The myth of human ecology. *Sociological Inquiry* 31(2): 128–39.

Schroeder, Emily Harper, Frederick C. Fliegel, and J. C. van Es. 1983. The effects of nonfarm background on orientation to farming among small-scale farmers. *Rural Sociology* 48(3): 349–66.

_____. 1985. Measurement of the lifestyle dimensions of farming for small-scale farmers. *Rural Sociology* 50(3): 305–22.

Schuler, Edgar A. 1938. The present social status of American farm tenants. **241** *Rural Sociology* 3(1): 20–33.

Schulman, Michael D. 1981. Ownership and control in agribusiness corporations. *Rural Sociology* 46(4): 652–68.

Schwarzweller, Harry K., ed. 1984. *Research in Rural Sociology and Development, Volume 1: Focus on Agriculture.* Greenwich, Conn.: Jai Press.

Scroggs, Claud L. 1957. Historical highlights. In *Agricultural Cooperation: Selected Readings,* ed. M. A. Abrahamsen and C. L. Scroggs, 3–56. Minneapolis: University of Minnesota Press.

Seidel, George E., Jr. 1986. Biotechnology in animal reproduction. In *Research for Tomorrow,* ed. United States Department of Agriculture, 68–72. 1986 Yearbook of Agriculture. Washington, D.C.: United States Department of Agriculture.

Sewell, William H. 1965. Rural sociological research, 1936–1965. *Rural Sociology* 30(4): 428–51.

Shannon, Fred A. 1957. *American Farmers' Movements.* Princeton, N.J.: D. Van Nostrand.

Shepherd, Geoffrey S., and Gene A. Futrell. 1982. *Marketing Farm Products, Seventh Edition.* Ames: Iowa State University Press.

Shryock, Henry S., and Jacob S. Siegel. 1980. *The Methods and Materials of Demography.* 4th Printing. Washington, D.C.: U.S. Department of Commerce.

Siegel, Paul M. 1984. Human ecology and ecology. In *Sociological Human Ecology: Contemporary Issues and Applications,* ed. M. Micklin and H. M. Choldin, 21–50. Boulder, Colo.: Westview Press.

Singh, Surendra P. 1983. Part-time farm operators and supply of off-farm labor in rural areas. *Journal of the Community Development Society.* 14(1): 51–61.

Slocum, Walter L. 1962. *Agricultural Sociology: A Study of Sociological Aspects of American Farm Life.* New York: Harper.

Sloggett, Gordon. 1979. *Energy and U.S. Agriculture: Irrigation Pumping, 1974–77.* Economics, Statistics, and Cooperative Service, Agricultural Economic Report 436. Washington, D.C.: U.S. Department of Agriculture.

Sly, David F. 1972. Migration and the ecological complex. *American Sociological Review* 37: 615–28.

Sly, David F., and Jeff Tayman. 1977. Ecological approach to migration reexamined. *American Sociological Review* 42: 783–95.

Small Farm Viability Project. 1977. *The Family Farm in California: Report of the Small Farm Viability Project.* Sacramento, Calif.: Small Farm Viability Project.

Smith, R. D., and D. E. Bauman. 1986. Bovine somatotropin: Research to improve milk production efficiency. *Animal Health and Nutrition,* December: 20–25.

Smith, T. Lynn. 1969. A study of social stratification in the agricultural sections of the U.S.: Nature, data, procedures, and preliminary results. *Rural Sociology* 34: 496–509.

———. 1972. *The Sociology of Agricultural Development.* Leiden, Netherlands: E. J. Brill.

Snyder, David B. 1986. Improving animal health through monoclonal anti-

242

bodies. In *Research for Tomorrow,* ed. United States Department of Agriculture, 94–98. 1986 Yearbook of Agriculture. Washington, D.C.: United States Department of Agriculture.

Soil Conservation Service (SCS). 1961. *Land-Capability Classification.* Agricultural Handbook No. 210. Washington, D.C.: U.S. Department of Agriculture.

_____. 1982. *Basic Statistics 1977 National Resources Inventory.* Statistical Bulletin No. 686. Washington, D.C.: U.S. Department of Agriculture.

Sonka, Steven T. 1979. Consequences of farm structural change. Report prepared for the Project on a Research Agenda for Small Farms. Washington, D.C.: National Rural Center.

Steward, Julian H., R. M. Adams, D. Collier, A. Palerm, K. A. Wittfogel, and R. L. Beals. 1955. *Irrigation Civilizations: A Comparative Study.* Washington, D.C.: Pan American Union.

Stewart, Robert E. 1979. *Seven Decades that Changed America: A History of the American Society of Agricultural Engineers.* St. Joseph, Mich.: The American Society of Agricultural Engineers.

Stinchcombe, Arthur L. 1968. *Constructing Social Theories.* New York: Harcourt, Brace and World.

Stockdale, Jerry D. 1982. Who will speak for agriculture? In *Rural Society in the U.S.: Issues for the 1980s,* ed. D. A. Dillman and D. J. Hobbs, 317–27. Boulder, Colo.: Westview Press.

Stokes, W. N., Jr. 1973. *Credit to Farmers.* Washington, D.C.: The Federal Intermediate Credit Banks.

Summers, Gene F., ed. 1983. *Technology and Social Change in Rural Areas: A Festschrift for Eugene A. Wilkening.* Boulder, Colo.: Westview Press.

Svobida, Lawrence. 1940. *An Empire of Dust.* Caldwell, Idaho: Caston Printers.

Swanson, Louis E., and Lawrence Busch. 1985. A part-time farming model reconsidered: A comment on a POET model. *Rural Sociology* 50(3): 427–36.

Tarver, James D. 1972. Patterns of population change among Southern nonmetropolitan towns. *Rural Sociology* 37: 53–72.

Taylor, David L., and William L. Miller. 1978. The adoption process and environmental innovations: A case study of a government project. *Rural Sociology* 43(4): 634–48.

Theodorson, George A., ed. 1961. *Studies in Human Ecology.* New York: Harper and Row.

Timmons, John F. 1979. Agriculture's natural resource base: Demand and supply interactions, problems, and remedies. In *Soil Conservation Policies: An Assessment,* ed. Soil Conservation Society of America, 53–74. Ankeny, Iowa: Soil Conservation Society of America.

Torgerson, Randall E. 1977. Farmer cooperatives. *The Annals of the American Academy of Political and Social Science* 429: 91–102.

_____. 1978. An overall assessment of cooperative market power. In *Agricultural Cooperatives and the Public Interest,* ed. B. W. Marion, 261–80. Research Publication 256. Madison, Wis.: North Central Regional Research Committee.

Tweeten, Luther. 1970. *Foundations of Farm Policy.* Lincoln: University of Nebraska Press.

U.S. Department of Agriculture. 1979. *Structure Issues of American Agriculture,* ed. Economics, Statistics, and Cooperatives Service. Agricultural Economic Report 438. Washington, D.C.: U.S. Department of Agriculture.

_____. 1984a. *Regaining Farm Profitability in America: A Cooperative Extension System Response.* Report prepared for the Extension Committee on Organization and Policy. Department of Agricultural Communications, Institute of Agriculture and Natural Resources. Lincoln: University of Nebraska.

_____. 1984b. *Cooperative Historical Statistics.* Farmer Cooperatives in the United States, Cooperative Information Report 1, Section 26. Washington, D.C.: United States Department of Agriculture.

_____. 1985a. *The Current Financial Condition of Farmers and Farm Lenders.* Economic Research Service, Agricultural Information Bulletin No. 490. Washington, D.C.: U.S. Department of Agriculture.

_____. 1985b. *Agricultural Statistics: 1985.* Washington, D.C.: United States Government Printing Office.

_____. 1986a. *Economic Indicators of the Farm Sector: Production and Efficiency Statistics, 1984.* Economic Research Service, ECIFS 4-4. Washington, D.C.: U.S. Department of Agriculture.

_____, ed. 1986b. *Research for Tomorrow.* 1986 Yearbook of Agriculture. Washington, D.C.: United States Department of Agriculture.

U.S. Department of Commerce, Bureau of the Census. 1930–1980. *U.S. Census of Population and Housing.* Washington, D.C.: U.S. Department of Commerce, Bureau of the Census.

_____. 1975. *Historical Statistics of the United States: Colonial Times to 1970.* Washington, D.C.: U.S. Department of Commerce, Bureau of the Census.

_____. 1981. Geographic mobility. *Current Population Report.* P-20, No. 368. Washington, D.C.: U.S. Department of Commerce, Bureau of the Census.

_____. 1983. Geographic mobility. *Current Population Report.* P-20, No. 377. Washington, D.C.: U.S. Department of Commerce, Bureau of the Census.

_____. 1984a. *1982 Census of Agriculture: United States Summary and State Data.* Washington, D.C.: U.S. Department of Commerce, Bureau of the Census.

_____. 1984b. Geographic mobility. *Current Population Report.* P-20, No. 384. Washington, D.C.: U.S. Department of Commerce, Bureau of the Census.

_____. 1985. Farm population of the United States, 1985. *Current Population Reports.* P-27. Washington, D.C.: U.S. Department of Commerce.

_____. 1986. Geographic mobility. *Current Population Report.* P-20, No. 407. Washington, D.C.: U.S. Department of Commerce, Bureau of the Census.

Walsh, Richard G. 1978. A critique and extension of cooperative theory. In *Agricultural Cooperatives and the Public Interest,* ed. B. W. Marion, 43–50. Research Publication 256. Madison, Wis.: North Central Regional Research Committee.

Webb, Walter Prescott. 1936. *The Great Plains.* Boston: Houghton Mifflin.

Whittlesey, Norman K., ed. 1986. *Energy and Water Management in Western Irrigated Agriculture.* Boulder, Colo.: Westview Press.

Wilson, E. O. 1975. *Sociobiology.* Cambridge, Maine: Belknap.

Wimberley, Ronald C. 1983. The emergence of part-time farming as a social form of agriculture. *Research in Sociology of Work: Peripheral Workers* 2: 325–56.

244

Wimberley, Ronald C., and Charles N. Bebee. 1980. *Structure of U.S. Agriculture Bibliography.* Bibliographies and Literature of Agriculture No. 16. Washington, D.C.: U.S. Department of Agriculture.

Wirth, L. 1939. Urbanism as a way of life. *American Journal of Sociology* 44 (July): 1–24.

Wittfogel, Karl A. 1957. *Oriental Despotism: A Comparative Study of Total Power.* New Haven: Yale University Press.

Wright, J. S., and D. W. Lick. 1986. Health in rural America: Problems and recommendations. In *New Dimensions in Rural Policy: Building Upon Our Heritage,* ed. D. Jahr, J. W. Johnson, and R. C. Wimberley, 461–69. Studies prepared for the Joint Economic Committee, Congress of the United States. Washington, D.C.: U.S. Government Printing Office.

Zahara, M., and S. S. Johnson. 1979. Status of harvest mechanization of fruits, nuts, and vegetables. *HortScience* 14(5): 578–82.

Zeichner, Oscar. 1939. The transition from slave to free agricultural labor in the southern states. *Agricultural History* 12(1): 22–32.

Zorbaugh, H. 1926. The natural areas of the city. In *The Urban Community,* ed. E. W. Burgess, 219–32. Chicago: University of Chicago Press.

Index